A SEASON OF FIRE

A SEASON
OF FIRE

▲ ▲ ▲ ▲

Four Months
on the Firelines
in the
American West

Douglas
Gantenbein

JEREMY P. TARCHER / PENGUIN
A MEMBER OF PENGUIN GROUP (USA) INC.
NEW YORK

Most Tarcher/Penguin books are available at special quantity discounts for bulk purchase for sales promotions, premiums, fund-raising, and educational needs. Special books or book excerpts also can be created to fit specific needs. For details, write Penguin Group (USA) Inc. Special Markets, 375 Hudson Street, New York, NY 10014.

Jeremy P. Tarcher/Penguin
a member of
Penguin Group (USA) Inc.
375 Hudson Street
New York, NY 10014
www.penguin.com

Library of Congress Cataloging-in-Publication Data

Gantenbein, Doug.
A season of fire : four months on the firelines in the
American West / Douglas Gantenbein.
p.   cm.
ISBN 1-58542-176-6
1. Forest fires—West (U.S.)—Prevention and control—Anecdotes.
2. Wildfires—West (U.S.)—Prevention and control—Anecdotes.   3. Forest fire
fighters—West (U.S.)—Anecdotes.   4. Wildfire fighters—West (U.S.)—
Anecdotes.   5. Gantenbein, Doug.   I. Title.
SD421.32. W47G36   2003   2003048356
634.9'618—dc21

Printed in the United States of America
1   3   5   7   9   10   8   6   4   2

This book is printed on acid-free paper. ∞

Book design by Lovedog Studio

For Jane

CONTENTS

A SEASON OF FIRE

Introduction

▲ ▲ ▲ ▲

A Season of Fire

On a warm afternoon in late August 2001, I stood on a dusty, wind-whipped Montana hillside and watched the annihilation of a forest.

From my vantage point I could easily see a column of smoke climbing like a giant mushroom from the mountains rising over Paradise Valley, 30 miles north of Yellowstone National Park. The column rose with such fantastic energy that even from six and seven miles away the smoke could easily be seen boiling upward, pushing higher and higher in swelling folds of hot gas and ash. The source of this awful sight was a firestorm ripping through a stand of dry, 150-year-old lodgepole pine trees. Lashed on by high afternoon winds, the fire front was moving steadily northward from its starting point, its flames—as tall as a 25-story building—devouring trees, deer, elk, squirrels, cows, and everything else that could not get out of its way in time. Streams filled with mountain trout were reduced to steaming, moist strips; granite boulders heated to the point they exploded.

This was the Fridley Fire, which would burn for two weeks more before fire crews packed up and went home. Set by lightning, driven by the wind, and finding drought-cured timber as its fuel, it was nature at its most devastating and furious. Against this, the best crews and equipment available to firefighting were all but helpless. The day I watched that enormous smoke column, for instance, the few fire crews then assigned to the fire weren't even attempting to halt the blaze. They were well away from the marching flames, spraying water and fire retardant on scattered ranches and homes in the hope of saving them should the fire reach that far.

As impressive as it was, the Fridley Fire was but one of the score or more fires burning that day. Indeed, it was almost impossible to stand anywhere in the West and not see a haze of smoke, or a tall plume rising from a fire that had "blown up." By the time I reached the Fridley Fire I had been chasing fires across the West for nearly three weeks, the longest of several trips spent learning about fires during a stretch that began the previous March. And I had found them everywhere.

Fire has perhaps become a defining characteristic of a region that has seen many earlier characterizations. When white settlers first arrived more than 150 years ago, there was the promise of land, and of a fresh start. Of gold, and quick riches. Of timber and salmon and almost limitless natural resources. Then there was the West of the mythic landscape, as the great national parks came to prominence in the nation's imagination—Yellowstone and Yosemite and the Grand Canyon. There was the iconic West of Hollywood, and the American cowboy. And, more recently, the "new West" of a lifestyle split equally between work at Microsoft or Cisco Systems or Novell, and climbing a 5.10 granite wall, skiing steep backcountry snow, or banging down a singletrack on a Klein mountain bike.

Into this mix, fire has forced its way. From late June through late

September, Idaho, Nevada, Utah, Montana, Wyoming, half of Oregon and Washington each, and most of California are completely in its thrall, fretfully awaiting the next dry lightning storm that might set 50 fires in a single night. In May and June, Arizona and New Mexico have their own nervous days, before summer monsoons there cool the fires. Fires cause towns to be evacuated, divert tourists, and kill wildlife and livestock—and sometimes people. Thousands of people spend their summers planning for them and fighting them, while tens of thousands of others hope to spend a summer free of fire. Fire has embedded itself in the summer consciousness of this region, like snow in the winter or stands of golden aspen in October.

Fire is not new to the West, of course. Core samples from trees that were seedlings when Columbus landed show the scars of fires that arrived like clockwork once a decade. Settlers traversing the Blue Mountains in northeast Oregon complained in 1850 about smoke obscuring the view. And fires were part of the landscape when I grew up in Portland, Oregon, during the 1950s and 1960s. I heard frequently about the Tillamook Burn, a series of fires that burned during the summer of 1933, reducing to ashes 235,000 acres in the Coast Range between Portland and the Pacific Ocean. On excursions to the coast, where my father loved to fish for salmon and we would catch boatloads of Dungeness crab, we drove through portions of the "the Burn." There, silvery spires flecked with black, charred marks stood above rows of 25-foot-tall Douglas-fir trees that, my mother told me, had been planted by schoolchildren in the years after the burn. And on Sunday-night Disney television shows, I watched as helmet-clad smokejumpers in seemingly faraway Montana leaped from DC-3s, and isolated fire-watchers spent their summer in mountaintop lookouts, scanning the horizon for the telltale curls of smoke.

For all of that, fires to me were more abstract than real. And that wasn't just because we lived in the suburbs of Portland. Forest fires during the 1950s and early 1960s were relatively rare and small. That began to change as the century neared its end. In 1960 about 1 million acres were consumed by wildfires. In 2000, eight times as much forest and brushland went up in flames. True, 2000 was something of an aberration—severe drought and swarms of lightning joined forces to start thousands of fires—but it clearly is part of a trend. On average, in fact, fires over the past decade have burned about 3 million acres a year. And many of them are hot, severe fires that annihilate a forest.

The 2000 fire year led me to think anew about fire, the West, and the way the summer's blazes have come to dominate the landscape. I decided to spend the next summer watching close-up a fire season as it unfolded from start to finish. This book is the result of that effort. To research it I spent the summer of 2001 crisscrossing the West, chasing fire. I trained as a novice firefighter, walked the devastation left by a fire with fire-behavior specialists, hung around fire camps that, after a fire broke out, emerged like mushrooms after a fall rain. I heard embers bounce off my hard hat, choked on smoke a few times, and got blisters from my logger-style boots.

I didn't get to every fire in the season. Not even most—there were just too many. But I got to plenty of fires, and talked to plenty of people in the fire world. From that I learned two things: First, although experienced firefighters can make upward of $20,000 in a summer, as far as I'm concerned they're welcome to every cent of it. It is hot, dirty, potentially dangerous work. "It's like aboveground coal mining," one fire manager said to me. And I agree. At least in a real coal mine you get an elevator to haul you up and down. On the firelines, you hike to the work site—maybe a mile or two over steep, uneven hills, with no trails—while lugging food, water, and heavy tools.

Second, I learned that fire—and fighting fire—is a far more complex issue than is often depicted. It's true, as is often said and as I
myself have written in magazine articles, that Smokey the Bear is indeed in part at fault for the current fire fix. As a kid, I knew Smokey
well: TV commercials featuring his face and stern warning that
"Only YOU can prevent forest fires!" had by 1968 made Smokey the
most popular advertising symbol in America. But it turns out that
fire is *needed* in many forests, and that Smokey has actually helped
turn American forests into giant piles of kindling.

Today, fire experts are questioning the notion that there might be
a "normal" fire year. Yet we have only a limited understanding of
what actually constitutes a "natural" forest, with its interplay of
growth, fire, and destruction, an interplay that despite the ferocity
of fire is as delicate as cat feet on a hardwood floor. We're beginning
to see how local and global climate influences the occurrence and
duration of fire: Weather in the West changes not only seasonally
but in long cycles that lead to 20-year periods of cool, damp weather
followed by 20 years of warm, dry weather. That doesn't take into
account El Niño or La Niña, the now-famous weather patterns that
wreak weather havoc globally, or the long-term impact of global
warming.

Experts are also starting to look at the human factor in the fire
equation. We've responded to the subtle dynamics of nature and fire
in a manner as wholly American as McDonald's, Disneyland, and
pickup trucks: by launching the equivalent of a D-day invasion and
attempting to bludgeon the problem into submission. The very word
"firefighter" sets the stage: This is a war, and by God we're going to
respond in kind. Today, the summer fire season has a counterpart for
just about every operation the military might conduct in Afghan-
istan, Iraq, or Somalia: airborne forces, ground troops, even an
intelligence unit with aerial surveillance and computer-generated

images of the adversary. Yet once a fire gets larger than about 250 acres and really starts to roll, the chance that firefighters can actually extinguish it is exactly this: zero. They must wait for the fire to become sufficiently quiet so that crews can dig a fireline around it, trapping the fire within a noose of bare earth and letting it burn itself out. Or fall rains finally douse a blaze that might have burned for two or three months.

During my summer spent chasing fire, I saw both why it's important to respond aggressively to fire and why sometimes it's best to respond with a little less vigor. There's a fierce debate on this issue, with a growing number of people arguing that the expense of fighting fires, the damage caused by the effort, and the relative paucity of the payback should lead us to dramatically scale back our firefighting efforts. I agree—to a point. But it isn't as simple as either "let 'em burn" or "stamp 'em all out." What might work in lodgepole pine forests doesn't apply to the ponderosa pine or Douglas-fir forests that dominate elsewhere.

The stakes are enormous. Today's fire patterns are symptoms of one of the great ecological problems in the United States. Even as the forests of the East—once all but wiped out by agriculture and development—return to something approaching their former glory, the forests of the West have become desperately ill. By some estimates as many as 100 million acres of Western forests are overgrown and fire-prone—an area more than half the size of the state of Texas. Most of this acreage lies within the 109 national forests that checkerboard much of the West. Once prized for their lumber, these forests now have far greater worth. They are the source of much of the West's increasingly scarce drinking water. They are the origins of the streams and rivers that nurture salmon. The green needles of their trees filter out pollution and create oxygen. As the West's cities grow, these forests offer a respite, a place to hike, climb, ski, or mountain-bike. Often, their very proximity to a town now generates its own economic activity, as "knowledge workers" who can commute via the Internet join small high-tech companies and other geographically independent entrepreneurs who choose to live near where they play as well as work. One forest health expert I talked with, William Wallace Covington of Northern Arizona University, believes that we have perhaps 15 years, perhaps as few as 10, to come to grips with the very real decay occurring in the West.

The fires of 2001 illustrated just about every facet of the complex decisions fires are forcing us to make. They also showed that we have many paths from which to choose in the years ahead. We're at a critical juncture in our approach to fire. Fires are so bad now, Covington notes, even a severe fire year such as the summer of 2000 may seem no worse than average. Long-term approaches are required, yet politics, the understandable alarm that erupts when a large fire begins to march, and easy access to a large and well-oiled firefighting infrastructure tend to emphasize quick fixes. But big fires don't take well to quick fixes. They tend to develop their own agenda.

In *A Season of Fire,* I've tried to show the strengths and weaknesses of how wildland fire is fought in the western United States. I've explored the ecology of fire, its habits, and its peculiarities. And I've examined the forces arrayed against fire. During my own season of fire, I saw the rhythm of the year, the preparation for the fire season, the unexpected—and in one case tragic—turns the year can take, how a relatively quiet fire season can suddenly explode when a single weather front sends lightning shooting down across hundreds of miles of dry forest. Fire is a troubling subject, but it's also a captivating one. It's a rare combination of terrible destructiveness and an almost uncanny force for renewal and regeneration. It is frightening; it is essential.

What I hope results from *A Season of Fire* is a better understanding of fire and better choices in how it is handled. We can't beat big fires. We never will. But we ought to learn their habits, how to manage them, and when to walk away and let one go. Because every summer, today and for years to come, will be a season of fire.

Chapter 1

▲ ▲ ▲ ▲

Smoke Signals

In May 2001, as the last of the thin winter snowfall disappears from the ice-carved summits of Glacier National Park, Steve Frye begins to expect the worst. Frye is 54, chief ranger of the park, one of the nation's most popular. He is of medium height and fit build, with a thick reddish mustache and calm blue-gray eyes. A ranger's hat or baseball cap usually covers a head that's mostly bald. His face is angular, with a square jaw and high cheekbones. Born in Minnesota, he retains a touch of that broad Midwest accent, and when he speaks it invariably is in calm, measured tones. That phlegmatic Minnesota air serves him well in the many tasks he faces: dealing with unruly visitors in one of the country's most popular national parks, raising two teenaged girls, fighting forest fires.

In May, it is that last task that worries Frye. He is the incident commander for the Northern Rockies National Incident Management Team, one of 16 such teams in the nation's huge wildland fire-fighting apparatus. As early as May, when fires often begin to break out in Arizona and New Mexico, Frye and his 20-person team may be called on to leave within hours for a forest fire. Once there, they'll form the administrative backbone for what in some cases is a weeks-long effort involving upward of 1,000 firefighters. Logistics managers arrange to feed the firefighers and equip them with Pulaskis—the combination hoe and pick that is the essential tool in the firefighting arsenal—gas-powered water pumps, and Gatorade. Fire meteorologists download data from satellites in an effort to forecast how winds and temperatures will shape the fire's growth. Line managers patrol the fireline, keeping crews on schedule as they punch line around the fire in an effort to encircle and snuff it. Fighting a wildfire is as close to a full-scale battle as one is apt to find in the continental United States. Frye is the general. He sets the tone for his lieutenants, applying a steadying hand when a fire blows up and makes a run, shooting flames 250 feet into the air as it marches through thick forests at the pace of a trotting human.

Frye has been facing fire for most of his life. His father was a seasonal ranger in Glacier National Park, and as a boy Frye spent his days wandering the back hills of the enormous, glacier-carved park. Back home, in Minnesota, he joined local fire crews in high school and by 1970 had joined the National Park Service as a seasonal employee, spending the summer in Glacier National Park's Swiftcurrent Lookout, a picturesque stone building completed in 1935 atop a windswept, bare piece of rock six miles northwest of the park's Logan Pass. By then the fire bug had him. He went on to work on fire crews during college, where he majored in psychology and philosophy ("excellent training for the Park Service," he says slyly), and once he joined the national park system he always stayed close to the fire business. He worked on the firelines as a grunt firefighter, then climbed the ranks of fire management. In 1995, he took command of his own management team.

Steve Frye (right), the leader of a Type 1 Incident Command team, confers with a fire analyst in the Fridley Fire camp.

During the previous summer Frye and his team had seen enough fire to last a lifetime. Frye was incident commander for a group of fires burning across the Idaho and Montana border. Called the Valley Complex, these fires were some of the worst in what turned out to be one of the most severe fire seasons in decades. Set by lightning in late July of that summer, the complex consisted of more than a dozen fires pushed together by strong winds. On August 6 the merged fires combined into a single megafire of 160,000 acres, a fire that burned 73 homes that night and threatened the towns of Conner and Medicine Springs. Firefighters were helpless to do much about the damage; the fire was too big, and with only a few hundred firefighters on the scene due to the enormous demands a hot fire season had placed on resources, Frye didn't dare ask his forces to be more aggressive. Crews were stretched so thin, in fact, that even managers pitched in. The night of August 6, as the fire neared Conner, Frye's fire-behavior specialist, Ron Hvizdak, pitched in to help a squadron of bulldozers punch some fireline through.

The Valley Complex burned through August, finally eating through some 212,000 acres of forest in what was one of the largest forest fires recorded in the United States.

In May, as Frye begins to make plans for the summer, it is much on his mind. It looks as if 2001 will be another good fire season—that is to say, a severe fire season. Firefighters all use the inverse of the word's real meaning—"looks like it'll be a good one," they say, meaning they hope for lots of chances to eat smoke, plus work lots of overtime. Firefighters are the same whether they work in the city or the forests. They want to protect people from the flickering flames, to test their mettle. In short, they love fire.

The immediate problem is drought. Forest fires play their hand with a few set cards and one wild deuce. The terrain alters little; a mountainside stays a mountainside, a ravine a ravine. The trees don't change much from year to year, either. But weather changes all the time, from season to season, day to day, from morning to nightfall. A wet winter can feed a big crop of grass and fine brush. A dry summer can turn that grass into perfect fire fuel. Add some dry lightning and wind, and no firefighting team on the planet can stop what happens next.

In the spring of 2001, drought forecast maps from the Climate Prediction Center, a branch of the National Weather Service, show a wide swath experiencing "abnormally dry" to "severe drought" conditions beginning in northern California, Nevada, Utah, and Colorado and blanketing almost all of Oregon, Washington, Montana, and Idaho. Those are, of course, the states with the most forest cover in the United States outside of the deciduous forests of New England.

That has fire forecasters concerned. Rick Ochoa, whom I meet in May while visiting the National Interagency Fire Center in Boise, Idaho, calls up a satellite picture of the West. The satellite uses sensors to measure the greenness of the countryside. And there isn't much. "You see this area here," he says, pointing to the Pacific Northwest. "It's typically very, very green. But it's not—it's dry for this time of the year." His pencil moves over to Idaho, Montana, and Wyoming. "Same for over here. This is where the fire season is going to be. You probably could draw a line from San Francisco to Salt Lake City, and everywhere above that it's going to be a hot season."

The drought looming in the spring of 2001 only exacerbates a problem that has long been building. Fire has shaped the West, and in turn it has shaped the Forest Service, the federal agency most responsible for managing the West's vast federally owned woodlands. Indeed, nearly a century ago the then-new Forest Service saw its primary mission as controlling wildfire. Fighting fires, Chief Forester Henry Graves said in 1913, was "the fundamental obligation of the

Forest Service and [one that] takes precedent over all other duties."
By 1935 the Forest Service had gone so far as to issue an edict that
all fires would be extinguished by 10 A.M. the day after they were discovered. If that didn't occur, then each succeeding day's work crew
was given the same task—get it out by 10 A.M. the day following.

The 10 o'clock policy came about during the Depression years,
when programs such as the Civilian Conservation Corps (CCC)
gave the Forest Service enough manpower to consider more than
stopgap measures. Thanks to the CCC, thousands of sturdy young
men now could be sent to fight fires. The impact of this muscle on
fire was considerable. Later, the incredibly novel idea of fighting
fires with airborne troops—smokejumping—extended the reach of
the Forest Service into wilderness areas that couldn't be touched by
firefighters who had to walk or drive to a fire. After World War II,
new 20-man crews were based across the West to supplement the
smokejumpers, and a full-time (at least for the summer) professional firefighting cadre emerged.

The approach summed up by the 10 o'clock program worked—
for a while. The annual acreage consumed by wildfires in the lower
48 states dropped from 40 to 50 million acres a year in the early
1930s to about 5 million acres in the 1970s. Then the line on the
graph began to move up. In 1961, for instance, a fire dubbed Sleeping Child, burning in western Montana, charred about 28,000
acres. It killed three firefighters and injured 75, and its size and ferocity shocked firefighters of the day, who were more accustomed to
thinking of very large fires as those burning no more than 300 acres
(a football field is slightly smaller than an acre).

But starting in the 1970s, and increasingly in the 1980s and
1990s, fires of 50,000 acres became routine, and fires of more than
100,000 acres were not unheard of. Plus, these were hot fires, fires
that in some cases destroyed a forest in detail, rather than just giv-

ing it a quick scorching that the forest shook off in a few years. Often they were "crown fires," which climb into the tops of trees, catch the wind, and leapfrog rivers, canyons, and firefighters in a terrifying conflagration.

A wildfire is one of the most complex natural disasters on the planet, the result of an interplay of almost infinite variability. Fire, of course, has three fundamental needs: heat, fuel, and oxygen—the classic fire triangle. In western forest fires, the heat source that starts a fire is often a lightning strike, propagated by the dry thunderstorms that are so common across much of the West during July, August, and September, the peak months of the fire season (numerically, human-set fires predominate, but lightning causes most large fires because of its tendency to spark dozens of fires at once). Lightning can reach a temperature of 50,000 degrees, easily hot enough to start a fire in the milliseconds it comes in contact with dry wood or pine needles. The fuel is the forest itself. The dried grasses in meadows or between standing trees make superb fuel, as do dried pine needles and small shrubs and trees such as Ceanothus and Gambel oak, both common in western forests. These materials are extremely sensitive to changes in humidity, and once dried out by the hot August sun are capable of reverting to that dry condition within hours after a rainstorm—"10-hour fuels," fire experts call them, referring to how long it takes for them to dry back out if dampened. Big trees, on the other hand—the so-called 1,000-hour fuels—usually contain a great deal of moisture, and can literally exhaust a fire by forcing it to expend energy to remove moisture from their live wood. When they're dry, however, they're so much seasoned firewood.

Finally, a fire requires oxygen. In the forests, a fire burning on a windless day may smolder for days without doing any real harm, choking on its own smoke and the carbon monoxide that it gives off.

But with a puff of wind such a fire quickly comes to life, its flame height increasing with its temperature. Once sufficiently stoked by the winds, and if it has found a ready supply of fuel, a fire may no longer need wind to sustain it. Instead, it becomes a "plume-dominated" fire, creating an enormous convection column—a smoke plume—above it. As hot air is sucked upward by the plume it creates a vacuum at the base, a vacuum that can be filled only by pulling in air from the fire's surroundings. It becomes, in effect, a firestorm. The power of such a fire is difficult to comprehend. As it burns it may generate temperatures of 2,000 degrees and consume 35 tons of fuel per acre. A big, 50,000-acre fire generates enough heat to warm 350,000 homes for a year. And the winds it creates may top 100 miles per hour. After such a fire, burned trees blown flat by the blaze's winds will show as well the effect of fire whirls— small tornadoes spawned by the fire. Sometimes, wind-downed trees will weave across the landscape in a crazy S pattern. The towering plume, meanwhile, may turn into a thunderhead—a "pyrocumulus" cloud. Moisture condensing out of the cloud generates an enormous amount of heat, far more than from the fire itself. This heat in turn creates giant downdrafts, which can blast a fire with tremendous influxes of oxygen, fanning the flames further.

The fire itself is a complex chemical process. An approaching fire prepares its own way by heating and drying fuels ahead of it, distilling some of the woody material in its path into burnable gases. Once an actual flame erupts, that distillation process continues. Oxidation generates heat and light—the visible fire—and creates water and carbon dioxide, both of which are essentially invisible. The smoke that marks a fire is the result of incomplete combustion, throwing off ash and soot. In a moderate fire, that smoke will be light gray or brown, the result of reasonably complete combustion that leaves relatively little soot. As the fire gains intensity, in its haste it loses its ability to oxidize most of the burnable material at hand, and the smoke becomes increasingly dark because of the heavy loads of soot. In the biggest, hottest fires, the furious flames are capped by a dense, boiling cloud of black smoke. But even then, the trees and grasses are not what is burning. The fire is heating them to the point where they begin to turn into gas—gas that actually fuels the fire.

What makes forest fires especially unpredictable is the environment in which they exist: the terrain, the winds and humidity, whether the fire front finds dried grasses or tall trees, whether a slope faces the sun or not. Each fire that burns is literally unique, and each moment it burns it behaves in a manner different from its behavior every other minute of its life.

Coping with wildfire today involves an organizational anaconda that winds from little Forest Service fire stations in remote stretches of Washington State to the Forest Service's huge Romanesque rockpile of a headquarters, located directly across the Mall from the White House. There, it has been a busy off-season. Following the 2000 fires, one of Bill Clinton's last major policy moves had been to throw his support behind what was called the National Fire Plan. The plan called for $1.8 billion in fire-related spending for 2001, with the aim of fighting fires, speeding rehabilitation of fire-damaged lands, and taking steps to reduce the threat of big fires in the future. That latter step was a major switch. Money had long been poured into firefighting on an almost blank-check basis. Now millions were to be spent on the less glamorous work of thinning out the dense thickets of brush and young trees that turned millions of Western acres into tinderboxes. Millions more were meant to help local communities "fireproof" themselves by taking steps to ensure that if a fire did approach homes it wouldn't find those weekend getaways or Web-enabled home offices surrounded by thick trees, topped with shake roofs, and bookended by stacks of nicely dried firewood for the woodstove. Which happens—a lot.

The National Fire Plan isn't a magic bullet. It calls for hundreds of new firefighters, but only enough to be adequate for a statistically "normal" fire year. The 2000 season had not been normal, and even those extra firefighters signing up for 2001 likely would not have helped much. So fire authorities are hopeful that the new teams will help keep fires under control more deeply into the season. But a few big thunderstorms in August will quickly stretch resources past the breaking point.

Meanwhile, the plan certainly is proving a boon for the Forest Service, allowing the biggest fire-oriented hiring binge since the early 1970s and putting it in a key position to determine the thrust of the plan and how its big pile of cash is allocated. The Forest Service is fast becoming, in short, the Forest Fire Service. Fire now accounts for nearly half its annual budget of just over $4 billion, and it has become the financial lifeline to an agency that was on the ropes for much of the 1980s and 1990s as steep cutbacks in logging on national forests gutted its timber-sale and road-building programs. (Amazing fact: The Forest Service was for years the number-one road-building entity in the United States, with 338,000 miles of roads—nearly 10 times that of the Interstate Highway System.)

In May, preparations for the coming season are well under way, and have been since October. Wildland firefighting is like making toys for Christmas—as soon as it's over, you start work on the next year. Across the West, those charged with protecting America's forests from fire have been hard at work for months, hiring crews, ordering equipment, stockpiling supplies, reviewing the prior year's fires to figure out how to do better. Now most of the firefighters—it is, after all, largely summer work, like mowing lawns or painting houses—are trickling in to their units from winter vacations or jobs running Sno-Cats at ski resorts. Many are firefighting veterans. In Logan, Utah, for instance, the Logan Hotshots were at work getting in shape for the coming fire season, most after wrapping up studies at colleges and universities scattered across the West. The "Logans" are among the toughest firefighters in the system—20-person teams that leave their home base in June or earlier and work 14-day shifts on fires until September or October. In May, at their Cache Valley compound in northern Utah, team members are lifting weights, running, taking fast "power hikes" over the steep northern Utah mountains, and reviewing the use of chain saws, water pumps, and Pulaskis. Veteran team members include Aicha Hull, a young woman from western Idaho whose dark brown pigtails and cherubic face belie the fact that she already has spent two years rappelling out of helicopters to fight fires before joining the Logans, and who is studying chemistry at the University of Nevada–Reno in preparation for taking her 3.9-plus grade point into medical school. There is John Scott, a handsome, sharp-featured young man who is a business and marketing senior at Boise State University. And Robert Harjo, a soft-spoken Creek-Seminole from Oklahoma, each ear bearing a silver ring, studying journalism and environmental science when not out digging fireline. The Logans saw some of the worst fires during the 2000 season—"just outrageous fire behavior," assistant team leader Rob Barnett puts it—and in May anticipate a repeat.

Other firefighters will see a big blaze for the first time in 2001. The National Fire Plan calls for hiring perhaps 5,000 new firefighters, a massive infusion of rookies into a job that can be full of danger. But firefighters tend to self-select. Timid people, or those not up to hard physical work, generally don't apply. One applicant is Matthew Rutman, a 26-year-old Californian. He is tall and lanky, with long black hair and a wispy beard. Rutman doesn't so much walk as lope; his long legs seem to leap out in front of him as he strides, letting him cover ground at the pace of a country farmer from the nineteenth century. He knows all about hard work after three years with the California Conservation Corps, cleaning debris from trails, chopping brush, hauling trash, even fighting some fires. He likes the hard labor. But the work also appeals to his strong sense of idealism. Rutman is acutely political, a staunch opponent of expanding global trade and one of the activists who helped shut down the World Trade Organization meeting in Seattle in November of 1999. But he also has a strong practical streak. So rather than waving placards, he also works actively to make life better, if only for a few people. In the spring he has just returned from Guatemala, where he works with local schools to help install computers. He's broke, and hopes a summer spent fighting fires will replenish his bank account enough so he can return to Guatemala in the fall with a shipment of computers and accessories he has wheedled out of people or salvaged. But he also applies late for openings with Forest Service firefighting crews. He hopes for a station in California, but instead is assigned to a Forest Service station at Lake Wenatchee in the central part of Washington State. He'll report for duty there after finishing firefighter "basic training" in mid-June.

The Logans, Rutman, and others expect a busy year. In national forests and national parks, where prescribed burns are taking place in an effort to burn off some of the fuel load, fat fallen logs are like kiln-dried lumber, and are burning down to white. In Montana, a fire jumps from treetop to treetop even though the grass on the ground is green—the trees haven't received enough moisture over the winter to pull it up into the treetops. By July the grass will be dry and brown too—and then look out. Near Lake Chelan, a long, glacier-carved loch in the north-central part of Washington, a fire breaks out in May that the three firefighters assigned to it think they'll have in hand in an hour or two by digging a fireline across the tip of the fire, like capping a T. But as they approach the fire, lugging Pulaskis, they hear the loud crackle of pine needles torching and the *whoosh!* of trees immolating in a few seconds. This fire has ideas. "That isn't going to work," one of them says to his companions of their plan. "We'll need to dig line all the way around this thing."

Word of fires such as that is filtering back to Boise, site of the National Interagency Fire Center (NIFC), where I'd met Rick Ochoa. The Center is the Pentagon of brushfire, one of many parallels to military action that have infiltrated the fire world, often with unfortunate results. Known as "Nifsee," the Center has evolved over 20 years from a regional to a national fire-management center. Its layout reflects its somewhat unplanned development; buildings are scattered over several acres near the Boise airport— meteorological buildings, offices, a supply warehouse and the Center's three-story, buff-colored headquarters, named the Jack F. Wilson Building after a former NIFC director.

Inside, next to the two-story room with desks that in July will be packed with dispatchers scanning two or three computer screens at once as they try to match fires with fire crews, I chat with Neal Hitchcock, the 36-year-old coordinator for the National Interagency Coordination Center. He is a stocky, bearded man who has worked as national coordinator since 1995. Like just about everyone in the fire world, he got his start as a summer firefighter while he was in college, then stayed with it rather than pursue his first love— wildlife biology. Now, rather than digging fireline, he spends 12-hour summer days trying to piece together a giant puzzle made up of firefighters, aircraft, fires, and whether a fire was burning near homes or not. I don't know what he was like as a younger man; in his late thirties, however, the work has given him a Buddha-like disposition, calm and unruffled.

Hitchcock is the chief traffic cop for wildland firefighting, in charge of keeping his eye on the big picture to ensure that firefighters, aircraft, and other firefighting resources get to the fires that pose the biggest threat, not just the ones that have the loudest fire managers. Hitchcock has a tough job—trying to prepare for something that when it happens is bound to be a surprise. The 2000 season had been a difficult one; for weeks, Hitchcock and his dispatchers simply had to sit and watch the maps light up with new fires. From July through August the fire center had been at what's called Preparedness Level 5—maximum alert. Every available fire crew, fire truck, and aerial retardant tanker was in use.

Still, Hitchcock views his work in rather prosaic terms. It is, he says, basically "risk management—it's trying to understand what sorts of risks you assume if you move two tankers from California to Oregon, or send a Hotshot crew from one state to another." That's weighed against the risk a fire poses if left unchecked, or if inexperienced firefighters are left to tackle a job that demands veterans. In addition to the usual unknowns, this summer would pose a new one: the inexperience of the new firefighters pouring into the field that summer, something that not only reduced their effectiveness but put them at risk. "You just can't expect people to become experts overnight," Hitchcock tells me.

Hitchcock's May preparations consist largely of attending meetings to plot strategy, training new dispatchers, and waiting for the first big fires to break out. On the western edge of the center's complex, things are more manic in the Boise fire cache—one of 11 fire supply warehouses and the supply center for firefighters throughout Idaho and Montana. Keeping as many as 1,500 firefighters in a single camp clothed, fed, and equipped, not to mention reasonably clean and healthy, is logistically a daunting task. Even in May, the big warehouse in Boise that serves as a firefighting cache for Idaho, eastern Oregon and Washington, and parts of Montana is still recovering from having been sucked dry the previous summer. In August of 2000, for instance, the Clear Creek Fire in northern Idaho consumed about 196,000 acres. Some 800 firefighters were assigned to the blaze. The Boise cache sent out 2,070 Pulaskis, 3,817 sleeping bags, 171 chain saws, 20,580 meals (mostly Army-issue MREs, for Meals Ready to Eat, which supplemented on-site catering services), and 10,897 100-foot lengths of hose. And batteries— lots of batteries, 340,528 to be exact, mostly AA batteries used in radios and flashlights. In fact, modern firefighting would not function without the humble AA battery.

Meanwhile, in the sleepy little town of Greybull, Wyoming, Elaine Sellars also is making plans for the season. Sellars owns a T shirt shop, and her summer specialty is selling custom-printed shirts to fire crews. Within a day of a fire's start and its official "naming," Sellars is on the scene, hawking shirts with the fire's name and often a clever illustration. She, too, is thinking it will be a busy year. Her business depends on it. The West's fire world, I discover, takes all kinds.

Chapter 2

▲ ▲ ▲ ▲

The Ponderosa Problem

A few weeks after visiting the fire center in Boise, I stop in Missoula, Montana. Missoula is the base for all sorts of fire-related stuff: a smokejumper base, dozens of fire-studying students at the University of Montana, firefighting support contractors, and more. It's also the location of the Forest Service's Fire Sciences Laboratory, perhaps the world's foremost center for the study of wildfire. I am there to meet Kevin Ryan, one of the premier fire experts in the nation.

Ryan's particular specialty is fire effects: the impact a fire has on a forest, how it changes a landscape, shapes it, enhances it, or harms it. It's a field of study that didn't even exist until recently. Now Ryan is much in demand, quoted in articles and called to testify in Washington, D.C. "Up until now, most attention to fires has been hero-worship," Ryan tells me, referring to the tendency to rush TV crews and reporters to the scene of the latest forest fire, then ignore the issue until smoke billows again. "But after last year, there's a real interest in trying to understand the scientific underpinnings of what's going on." Maybe, he says half jokingly, the motivation also comes from the fact that in the previous year forest fires had almost taken out two national laboratories for weapons research—the Los Alamos National Laboratory in New Mexico, and the Argonne National Laboratory in Idaho.

He says this to me as we leave the fire lab, located in a two-story building adjacent to the Missoula airport, and head north in a Forest Service–green Ford Expedition. The vehicle—complete with CD player, air-conditioning, and cushy captain's chairs up front—had caused some Russian foresters visiting the lab no end of amazement. "They just couldn't believe we'd take a vehicle this nice out into the woods," Ryan tells me, a little embarrassed himself at its opulence.

Ryan is 55, with silver hair, a matching beard, and deep-set brown eyes. He didn't mean to get into fire science—tree physiology was his first love. But while studying forestry at the University of Colorado in the early 1970s, he was picked out by Jack Barrows, an influential professor at the school and one of the early specialists in the science of forest fire. In 1954, for instance, Barrows had published an exhaustive study on lightning strikes in the Rocky Mountains and their correlation with fires. "Barrows drafted me into fire science," Ryan says. "I've been working at it ever since." But he's stayed in close touch with his passion, developing a seemingly simple test that can tell if a fire-damaged tree will live or die by measuring an enzyme inside the bark.

We drive north from Interstate 84, passing new subdivisions sprouting outside of now-hip Missoula, and up a twisting gravel road. With us is Mick Harrington, a colleague of Ryan's and himself a fire-effects specialist. Harrington also is 55, mustached; he worked at the Fire Sciences Lab as an undergraduate at the University of

Montana, then joined the lab full-time in 1987, focusing much of his work on the ponderosa pine ecosystem.

A few miles farther and the paved road ends. We enter the Rattlesnake National Forest, which stretches north of Missoula through the foothills of the Rocky Mountains. The road winds up through the cool gray-green forest, deep in shade on this cloudy day. After about 30 minutes we arrive at a thick stand of ponderosa pine, Western larch, and Douglas-fir. It looks fine—the sort of forest that one sees throughout the West. Dense and dark, the way a forest should be. But looks, it turns out, are deceiving. "Our view of the past," Harrington remarks, "is clouded by the present." This forest, which seems so healthy, is in fact a mess. "The trees probably have never been so crowded and dense here," Harrington tells me, as we leave the car and walk into the forest over a thick, spongy layer of needles and shrubs. "But we've gotten used to it—this idea that the forest should be just packed with trees."

In the forest that Ryan, Harrington, and I are visiting, fire once moved through every decade or so. These were not the big fires that now dominate headlines, but small, low-intensity fires that functioned like giant Weed Whackers. They burned off the grass and underbrush and killed many of the seedlings. Ponderosa pines, the tree that dominated this forest until the past century, survived these fires easily, its thick bark shrugging off the flames and its vulnerable needles well above the height of the flames.

The resulting forest was typically open and parklike, with big, mature, widely separated trees. The trees' canopies shaded the ground, and they stood far enough apart that each tree had plenty of room for the big root systems needed to find water in the arid West. But these forests began to change almost as soon as white settlers arrived in large numbers beginning around 1850. Cattle and sheep that came with the new arrivals mowed through the grasses and flowering plants, removing the fuel that summer lightning turned into frequent, relatively minor fires that swept clean the forest floor. Without these fires, and with less grass to compete against, seedlings of pine and other conifers that otherwise would be lucky to survive suddenly found perfect growing conditions. Forests that had densities of perhaps 60 or 70 pines per acre now saw 150 to 200 crowd in. Sometimes the trees grew so thickly that they formed impenetrable thickets, "dog-hair" stands.

Initially, foresters saw these thick tree stands as the future of forestry, much as a farmer preferred great masses of growing corn to scattered stalks. In Arizona, pioneering Forest Service scientist Gus Pearson in 1908 helped establish the Fort Valley Experimental Forest, where among other things he hoped to show the benefits of a fire-free forest. Pearson's objectives were purely economic—from its inception, the Forest Service has sought to manipulate the environment in a way that creates the greatest amount of dollar value. Fire was seen as the enemy of that goal. Not only did fire destroy young trees, eliminating a future "crop," it scarred larger trees. Ryan points to a nearby pine that has a semicircular mark at its base, as if the bark has turned in on itself. "That's a 'cat face,'" he says, referring to the mark, actually a scar caused by a past fire that some say resembles a feline. "And that's also the most valuable log—the one cut from the butt of the tree. So the thought back then was that fire was damaging the most valuable part of the tree."

In the forest where Ryan, Harrington, and I stand, the terrain is too steep for sheep or cattle. But after loggers came through in 1919, taking most of the largest trees, fire was largely removed from this landscape. That was as unnatural as taking away sunlight. Ryan unfolds a poster on the hood of the Ford, showing the cross section of a tree that had grown near here since around 1300—until it was logged 82 years previous. He points to dark spots on some of the tree's rings, telltale marks from long-ago fires that are scattered across the trunk at surprisingly regular intervals. Harrington provides commentary. "Up until 1919," he says, "the maximum interval between fires was 35 years. Sometimes fire came through every 5 or 10 years. But we haven't seen any fires since this area was logged. That means we've lost anywhere from three to six fire cycles, and this crowded forest is the result."

Too many trees—and often the wrong kind of trees. Two hundred years ago, Ryan and Harrington tell me, this forest would have had far more ponderosa pine. Now it's much more of a mix, with Douglas-fir and grand fir in particular filling in much of the forest, their shorter needles, packed more densely on the branches, in sharp contrast to the long, spiky needles of the ponderosa. Crowded "mixed-conifer" forests such as this, where Douglas-fir and other species have shouldered their way into forests once dominated by the ponderosa pine, are among the most fire-prone in the West.

Moreover, in a forest such as this, nobody is particularly happy. The Douglas-fir are too numerous for their own good, and have found terrain where they were able to take root but not flourish. Same for the grand fir. Both trees tend to get just enough water to survive, but are stressed and vulnerable to disease and insects. Western larch, meanwhile, can like the ponderosa usually survive a fire— even one that strips it of needles—because those needles emerge from hard, tough bumps on its branches. But although it looks like an evergreen, with long, spiky needles, the larch sheds its needles each fall. Growing them back in the spring requires more water and nutrients than is required by the Douglas and grand firs, trees that keep their needles anywhere from six to 12 years. "It's tough to have to undergo that needle construction when your competitors don't," says Ryan. "For the larch, fire is a way to keep nutrients on the site and water on the site, and to keep it happy as a clam."

Overgrown thickets of trees such as these ponderosa pines in Arizona are a significant factor in forest fires. (MARTOS HOFFMAN)

Nor do these forests create good wildlife habitat. The berry- and seed-producing shrubs and grasses, although tall, are starved for light as well as water under the thick canopy, so they produce less crop. Small mammals such as the tassel-eared Albert's squirrel suffer, as do birds such as the hairy woodpecker. Their problems move up the food chain to species that eat them, and down to insects and other pests that may suddenly explode in the absence of enemies. "It's just not a very productive forest," Ryan says, a little gloomily.

But it's the ponderosa, *Pinus ponderosa,* that suffers most. If there is a hero in this tale—or perhaps, more accurately, a victim—it is the ponderosa pine. Today, from Canada to Mexico, from the east slopes of the Cascade Mountains in Oregon and Washington to where the Rockies flatten out into the Great Plains, the ponderosa pine is the tree that exemplifies the forests of the West. Almost non-existent 15,000 years ago, the ponderosas moved in from southern North America as the glaciers of the last Ice Age retreated and the rocky, sandy mountain soil warmed and dried. Also called yellow pine and bull pine, ponderosas can reach more than 200 feet in height, often living more than 500 years. After one Arizona tree was cut, a naturalist counted 1,047 rings; when the Viking Leif Ericsson discovered North America and called it Vinland, that tree was a new seedling.

Lewis and Clark found the ponderosa's cones, washed down the Missouri River, and wondered what tree dropped them. When the explorers finally encountered the ponderosa, they made canoes from its logs for their trip down the Clearwater River, and were intrigued by the Indian practice of stripping off part of the bark to get the soft layer of cambium. "Along the road," Clark noted in his journal, "we observed many of the pine trees peeled off, which is done by the Indians to procure the inner bark for food in the spring."

Scottish botanist David Douglas named the tree in the middle of the nineteenth century, a half-century after Lewis and Clark encountered it. Douglas greatly admired the tree, calling it "very elegant" and "highly ornamental" in his journals. Douglas's appellation for the big tree was fitting. As Utah writer Alexandra Parker noted in her tribute to the ponderosa, *Graced by Pines: The Ponderosa Pine in the American West,* Douglas used a form of the Latin root *ponderosus,* meaning "heavy, weighty, significant," or, in the verb form, "to mentally weigh, to reflect on." Wrote Parker: "A walk through a grove of mature ponderosa pine reveals the aptness of this title."

Yet the ponderosa pine also is the most threatened tree in the West. That may seem ironic—anyone driving along Interstate 84 as it traverses Washington, Idaho, and Montana will see millions of ponderosa pine. But like the forest I stand in with Ryan and Harrington, these pine forests are aberrations—green perversions of their former selves, the product of accidental and deliberate efforts to eliminate fire. Today, perhaps only a few thousand acres of ponderosa pine forest remain in something like their original state. The vast majority—estimates range from 50 million to 100 million acres—are in poor health. In some cases the ponderosa have been crowded by fir-tree interlopers. Both Douglas and grand firs have always been part of the mix in most ponderosa forests, but strictly as marginal actors. Douglas-fir, for instance, typically stuck to sheltered draws and ravines, where it tended to be colder in the winter and wetter in the spring and fall, conditions that favored the Douglas-fir just a little over the ponderosa. The Douglas-fir can't withstand much fire, so the regular blazes once found here kept it in check. But when that natural enemy left, the Douglas-fir crept out of its localized stands and began to march across much of the forest. Once established, it quickly began to crowd the ponderosa pines. It did so simply by outseeding it. The ponderosa is a frugal tree, relying on its longevity to ensure that it will produce sufficient progeny. It needs a very specific set of circumstances—moisture, a good seed crop, and exposed mineral soil where the seed drops—to produce seedlings. It doesn't even drop seeds every year, often waiting for years for a wet spring and summer. The profligate Douglas-fir, meanwhile, happily lays down seeds every year.

Worse, the ponderosa now is vulnerable to fire in a way it never was before. That's because the overgrown forest conditions create big, hot fires that even the tough ponderosa can't handle. So now those ponderosa pines that the loggers missed in 1919, and that survived perhaps a dozen fires in their lifetimes, would almost certainly die in the first fire that came along. Such a fire might even mean the end of the ponderosa pine in this forest—certainly any semblance of a ponderosa forest in anyone's lifetime. In 2000, parts of the Bitterroot National Forest—a classic ponderosa pine forest—burned so severely that the forest floor literally was sterilized. To regenerate, seedlings will have to find good ground to sprout near a surviving tree, grow 30 or 35 years to maturity, then scatter their own seeds out 50 or 100 yards from themselves—and then only as other biological forces work to heal the damaged soil. It would be a slow, slow process, likely requiring hundreds of years

The absence of a true ponderosa pine forest also means the absence of a singularly appealing ecosystem. In a true, mature ponderosa forest, grasses such as Arizona fescue thrive, as do flowering plants such as lupine. Mule deer and Rocky Mountain elk graze on this thick ground cover, while up in the trees the tassel-eared Albert's squirrel busily chews on the ponderosa pine's cambium and sends piles of needles to the ground beneath a tree that it finds particularly tasty. Almost entirely dependent on the ponderosa, the squirrel also uses the tree for building its nests and for shelter from predators. Several bird species are common in ponderosa forests, including Steller's jay, brown creepers, white- and red-breasted nuthatches, juncos, red-shafted flicker, and the Western tanager, a summer visitor from the tropics whose orange, yellow, and black markings contrast with the green of the pines like a Vegas showgirl in downtown Billings, Montana.

The ponderosa pine also seems uniquely in tune with human beings. Its forests are a delight; the ample crowns of the trees provide shade from the hot sun, their widely spaced trunks allowing cool mountain breezes to blow through, the clean forest floor cushioned lightly with needles—yet easily traversed on foot. You don't need a trail in most ponderosa pine forests; you simply point in the direction you want to go and walk, changing course only occasionally to skirt a trunk. One popular saying is that it once was possible to drive a Model T from Bend, Oregon—in about the dead center of the state—to Klamath Falls, 160 miles to the south, right through the pine forest. And the trees themselves are beautiful, with deeply grooved, cinnamon-colored bark flecked with black and dark brown, and masses of blue-green needles. On a clear August day few things more closely characterize the grandeur that once defined the entire West than the inimitable palette created by the green of the trees, the deep cerulean blue of the sky, and the tawny hues of the dry grasses that flourish in gaps in the trees' canopies. Most days, you also can smell the distinct scent of pine in the air, a product of terpenes—an organic compound that in other plants creates the smell of peppermint and citronella—in the pitch. "Press your nose deep into a resinous fissure and breathe deep," Parker wrote. "In that fragrance lies the essence of this land."

Yet the ponderosa pine forest is more than an esthetic pleasure, like a Renoir painting. In some way, humans carry in their brains an image of "forest," and the ponderosa pine forest is that image. Early humans needed certain things to survive—shelter from the weather, abundant game, an environment in which they could see great distances, making them safe from ambush by wild beasts or human rivals. The African savannah provided such a venue, with its broad grasslands punctuated by stands of acacia and flame trees. In the New World, the ponderosa pine forest provided an analogous environment, and it is no wonder that Native Americans populated it so densely—Crow and Navajo, Cheyenne and Salish. All knew the ponderosa pine well, and all had their own names for it. These tribes knew what they were looking for when they got here, and the ponderosa pine forest fit the bill perfectly. In more recent times, Terry Daniel, a professor of psychology at the University of Arizona, has used the ponderosa pine as a gauge of human appreciation of forest beauty. He found that people uniformly like the ponderosa pine forest type—open yet shaded—when compared with either more densely wooded forests or more open terrain.

It certainly is my favorite forest type. But like many in the West, I also learned to love something that wasn't all it seemed. In north-central Washington State, for instance, there hides a collection of deep-blue mountain tarns surrounded by peaks hewn from salt-and-pepper granite. Collectively, the area is known as the Enchantment Lakes. It's a fitting term; the place feels like a Lost World, lifted up from the surrounding hills. Also fitting, I suppose, is the fact that there is no easy way to get there. Beginning in 1974, with my first visit to the Enchantments, I've always hiked in along a trail that climbs some 6,000 feet and covers 12 miles before it finally tips over a granite ledge and deposits me, exhausted and wheezing, next to the first lake, Lake Vivianne.

The lakes themselves are beautiful, as are the sharp, triangular edges of adjacent Prusik Peak (so named for a mountaineer's knot that allows one to ascend a rope without having to grip it barehanded), the big noble brow of Little Annapurna, and the rocky profile of McLellan Butte. But the hike in itself is exquisite, although brutally arduous. A few miles from the trailhead, for instance, the trail traverses through a grove of tall, brown-barked ponderosa pines. Here the afternoon breeze would blow through, warm but dry, and I could sit along the trail, getting the weight of my always too-heavy pack off my back, and look through the trees at glimpses of Icicle Creek far below. Many of my best memories of the hike into the Enchantment Lakes are of moments along the trail, eating M&Ms and gulping water, inhaling the piney scent.

But in August 1994 two men were working along Icicle Creek Road, a few miles upstream from the Enchantment Lakes trailhead. One of them set a hot chain saw on the ground, and within minutes the dry pine needles beneath it caught fire. The blaze grew quickly, and when fire engines arrived 20 minutes later it was already out of control, running from the ground up into the tops of the trees, and then from treetop to treetop. The Rat Creek Fire, as it was called, burned for much of August, scorching more than 40,000 acres and destroying a half-dozen homes. Among the territory that was badly burned: the forested stretch where I loved to sit and look down through the trees at the distant river. What I didn't realize during my half-dozen treks up the Enchantment Lakes Trail was that most of the forest the trail traveled was not what it seemed. It *seemed* perfect—thickly wooded, shady, green. But in fact it was a mess. When fire arrived in 1994, a forest that had once seen fire as a regular visitor could not withstand it. Today, along the trail I so enjoyed, blackened and bare trunks stand like silent soldiers, watching over a forest that no longer exists.

A similar fate may await much of the West. In the forest Harrington, Ryan, and I walk through, any fire that breaks out will be far more difficult to control than it once would have been, and is apt to commit far more serious damage. Eighty or 90 years ago, most fires were pretty easily extinguished by a few rangers on horseback, who sometimes would just walk up to a fire and beat it to death with a blanket. Nobody teaches that technique these days; almost any fire that burns now has the potential to take hundreds of acres in a day, sometimes thousands.

We head back to the Expedition. "The guys who thought it was wise to take fire out of forests thought they were doing the right thing," Ryan says to me. "They were trying to do some good." But here, as elsewhere across the West, the law of unintended consequences had found fertile ground.

Chapter 3

▲ ▲ ▲ ▲

Red Card

By early June, smoke is blotting the horizon in some parts of the West. Fires are burning in California, Arizona, and Nevada, and drought conditions persist throughout much of the West. It is dry as hell from Arizona to British Columbia.

June is a transition month in the fire world. Fires typically don't hit the entire West at once; instead, they pop up first in New Mexico and Arizona in May and June, then roll northward as the days lengthen and heat up. June also is a big fire month in Alaska, of all places—that state's dry season is in May and June, and its vast stands of spruce trees burn readily until summer rains begin. By July the southern parts of the West usually see an end to their fire season, as monsoon rains moving up from Baja pour rain down each afternoon across many forested areas. But these clouds also will continue northward, now dry, and become lightning storms that can spark fires in Nevada, northern California, eastern Oregon and

Washington, Montana, and Idaho—places where the hot July sun has by then thoroughly dried out the forest.

In 2001, it looks as if Oregon, Washington, Idaho, and Montana will be hit particularly hard by fires. New Mexico and Arizona are largely off the hook—late-spring snows and rain have dampened the fire season there, although also setting the stage for a severe fire year in 2002 by allowing shrubs and grass to flourish, creating the volatile "fine fuels" that fires love.

So in the northwestern part of the nation, fire managers are working hard to get new firefighters trained and ready. The National Fire Plan has poured millions of dollars into the hiring pot, allowing firefighting agencies to add more than 5,000 new firefighters nationwide. But as Neal Hitchcock had told me in May, it is going to be a headache to get them trained and effective in time for the fire season. That is particularly the case in the northwest. The fire threat already is high, but many firefighting classes aren't scheduled until mid or late June.

Early on a sunny, mid-June morning, I roll my Subaru Outback into the parking lot at Entiat High School, overlooking the big Columbia River in north-central Washington State. Near me, mint green Forest Service Ford F250 crew cabs are stopping as well, and from them pile sleepy-looking 20-somethings in forest green Nomex pants and yellow-orange Nomex shirts. Self-conscious in jeans and a T-shirt, I hop out of my car and walk to a corner of the parking lot, where several people are setting up card tables and taking thick stacks of training manuals from cardboard boxes.

School is in—Fire Guard School. At dozens of locations across the West, such as Entiat, crowds of new firefighters are swarming into local high schools and junior highs to earn their basic certification as wildland firefighters: a "red card," so named for the red ink on the white paper card, although what it actually says is the prosaic-sounding "Qualification Card: Incident Command System." In three days, the 150-odd people enrolled in my class are slated for certification as basic wildland firefighters, ready for assignment to any one of the scores of Type 2 firefighting squads in the western United States.

Type 2 squads are pretty low in the firefighting hierarchy. With a Type 2 certification and a red card, a firefighter is basically qualified to begin his or her climb up the big firefighting ladder that might lead to a post with a Hotshot crew or smokejumping outfit—the Type 1 teams, cream of the crop—or on a career path with an agency such as the National Park Service, where they might work as an FMO, a fire management officer. Still, a Type 2 firefighter with a good crew could expect plenty of action—in some cases, even more exciting stuff than a Hotshot. Hotshots, 20-person firefighting teams that spend the entire summer commuting from fire to fire, usually show up at a blaze several days after it has started. By then, most fires also have assigned to them an incident management team, a collection of fire managers who plot strategy and devise tactics. Each day the Hotshots are assigned a section of the fire to patrol, and sent to work on the most active stretches of the fire or in the toughest terrain.

On big fires, with Hotshots around, Type 2 crews typically work as mop-up crews, or stand around pointing a hose at a barn that might be threatened by flying embers if the fire makes a run. But many newly minted firefighters are assigned to "initial attack" crews posted to local Forest Service, Bureau of Land Mangement, or National Park Service jurisdictions. As such, it's their job to make a first run at a fire. Experienced firefighters almost always lead initial attack crews, of course, and a local chain of command will include a fire management officer who is charged in part with knowing the terrain and fuels in a specific area and formulating tactics and strategy for fighting new fires.

But initial attack is in some ways the most precarious task in fire-fighting, because small fires are the most dangerous fires. Big fires are like an aroused rattler—noisy and show-offy. With their towering smoke plume, 300-foot flame heights, and thunderous roar, big fires don't sneak up on anybody. But a small fire can. It can stroll lazily along the forest floor, looking perfectly innocuous, then hit a patch of dry grass or brush, catch a gust of wind, or find a slope to climb, its rising flames fingering up the hill to find new fuel, climbing faster and faster. With few exceptions, nearly all of those firefighters actually killed by a fire—rather than in an airplane or helicopter crash or after a heart attack, all while in support of a big blaze—have died in small fires that grew out of hand.

Most of the would-be firefighters joining me are from small central Washington towns such as Leavenworth, Ellensburg, and Yakima. Entiat itself is a tiny burg, really just a collection of houses with a few gas stations and small grocery stores on Highway 97, about midway between the city of Wenatchee and Lake Chelan, a popular summer tourist destination. Entiat is hot, windy, and isolated, yet also a place that has produced scores of firefighters and is the base for the Entiat Hotshots, one of the crews that form the backbone of the firefighting world. In fact, the vast majority of those in the firefighting ranks come from small towns. In part that's due to simple geography—little towns such as Entiat are right on the edge of fire country, and Entiat itself has been threatened by fires several times in recent decades.

And once people spend some time on fires, word gets around. For the most part, the young firefighters I meet over the summer have gotten into the work because they knew somebody who also is a firefighter. In my fire class, for instance, is a young, lean man named Nick Dreis. Dreis, 21, had grown up some 50 miles away in the town of Leavenworth. He liked to travel, and after hearing stories from his Leavenworth pals—several of whom now are based in Entiat as members of the Entiat Hotshots—about how good the money could be, he decided to give it a try to earn some cash for his journeys. Besides, he is an avid outdoorsperson who likes to rock-climb, ski, mountain-bike, and hike, and an outdoors job that offers a chance to fling his muscles around a little has more appeal than the kitchen jobs he held in Leavenworth, or schlepping concrete for his father, a mason. Matthew Rutman also is in my class, back from Guatemala and anxious to start making some money. He's in my training squad, a dozen of us assigned to a single team leader and a corner of the football field for setting up our tents. Rutman stands out from most of the other people in the classes. He's a little older than they, and has well-formed opinions on matters that go far beyond forest fires—he'll readily talk about global trade, for instance.

South of us, closer to Yakima, a Guard School held the week before had included newcomer Rebecca Welch. Welch is a complete rookie at this sort of thing. A laconic, blond-haired, sturdily built young woman from Lancaster, California, she has recently earned her communications degree at the University of Sioux Falls in South Dakota, and like many young people has been casting about for ways to avoid getting a real job. The previous fall her father had read about the campaign to hire new wildland firefighters, and encouraged Rebecca to think about it. "No, Dad—why would I want to do that?" she said to him, in perhaps the reflexive negation most young people feel when given advice by a parent. But the idea stuck with her, and after she read some magazine and Web articles by women firefighters who enjoyed the challenge of the job and the chance to make a difference in people's lives, she changed her mind. The work also gives Welch an opportunity to see if her athletic nature—she competed in soccer, basketball, and track in high school and college—will serve her well in the woods.

Indeed, fighting wildland fires has a strong competitive component. In the eyes of many who join firefighting ranks, a forest fire is
an adversary to be bested, and a test for their young adulthood.
There's also a strong moral element to firefighting, a chance to do
good. Young people are naturally idealistic, and after years of Earth
Day rhetoric they typically feel an almost subconscious urge to help
the environment in some way. Combine that with the still-common
Smokey the Bear message and that idealism meshes with competi-
tiveness to make a firefighter.

Women, in particular, seem to feel that firefighting offers a
chance to work in an environment that remains somewhat ex-
ceptional. Jean Pincha-Tulley, a fire management officer with the
Forest Service in California's Tahoe National Forest, remembers
joining a fire crew in 1978 and hearing constantly from her 19 male
compatriots that women couldn't handle the job. But good work
from trailblazers such as Pincha-Tulley, plus changing attitudes
toward women as a whole, opened doors. By the spring of 2001
Welch and others are hardly alone as women on a fire crew, with
women comprising 25 to 30 percent of wildland firefighting crews
and an even larger proportion of fire management jobs. "The only
thing I can think of that compares to this work is combat," Camille
Johnson, an Ohio native who worked that summer of 2001 on
Welch's crew and has been fighting fires for more than 10 years,
tells me. "I've worked day after day, for hours and hours, going physically all-out. You hit a wall, you're so tired, but you just keep going."

There's a reason for that allure, whether the one who falls under
its spell is male or female. Fire is literally fascinating—a word derived from the Latin *fascinare,* meaning to enchant, or even to be-
witch. That's because fire shows us just enough of itself to be
tantalizing, but not so much as to reveal its true nature. It's at once
too fast for the eye to follow, and too slow.

Fires both large and small are characterized by their intriguing flicker. We *think* we see the fire, but at any one time its glimmering spears of flame occupy as little as 20 percent of its apparent space. The effort to visualize the entire fire becomes an end in itself, and I'm not alone in having spent many hours contentedly sitting by a fire, staring into it. The same principle is at work in television beer advertisements that induce young men to buy their products by interspersing quick shots of buxom women with longer images of the can. In the same way, a fire shows just enough to encourage the viewer to watch carefully in the hope of seeing a complete picture.

Big fires, however, play a second visual trick, one with more serious ramifications. Such fires, called "pool fires" because they often are studied by igniting pools of flammable liquid such as ethanol, move with a sinuous, wavelike motion, caused by cool air drawn in by the flames and blowing over its surface. In the lab, that wave motion will be extremely regular, occurring every few seconds. But in a forest, in a much larger fire, the wave motion becomes both more irregular and less frequent, making it that much more difficult to discern. The fire may literally be creeping toward someone with intermittent footfalls, but like a cat stalking a mouse it does so slowly enough so that the eye can't register the motion.

The *frisson* of danger fire offers is something that always has been appealing to young people—but perhaps even more so to a generation raised on ESPN's "extreme" sports. Going into the 2001 fire season, 765 fire-related deaths had been recorded since 1910. Many of those killed were young people, drawn by the nature of the work as well as its seasonal schedule, which dovetails nicely with college or winter ski trips. Still, the thought that people in their teens, or just out of them, do some of that dying disturbs some in the fire business.

Firefighting's very real risks, however, are paired from the outset

with the idea that the work is a blast. An hour after I check in at Entiat, for instance, we are ushered into the school gymnasium for our
opening pep talk from senior officials with the Okanogan and Wenatchee National Forests, which had already hired many of those in
the school. "I hope you'll learn a lot here," one of them says. "And
this summer, we hope you'll have a chance to work hard and have
some fun!" We're already assigned to training squads, and a few
minutes later troop down hallways to designated classrooms on our
way to becoming firefighters.

Over the next three days we learn how to recognize dangerous
weather and wind conditions that can fan a fire; how to read section
and township maps so we know where we are around a fire; how to
recognize different fuel types; and how to coordinate the work of
multiple firefighting teams. Wildland firefighting has little in common with its urban counterpart, where heavily armored firefighters
charge into a burning building, hoses jetting water. So mostly we
learn about the primary objective of wildland firefighting: digging a
ditch. True, that ditch is given a slightly more technical term—the
"fireline," or more commonly, simply "the line"—but it's a ditch
nonetheless. Just about the entire objective in wildland firefighting
is to encircle a fire with a strip of bare earth maybe two feet wide. If
we can do that, and maybe use a chain saw to take out trees that are
close to the line and whose branches might pass the fire over it,
many fires will grind to a halt once they hit it, or at least pause long
enough for firefighters to extinguish encroaching flames with dirt or
water.

With the ditch as the basic weapon in the firefighting arsenal,
basic tactics take on one of two variations. Most common is an "in-
direct" attack—digging a fireline well in front of a fire, sort of a trip-
wire it eventually will wander up against. In some cases, firefighters
will set a backfire, burning out the area between the new fireline

and the approaching fire, using a small and (with luck) manageable fire to deprive the bigger flames of fuel. Or they'll start work at the base of the fire, its origin point, and dig line along its sides, slowly pinching in on the head of the fire until, like a snake pinned by its neck, it has no place to go.

In either case, the work of digging a line always begins from an "anchor point"—an unburnable area such as a road or rock field—and uses that as the starting place for digging line. With good planning, a series of anchor points can be strung together like stones on a necklace, reducing the amount of line needed. We also learned how to identify a "safety zone," an area where we could retreat if we lost control of a fire. In a safety zone, the fire would pass harmlessly around us. A large rocky area, a stretch of forest or shrub land that already had completely burned (putting us "in the black"), or a marshy area all could be construed as a safety zone.

The word "safety" is mentioned often, but usually in a tone not that different from the drone already coming from instructors who may have been excellent foresters or fire managers but who had refined to its final degree the art of packaging interesting material in such a way as to inflict maximum boredom. The classes are, in a word, dreadful. One instructor talking about the effect of weather on fires continually stops and hesitates before proceeding to explain basic concepts such as the interaction between wind and terrain, prefacing his remarks by saying, "I really don't understand this all that well." Another complains about the lack of time allotted for his topic, then spends the next hour giving an almost incoherent explanation of firefighting tactics rather than focusing on a few key points. We even are treated to a lengthy session on how the incident command system works—a topic relevant perhaps for managers-in-training, but completely beside the point for firefighters at the very bottom of the firefighting chain. This talk is enlivened by a ponytailed Washington

State Department of Natural Resources firefighter named Ed James, an eccentric sort who introduces himself in the Yakama Indian tongue and peppers his talk with anecdotes about managing fire crews made up of inmates. Moreover, James makes it clear he has priorities. "If you're not safe around a fire," he says several times, "you won't work for me." And I believe him.

Despite the uneven signals, we have repeatedly drummed into us the "standard fire orders," the 10 Commandments for firefighters. And there are, in fact, 10 of them—each starting with a letter that matches a letter in the words FIRE ORDERS, in this manner:

F   Fight fires aggressively but provide for safety first.
I   Initiate all actions based on current and expected fire conditions.
R   Recognize current weather conditions and obtain forecasts.
E   Ensure that instructions are given and understood.
O   Obtain current information on fire status.
R   Remain in communication with crew members, your supervisor, and adjoining forces.
D   Determine safety zones and escape routes.
E   Establish lookouts in potentially hazardous situations.
R   Retain control at all times.
S   Stay alert, keep calm, think clearly, and act decisively.

Quite a mouthful. To add to memorization problems, firefighting agencies also had decided that the 10 orders didn't cover all the bases, so they'd added a list of 18 "watch out" advisories, which were seen as yellow flags to the fire orders' red ones. These included fighting a fire that wasn't well scouted, working with unburned fuel between a crew and the fire, working at the head of a fire (in its path, in other words), weather that was getting hotter and drier, uncertainty over escape routes, and fatigue.

The clear goal is to avoid a situation where a fire might trap firefighters. But in the event that happens, there is the fire shelter. Carried by every firefighter since 1978, the shelters come in a canvas pouch a little larger than a typical hardbound book. Made of a thin, fabriclike layer of fiberglass glued to reflective aluminum, the shelters are shaped like a small tent, open at the bottom except for small flaps that form a partial floor. To get inside, the user steps on the back wall of the shelter, pulls the rest of it over his or her head like a jacket, falls to the ground, and forms a cocoon by holding the inside flaps against the ground. The shelters are extremely effective against radiant heat—the heat one feels when holding cold hands out toward a woodstove. But they're only marginally effective against conductive heat, the heat you'd feel if you touched that same stove. Worse, if temperatures get much above 475°F the glue that bonds the protective aluminum to the fiberglass body begins to melt, and the entire shelter literally falls apart. As an additional insult, the vaporizing glue emits toxic fumes. At 1,200 degrees the aluminum itself melts. Many fires hit 1,600 degrees—some go even higher.

Within the firefighting corps there's a clear ambivalence about the shelters. They have saved scores of lives—250 or more, in the estimates of fire experts who have tracked fire "entrapments," the clinical term for when terrified firefighters are overtaken by a rampaging fire. But they're also derisively termed "shake 'n' bakes," and some firefighters I talk with disdain them as something no experienced firefighter would ever need. "If you have to get in one of those," a veteran smokejumper told me, "you've screwed up, bigtime." It didn't offer much reassurance in 2001 to learn that the newest models of the shelter have been assembled with a faulty plastic pouch that holds them inside the canvas belt mount; a too-hasty pull on the plastic tab that opens the pouch would leave you with a tab in one hand, a still-wrapped shelter in the other.

Moreover, training in using the shelters is at best cursory. The logic seems to be that if you have to use a shelter, you've failed at some point, so we're going to train you not to fail so you won't use a shelter. I even hear some reports over the summer of squad leaders who forbade training with shelters, for fear that firefighters might become too comfortable with the idea of using them.

On the afternoon of our second day in fire school, however, we practice with the shelters—actually, with dummy shelters made of cheap garden tarp material, the real things being too expensive ($100 each) and flimsy for practice. Before that session we watch a video about using the shelters. They are a last resort—it is always better to reach a safety zone, or try to outrun the fire. The video also instructs us to avoid deploying the shelters in areas where it won't seal well against the ground—preferably on flat earth stripped of burnable grass or debris. Roads are ideal, so long as you are careful not to set up in the middle of the road, where firefighters in a fleeing truck might do to you what the fire could not. And it emphasizes removing packs before getting into a shelter; most firefighters carry "fusees"—sort of modified highway flares that are used to set back-fires. These, obviously, might prove an unwelcome presence in a shelter designed to keep fire *out*.

A few minutes later we have our chance to try one out. In the drill, we run across the school football field, shelter in hand, then stop, unfurl the shelter, and climb inside. The objective is to be inside within 20 or so seconds, after which the instructor tries to rip the shelter off you, imitating the effect of the high winds caused by a big fire. I climb into mine and fall to the grass, wrapping the tabs along the sides of the shelter under me and trying to use my feet to pin down its tail. I lie there on the warm grass and feel the hot eastern Washington sun beat against the surface of the shelter. Maybe 90 degrees out, I think. I try to imagine 500 or 600 degrees, and the sound of a fire as it crackles and crawls toward me. I can't. We had been warned that temperatures inside the shelter could easily approach 200 degrees during a burn-over, but that no matter how awful things were inside, what was outside was far worse.

That night we hold relay races in which a team member can start to run toward the finish line only after a preceding team member has passed the "baton" by successfully getting inside a fire shelter.

In between practicing with the shelters and running races with them, we get our first exposure to the tools of the trade. Our first task is learning to handle a Pulaski, the basic firefighting tool, a combination ax and mattock. With a Pulaski, a firefighter can chop small trees or brush with the ax edge, or use the mattock to dig down to bare earth. It is named for forest ranger Edward Pulaski, a participant in one of the most celebrated stories in firefighting lore.

In 1910, Pulaski was a 40-year-old forest ranger in the brand-new Forest Service. He had quit school at 15 to make a living, and had drifted west from his native Ohio, working in mines and the woods before landing a job in 1908 as the Wallace District Ranger in Idaho. On August 20 of that year, Pulaski was leading a crew of 150 men as they attempted to battle one of the dozens of huge fires that had erupted across the West that summer, fires that shaped firefighting policy for decades to come. The men were cutting firelines on the divide between Big Creek of the Coeur d'Alene River and Big Creek of the St. Joe River when the fire mushroomed in size, generating winds so fierce, he later told his wife that men were blown from their horses' saddles. Some of his crew were able to flee, but 42 of them, along with Pulaski, were trapped by the flames as they attempted to head down toward Wallace, about 10 miles away.

Pulaski knew of a mine in the area, and he and his crew ran for its tunnel. Even as they did, one man was killed by a falling tree, another when the fire overran him. Once the crew was inside, Pulaski directed them to lie facedown on the floor as he stood at the mine entrance, using his hat to throw water on embers and hanging wet blankets at the mine entrance. "The men were in a panic of fear, some crying, some praying," he wrote in 1923. "Many of them soon became unconscious from the terrible heat, smoke and fire gas. . . . I, too, finally sank down unconscious. I do not know how long I was in this condition, but it must have been for hours. I remember hearing a man say, 'Come outside, boys, the boss is dead' . . . I replied, 'Like hell he is.'" Pulaski had saved all but five of his men. He paid a price, though—he was badly burned and partially blinded.

The experience, the story goes, convinced Pulaski that firefighters needed a better tool. That winter, he forged a mattock and an ax blade together, each tool facing opposite the other. Mounted atop an ax handle, the "Pulaski," as it became called, could be used to chop roots or trees, or dig a fireline, or dig a hole for planting a seedling. It's a nice tale, and not entirely inaccurate. But according to Stephen Pyne, a fire historian at Arizona State University and the author of several books on fires, similar dual-use tools had been employed during the 1870s. So perhaps Pulaski had seen such a tool and forged a copy that winter. Or it was an idea sufficiently obvious that it made sense to have several inventors. Either way, Pulaski brought the design to the attention of the firefighting community, and by 1920 it was made standard equipment. It was so nearly perfect that it has hardly changed a bit since then.

On the firelines, several other hand tools complement the venerable Pulaski. We also use a "combi," a small, sharp-edged shovel that can be turned at 90 degrees to the handle to scoop earth loosened by the Pulaskis. A big rake, called a McCleod, removes loose pine needles and leaves. Finally, shovels help "hot-spot" a fire, with dirt tossed on the fastest-burning portions. Working caterpillar-style, our team combines with another to dig a fireline about 400 yards up a hill, both for practice and as a backup line in case our practice fires, scheduled for the next day, escape. The day ends with a lesson on gasoline-powered pumps, great tools if water is handy. Our team faced off with another for a pump-starting competition: The winning team's boss got to hose down the losers' boss. Alas, our good-natured crew boss, a 22-year-old University of Washington English major named Aaron Schmidt, got soaked when we flooded our Mark III pump by closing its choke before it had fully warmed up, dousing the spark plug with more gasoline than it could handle.

The next day is the real deal. We are driven into the hills near Lake Chelan, issued tools, and marched up a dirt road to stations spaced about 100 feet apart. There, a sociable fire management officer named Janeen Turvo, who works for the nearby Chelan Ranger District, uses a "drip torch"—a metal can with a spout and a slow-burning wick used to drop a burning mix of diesel fuel and gasoline in order to start a backfire—to set a small brush fire. Once "our" fire is burning briskly, we dig a fireline from a nearby dirt road in case we need an escape route. As we near the blaze, flames lick up four or five feet as they hit a pile of branches and dried needles. I'd always viewed forest fires as big campfires—warm, but not unbearable. From even 20 feet away, however, the heat from our tiny (30 feet diameter) fire is astonishing, rolling over us in waves. Despite the heat and exertion of flailing away with my combi, I'm not sweaty—my sweat dries instantly. At times the wind shifts, blowing hot gray smoke into our faces and forcing me to leave the line occasionally to get out of the choking cloud. This, I think, is *nuts!*

It takes us 30 minutes to encircle the blaze, and when it hits bare earth it promptly dies. Then comes the part TV newscasts don't show: mop-up. After torching unburned areas inside the fireline, we walk into the blackened, still-hot circle, beating out small flames and digging up smoldering embers—an incredibly dirty, frustrating process, one that ends only when we have crawled across the burned area and "cold-trailed" the fire by searching for warm spots with the backs of our bare hands. One lanky teenager named Jeff always lets us know he's found one by leaping up and yelling "Yeow!" After three hours, our fire is officially out. Soot-covered and tired, we hike back to our trucks. Behind us, a few curls of smoke emerge from the blackened earth we supposedly had beaten cold. With disgusted looks on their faces, some veteran firefighters on hand to help out move in to finish off what we haven't.

As we walk back to the vehicles for a ride back to Entiat and a quick written test to cover what we've learned, we step over and around charred logs scattered throughout the meadowlike area where we were working. In the summer of 1994, when the Rat Creek Fire was burning south of here near the trail to the Enchantment Lakes, the Tyee Fire had ripped through our practice site. Miles away I can see hills littered with the blackened sticks of burned tree trunks, waiting for a strong gust of wind to blow them down.

Chapter 4

▲ ▲ ▲ ▲

Thirtymile

By early July I am anxious for some fires to start. A perverse thought, but one that I really can't help. June is pretty quiet, and I've been busy getting my firefighter training and watching smoke-jumpers fall out of airplanes during a visit to the big smokejumper base in McCall, Idaho. But by July 8, a dozen large fires of 500 acres or more are burning in California, Montana, Washington, Oregon, and Colorado. One of the worst fires so far is called the Martis Fire, which starts June 17 in a forested, mountainous area southwest of Reno, Nevada. The fire burns briskly through stands of piñon juniper and ponderosa pine, and within a week torches more than 14,000 acres. But without much else going on, fire managers are able to mount an all-out assault. At the peak of their attack, about 1,000 firefighters are grubbing out a line around the fire, backed up by 61 fire engines, a dozen bulldozers, and a dozen heavy helicopters. The tone for an expensive fire season is set early, with more than $11 million spent on what later in the season will be regarded as a moderate fire. Still, with severe drought persisting, fire managers continue to act wary. Talking to reporters when the Martis Fire is about 75 percent contained, incident commander Pat Murphy sounds a note of caution. "I've been involved in wildland firefighting for nearly 35 years, and I can't remember a summer where I've seen vegetation so dry," Murphy says.

Fire managers also are sweating it out in Oregon and Washington, two states that had largely escaped the big fires of 2000 through dumb luck more than anything else. Although these states are best known nationally for the wet weather experienced in Seattle and Portland, much of their terrain actually is typical of forested areas found as far away as Arizona and New Mexico. The ponderosa pine dominates, and like ponderosa pine forests elsewhere, most of the pine timberland here has become overgrown and dog-haired in the past 50 years. Century-old photos taken around Entiat and other central Washington towns show a mosaic of tree groves and wide grassy meadows. By the 1990s those meadows had filled in with trees.

As July progresses, things begin to pick up. In the Naches Ranger District, a Forest Service station east of Mount Rainier, the fire crew to which Rebecca Welch has been assigned keeps busy clearing brush from parking lots and removing fallen logs that block trails. Then, on July 2, their first real fire breaks out. It is a fairly small, 250-acre burn called the Woodshed Fire; Welch nonetheless finds the experience thrilling. Her crew responds at 2 P.M. to the lightning-set fire, digs line around a portion of its perimeter, then patrols the firelines all night to ensure that glowing embers don't blow over the line and spark new fires. The next evening, Welch excitedly calls her parents in Lancaster, California. "This was the coolest thing!" she tells them. "I want to fight fires forever."

A week later, Washington State sees its first "project fire" of the year, the term used for a fire that eludes initial attack and becomes a multiday effort. In that case, command teams roll in, resources such as helicopters and extra fire engines arrive, and the regional fire center in Portland or even the big fire center in Boise keeps track of things and dispatches extra crews and hardware as needed. This new fire, called Libby South, burns across wooded ridges a few miles from the Columbia River, in the northern part of Washington some 50 miles from the Canadian border.

Libby South is a human-caused fire—although not one that got its start due to a careless match. Instead, a Washington State Department of Natural Resources crew had been assigned to clear debris from a logging road in case fire engines needed access if a fire broke out. The truck's catalytic converter, hot from the drive and probably topping 600 degrees, ignites the grass. Temperatures are well into the 90s and humidity around 10 percent, so the new fire burns hot and fast. By 8 P.M. on July 9 it has ripped through 800 acres of ponderosa pine and Douglas-fir growing in steep, rough terrain, and it keeps going even as night falls and temperatures cool. By the next morning, the Libby South has spread to 1,400 acres. Fire crews from around the eastern half of the state scramble into action. Soon 400 firefighters are digging line around the blaze, supported by two helicopters and 40 fire engines.

Still, it is clear that more firefighters are needed if the fire is to be held; conditions are more like August than July, and fire managers are intent on keeping in check as many early-season fires as possible. Soon after midnight on July 10, phones ring in crew quarters in Naches, Leavenworth, and Lake Wenatchee. Among those awakened is Welch; Rutman already is awake, as he's heard from his boss there is a good chance of action. Rutman even had been taken off duty around the lake and put on the fire crew so he could get some experience.

Leavenworth, where teams are told to meet, is a town of about 2,000 full-time residents and many more part-timers that has managed to survive the loss of its logging industry by capitalizing on its mountainous setting to remake itself as a faux-Bavarian village, complete with signs in a bastardized German ("Wilkommen zu Leavenworth") and thick encrustations of "Alpine chalet"–style architecture along its main street. The effect is appalling, but it's hard not to admire the sheer pluck it took to pull off the transformation from dingy timber town to gingerbread fantasia. And it works— Leavenworth is a tourist mecca, and its streets and downtown parks are jammed from May through October as people pour over Highway 2 from Seattle to attend its Oktoberfest, Sausage Fest, art festivals, and more.

But the streets are dark as the vans from Naches and Lake Wenatchee pull into the complex of clapboard-sided buildings that comprise the Forest Service's Leavenworth District Ranger Station. Not long before they get there, a 26-year-old ex-schoolteacher named Pete Kampen arrives at the station to find two of his crew members: Thom Taylor, a gravel-voiced squad boss from the Leavenworth station, and Nick Dreis, who'd been in Fire Guard School with me. Taylor and Dreis are flaked out in a grassy area in front of the station's main building, trying to get a few quick snatches of sleep. Soon the Naches and Lake Wenatchee groups appear. This disparate group is now known as Northwest Regular Crew No. 6. In command is Ellreese Daniels. His deputy is Kampen, who is training to become a crew boss.

After standing around for a short time in the warm, pine-scented air, the sleepy firefighters pile into two vans and head east on Highway 2 to the town of Wenatchee, past night-shrouded apple and cherry orchards, then north on Highway 97 along the Columbia River. As dawn breaks, they turn west at the base of the Methow

Valley, and not long afterward see a thick haze of smoke rising from the steep, crenellated ridges that climb sharply to the south. The Libby Fire. An acrid smell fills the vans, and the crew members feel a rush of adrenaline that helps clear their bleary eyes. "This is a *real* fire!" Welch says to herself. With her in the vans are several fire-fighters she knows from Naches. Among them: Karen FitzPatrick, a tall, auburn-haired 21-year-old from the eastern Washington town of Yakima. FitzPatrick had been working summers in a coffee stand in Yakima, but had quit that to join a fire crew so she could save money for college. A deeply religious young woman, she also has a built-in nose for fire. A few years previous, she'd jumped over the fence bordering her family's home west of Yakima, dragging a garden hose with her, and largely extinguished a brush fire that erupted on the dry hillside. This at 2 A.M. In silk pajamas. Welch doesn't know FitzPatrick real well, but she has become friends with Jessica Johnson. Johnson is 22, but already an experienced firefighter. She worked as a volunteer for the West Valley Fire Department, just outside of Yakima, where she impressed Deputy Chief Dave Leitch with her moxie and willingness to take on any task. Johnson spent the previous summer working for a state-run fire crew, but thought she'd get more action with a Forest Service outfit.

Welch likes her crew boss—a tough, 30-year-old firefighting veteran named Tom Craven. Craven looks like a tough cookie, with close-cropped hair and broad, sloping shoulders that he used to bull over defenders while playing football at Central Washington University. He took a shot at the NFL, but that didn't pan out, and now he's fighting fires. But he enjoys the work, and the firefighting camaraderie reminds him of life on a football team. His crew members adore him; he's young enough to kid around with them, but old enough to command their respect. Among those ready to do what Craven orders is Devin Weaver, a good-looking kid who just turned

21, with close-cropped brown hair and a big grin that carves deep furrows in his cheeks. He loves the outdoors, loves to hunt, golf, and hike. Weaver is also from Yakima. In the fall he'll be leaving Yakima for Seattle, where he has enrolled at the University of Washington and intends to study engineering. The move has him worried; he's a bit of a homebody, and since the eighth grade has helped work in his father's silk-flower factory. The experience bonded the young Devin deeply to his father, Ken, and Devin does not feel the strong urge to break free of his parents. Plus, like many people in the eastern part of Washington State, Devin thinks of Seattle as both alluring and frightening.

At the Forest Service station in the town of Twisp, the crews meet a fire management officer who has some bad news. They aren't going to Libby. Instead, they're assigned to drive farther west and north and past the old mining town of Winthrop and into a valley cut by the Chewuch River, which flows down from the remote Pasayten Wilderness before emptying into the Methow River and finally joining the mighty Columbia. A campfire has escaped a rough pit made to enclose it. The fire started perhaps as early as two days before, a Saturday, and has burned about five acres. A Canadian fire patrol plane flying reconnaissance over the Libby Fire spotted smoke from this new start the previous afternoon. Local fire managers, although focusing on the growing Libby Fire, are anxious to make sure this new smoke doesn't get far—they know the fuels in the valley are dry and flammable, and fear a big fire if this little smoker gets rolling.

Rutman, along with the others, is deflated by the new assignment. He had anticipated some real fire action. Instead, the little fire up the Chewuch is being described as a mop-up action. Firefighters from the Entiat Interagency Hotshot crew, based in the town where many of us had attended fire classes, have been working the fire all night. With Hotshots—the best wildland firefighters in the West—on the job, that probably means there won't be much left for Northwest Regular Crew No. 6 to do. That could mean hours, if not days, of the worst kind of drudgery—"cold-trailing" a fire to make sure it is cold as stone. For firefighters, the sight of flames shooting into the air is what gets them excited; grubbing around in wet, muddy ash for warm embers is as scintillating as day-old oatmeal. Nick Dreis, meanwhile, frets that a short work assignment might have them back home by the end of the week. Fire crews, once assigned to a blaze, can stay for as long as 14 days before taking a mandatory rest break. During that two-week period, however, they can work long days, with lots of overtime. Once rotated off a fire, a crew goes to the bottom of a list and must wait for its turn to come up again.

By 9 A.M., the combined crew reaches the Chewuch fire, by then labeled the Thirtymile Fire after a mile marker on the road. The crew organizes its gear while Daniels and Kampen meet with Pete Soderquist, the fire management officer for the area, and Marshall Brown, the supervisor of the Entiat crew. The Entiats are beat; they've been at the fire since midnight after getting maybe 30 minutes' rest before they were called into action. The fire started just south of the road and jumped the Chewuch River, burning through stands of lodgepole pine and alder that grew thickly in the damp soil near the river. But the Hotshots worked hard, digging line most of the way around the two or three spot fires that had spread from the origin point. As dawn breaks, it seems the Entiats have whipped the blaze. It has generally fizzled, burning in a half-dozen small spot fires that cover perhaps three acres in a five-acre area. An occasional tree torches with a sizzle, but otherwise, in the cool morning air, the fire mostly smolders harmlessly.

The Entiat Hotshots are a reminder of the Forest Service's longtime machismo when it comes to fire. Founded in the early 1960s as a local fire crew, the Entiats were for years known by the un-PC name of "the Bushmen." Their crew building still has tucked away inside it some less-than-enlightened hand-painted signs from that era. Rechristened the Entiat Hotshots in 1983, the crew has retained something of an aura as a hardworking, hard-partying bunch. Its former supervisors include George Marcott, the fire management officer in the Naches district, and Gabe Jasso, who is scheduled to fly as an aerial observer over the Libby and Thirtymile Fires on July 10. Marshall Brown, a stocky man in his early forties with a thick Fu Manchu mustache, has been the crew superintendent since 1998. During the night, Brown is so confident that his crew can lasso the Thirtymile that he turns down the offer of help from a local fire engine. Still, he also has ordered in two Mark III pumps and 1,500 feet of hose to help the morning crew, and asks the dispatch center to assign a helicopter to work the fire with water buckets after daylight.

The Northwest Regulars are briefed for about 45 minutes on the night's work and what is expected of them that day. Daniels and Kampen have in hand the exact location of the spot fires, each of which has been cataloged by the Entiat crew using global positioning satellite beacons, one of many high-tech tools finding their way into firefighting. The plan is to use the pumps and hoses to wet down and cool the fires, then dig line around them. There are hints the task will prove harder than initially thought, and Soderquist and Eldon Thomas, the assistant fire management officer, call the Libby fire base to check on the availability of additional Hotshot or regular firefighting crews to help out. Unbeknownst to apparently everyone at the fire, the foreman of an engine crew that arrived at the fire before the Hotshots has radioed to the Okanogan Dispatch Center, in a Forest Service office east of the Methow Valley, that the fire has some real potential. "It will grow tonight," he says, according to radio logs. "It will not hold; will hit slope and get larger." Word of this comment is not passed to the newly arriving Northwest Regular Crew No. 6. The Chewuch Valley certainly seems like a place where a big fire could get rolling. In addition to a heavy fuel load, its V-shaped profile makes a natural funnel for wind, as do the numerous side gullies that ripple the valley walls. And if a fire hits the valley's steep, sunbaked sides, covered in grasses that already are well cured and dry, it could climb easily to the tops of the ridges.

By 10:30 A.M., as the newly arrived firefighters complete their briefing, temperatures warm into the 80s. But winds are calm, and from the road there is no sign of the fire, just a pall of smoke over the trees and wafting through the forest. As the Northwest Regulars go to work, a fire investigator pulls up and begins sifting through the fire's ashes. He pulls out a charred hot dog and offers a piece to Rutman. "No, thanks," Rutman, a vegetarian, tells him. The investigator strings yellow crime-scene tape around the illegal campfire.

The crew finds some fallen logs and steps briskly across Chewuch River, about 20 feet across and two or three feet deep. Rutman works as a "swamper" for Dreis, who is running a Stihl 044 chain saw, a powerful but light saw that's popular with fire crews. The sawyer is the highest-ranking job on a squad, one that Dreis has gotten even as a rookie because of his experience running a saw on his parents' property and elsewhere in Leavenworth. His job is to cut a firebreak through the trees and brush, trimming as much as he can to the ground to deprive the approaching fire of fuel that will allow it to climb into the treetops. Rutman trails behind him, throwing what is cut as far from the fireline as possible. Thom Taylor moves in front of the two, scouting the best route where the most can be cut with the least effort while also watching for snags—dead trees—that can fall silently on the firefighters. Behind the vanguard comes most of the rest of the crew, hacking line with their Pulaskis, combis, and shovels. Welch chops away with a combi. Another crew member, Donica Watson, hikes about 100 yards across the valley bottom and posts on a rocky slope as a lookout.

It is hard work. Dreis breathes heavily, and takes time when refueling his Stihl saw to catch his wind and drink some water. Rutman also labors, but focuses on his job. The two say little to each other. Behind them, the rest of the crew is also intent on its work, heads lowered, chopping at the ground and the shrubs. In the warming air the fire is becoming more active. Sometimes they are able to cut line as close as four or five feet away from the flames, which sizzle and pop in yard-high brush, occasionally setting off an entire tree. But at other times they must move 20 or 30 feet away from the growing flames.

Progress is good, but problems crop up. Jodie Tate, a slim young woman who also worked with the Naches crew, has trouble keeping the Mark III pumps running. The pumps are generally reliable, but as we had found in Fire Guard School when trying to win the water-pumping contest, they're vulnerable to flooding. And when the pumps are working, some of the canvas hoses burst, cutting water pressure at the nozzle to a pathetic trickle. On the fireline, meanwhile, heads pop off three Pulaski handles, while on a fourth the handle splits. Pete Kampen, who has assumed responsibility for tactics while Daniels handles the radios, pulls Tate off the pumps and puts her to work digging line in an effort to get as much line punched as possible. The ground is stony and rooty, making digging difficult.

Tate notices how dead branches strewn on the ground crunch loudly underfoot, and begins to wonder if the crew should even be in there. By late morning the thermometer tops 90, and she hears on a radio that the relative humidity is dropping below 10—insanely low. Meanwhile, the fire is rapidly coming to life, burning briskly even through the green alder sprouting in the usually marshy areas where the river ran high during the late spring, when snow melted in the mountains above and came pouring down the rivers. Rutman is surprised at how well the fire burned even through these trees, and estimates the flame heights are consistently hitting three and four feet along the ground. Occasionally the fire hits a pine or fir tree, which bursts into flame with a characteristic *whoosh*, followed by a crackling sound. At around 11 the crew has to scatter when a big pine catches fire, the entire tree disappearing in a tower of fire. But overall those on the fireline feel good about themselves; they'd formed up from three disparate crews and are starting to kick this fire's ass.

The fire, meanwhile, is kicking back, starting new spot fires and threatening to hit the east slope and run uphill. At 12:08 Kampen requests that a bucket-toting helicopter, staged at the smokejumper base in Winthrop, take off and offer support. Twenty minutes later he radios Okanogan Dispatch, requesting extra crews for the fire. The nearest crew is the Entiat Hotshot gang, which has moved to a Forest Service campground two miles downstream and is trying to get some sleep despite the stifling temperatures. The dispatch radio operator raises crew supervisor Brown at about 1, asking him to get his 'Shots back on the line. Brown delays as long as he can; his crew, as well as he himself, have been without sleep for some 24 hours. But at 1:30 he rousts the complaining crew and they drive back up the road to where Northwest Regular Crew No. 6 is laboring as hard as it can.

For about half an hour, the combined crews work flat out, trying to finish a line from the east side of the river to a rocky area near where the valley floor begins to climb. But they can't make it—the fire is burning aggressively toward them, jumping the line in places

and tossing fire bombs out into unburned forest to start new fires.
Kampen and Daniels realize the fire is getting away. They pass the
word to the squad bosses to pull the crews out and retreat to a safe
area on the west side of the Chewuch River, the side the road traverses. "We need to get out of here," Tom Craven tells his crew, suddenly serious, a shift from his usual fun-loving personality. The crew
members trot back to the road, where a broad clearing provides a
buffer from the fire, which now is making short, fast runs into the
cliffy area across the valley.

Here the crew again relaxes, even enjoying the show as the fire
crackles a few hundred yards away. Welch eats lunch, and is taking
a nap when Jason Emhoff gives her a kick. "You're *so* lazy!" he says
teasingly. "Shut UP!" she shoots back. Other crew members fish
bastard files out of their packs and set to work sharpening combis
and Pulaskis worn dull by the tough digging. Dreis sharpens his
chain saw and chats with Leavenworth friends working for the Entiat Hotshots; he hopes to join a Hotshot crew himself after a year
or two learning the business. Matt Rutman has a disposable camera in his pack, and pulls it out to take some pictures. The fire
now forms an orange wall not 100 yards distant, shooting 50 and
60 feet up. To Rutman, it is one of the most awesome sights he has
ever seen.

While the crew eats and rests, the Thirtymile Fire begins to grab
attention up and down the Chewuch Valley. At about 12:40, a helicopter working the Libby Fire is diverted to Thirtymile. It finds a
place in the river to use as a dip site for its big bucket, but is told by
Okanogan Dispatch to hold off—the Chewuch harbors endangered
bull trout, and there are concerns that the bucket might snare some
of the rare fish. The chopper lands at Eight-Mile Camp, a ranch
down the road from the Thirtymile Fire, and its pilot waits for or-

ders. At 2:38, he lifts off and begins dropping water on small spots south of the main fire. The helicopter is joined by a single-engine fixed-wing retardant bomber, although the pilot of the bomber finds the canyon tight for maneuvering, dropping a load on some timber near the Thirtymile Fire that is cut loose high and spread out too much to do any good. Two heavy fixed-wing tankers are called in as well, but by 4, they report, the fire is burning too hotly for them to fight it effectively. What had been a few small spots burning over a few acres is now at 50 acres or more, and growing quickly. At 4:03 P.M., a lookout on First Butte, in one of the many 1930s-era fire lookouts still used, radios that the Thirtymile Fire now is forming its own thunderhead—a giant plume of smoke.

Up the road, at a trailhead, Bruce and Paula Hagemeyer can see the growing smoke. Bruce is a contractor in Thorp, south of the Okanogan area, and the couple had driven up that morning for some camping. Earlier in the day they had passed the crews working the Thirtymile, but the fire seemed under control and no one told them to stop. But now they grow worried, and get into their pickup truck to drive back down the road. There is no other way out but to go back the way they came.

Meanwhile, where the fire crews rest and warily watch the mushrooming fire, Barry George, an assistant fire management officer for the Okanogan National Forest, drives up and gets out to talk with Ellreese Daniels. The fire is burning east of the road; "I'd like to keep it there," George tells Daniels. George also asks Daniels if he wants to remain in charge as incident commander. Daniels does.

A few minutes later, one of the engines patrolling for spot fires farther up the road radios to Daniels's crew, asking for some help. Craven's squad drives up to lend a hand, and is followed a short time later by Taylor's group. Kampen drops off that second group and turns the van around to drive back to the lunch spot. Dreis, peering out the window as he is taken to the new spots, notices a fire engine working a smoking spot that had jumped to the west side of the road. He is surprised to see a spot fire there, and wonders why they didn't stop to make sure it was out.

The fires the crews have been dispatched to help with are about a quarter mile from where they'd stopped for lunch. But there isn't much there—just some warm, wet ash that has largely been drenched by the crews on the engines. Still, Rutman and others begin dutifully digging a fireline around one blackened spot that is so small they can link hands and encircle it. "This is pathetic," Rutman says to himself. The engine and its crew leave, driving south to help downstream. It is 4:20 P.M.

By then the fire is moving quickly. It has crawled out of the damp streamside area into hillside timber cooked dry by the baking heat and Saharan humidity. Once it hits the 50-acre mark, it grows fast, expanding to 100 acres within 15 more minutes, by about 4:15. It runs up the eastern side of the valley almost to the top of the ridge, roaring through ponderosa pine and Douglas-fir and sending up the big plume the First Butte lookout had spotted. As the superheated gases within the fire rise, they pull in air from around the fire in the early stages of a plume-dominated burn. And the radiant heat from the fire increases markedly, preheating shrubs and wood dozens of feet away so that when the flames finally touch them they readily join in. Each step the fire takes makes the next level of intensity easier to reach.

For Northwest Regular Crew No. 6, mistakes are beginning to add up in the same way. Kampen and Daniels had not clearly defined the role each was to take, so communications between themselves and the crew members are confused. And while the dry, hot weather has been impossible to ignore, its influence on the fire's potential has not been fully taken into account. Everyone seemed aware of it, but no one talked about it. Now, in confusion that begins to surround the Thirtymile Fire like a fog, compounded by fatigue, radio static, and bureaucratic inertia, they make the mistake that puts them over an invisible line. By traveling up the road to help with the new spot fires, 14 firefighters have stepped into a trap.

Chapter 5

▲ ▲ ▲ ▲

Trapped

The next day, July 11, my morning copy of the *Seattle Post-Intelligencer* bears this headline: "Four Killed Fighting Raging Wildfire."

An hour later I'm speeding east on Interstate 90, north over Blewett Pass, then past Wenatchee and up the Columbia River. By then, I know a little more from morning television and radio—a fire had blown up, trapping a team of firefighters and killing four. A Forest Service team is heading in from Washington, D.C., to investigate. And now two big fires, not just one, are burning in the Methow Valley area.

As I near Twisp, a small town in the Methow Valley where the attack on the Libby South Fire is based, I see smoke rising from ridges to my left, and helicopters darting here and there dropping buckets of water. I figure that's the fire that caught the crew. In Twisp, inside the ranger station, I run into Ron DeHart, a Forest Service public information officer whom I know. I ask him, stupidly, how things are going. DeHart, an affable man with neatly combed hair that hints at his previous career in television news, puffs his cheeks and blows air out in a *whoosh*. "Rough," he says, shaking his head. "This is unbelievable. It was supposed to be a little mop-up operation." DeHart points out the location of the catastrophe on a large map of the area hanging on a wall. "That's where the Thirtymile Fire is burning," he says. It is the first time I've heard the name—it isn't the Libby South Fire that has caused the tragedy.

TV and newspaper reporters are swarming into the Libby South fire base, a few miles north of Twisp, overwhelming media contacts and then fanning out to talk with the wary firefighters who are beginning to pour into the area from across the Pacific Northwest. The Thirtymile Fire burned nearly 8,000 acres the previous day, and that—combined with the fact it has killed four firefighters—has pushed it to the top of the national priority list. No longer a "mop-up," the full weight of America's firefighting elite is now going to fall upon this fire and kick the living hell out of it. Even then, not 20 hours after the tragedy, a strange air of catharsis is building. There seems to be a determination to punish this inanimate fire for the awful thing it has done.

Gary Locke, the governor of Washington State, flies in on a helicopter that afternoon, tours Libby South fire base, and gets a briefing from fire managers who are focusing now on the Thirtymile. "Everybody is shaken up over the tragedy that occurred," says Locke, a compact, black-haired man, the only governor of Asian descent in the United States, as reporters cluster around. "Firefighters are a very tight-knit group of people. The ones that we lost were really just in the prime of their life, graduates of high school, going off to college, people in college looking forward to studying, getting a degree, and actually joining the fire service or the local fire departments, so this is quite a tragedy." Then he says something I think is utterly inane—something about how he hopes it will rain soon and end the drought, but not on a weekend, when Washington residents want to get out of town and enjoy the outdoors. That night, in a Winthrop hotel room, I'm kept awake by the constant rumble of trucks moving through town en route to Eight-Mile Camp, a rancher's field designated as the fire base for the more than 1,000 firefighters heading this way.

The next morning, at a press briefing in Twisp, we meet Jim Furnish, who has arrived from Washington, D.C., the day before to lead the investigation. Furnish is an instantly credible source in what has been a sea of confusion. Tall, balding, with deeply set eyes under a broad, high forehead, Furnish is deputy chief for the agency. For several days Furnish is consumed with interviewing survivors, holding press conferences, coordinating the work of his investigation team. But a week later, after a short trip home, I am back in Twisp. From the Twisp ranger station I call Furnish, who is holed up in a hotel in Omak along with a dozen other Forest Service fire experts—specialists in fuels, weather, crew management, and fire-suppression tactics—to begin sifting through their reports on the fire. "Come on over," he tells me. "I could use some lunch."

I meet him in a conference room in the basement of the hotel, Its walls plastered with maps and photos of the fire scene, a small TV monitor in the corner playing a taped interview of one of the crew members. We get into my Subaru wagon and drive into town, to a quiet restaurant called the Breadline Café that serves a surprisingly cosmopolitan array of salads and sandwiches for such a remote place. It's surprising as well to notice the narrow gap between fortune and failure. Winthrop, like Omak a onetime logging and mining center, is flourishing under a crush of tourists. Omak, just one mountain ridge farther east, is a dusty, hard-bitten town, with hardly a hotel in sight.

Furnish is a career Forest Service guy who has worked in a half-dozen national forests, held desk jobs and field jobs, and was a self-admitted veteran of the "old" Forest Service that saw its job as pulling as many logs out of the national forests as possible. In recent years, however, he's had a change of heart, even writing an article for *Forest Magazine,* the house organ for the Eugene, Oregon–based Forest Service Employees for Environmental Ethics, an organization composed of current and former agency employees who take a dim view of its common forestry practices. He senses that his assignment to head the investigation is almost ordained, a chance to bring to bear his decades of experience. "It seems fitting that I do this now," he says to me as we drive under a leaden overcast, the remnants of a wet front that had largely stalled the Thirtymile Fire a few days before. "I think I can bring some perspective to this investigation. Plus, I'm retiring soon, so I feel like I can speak my mind."

The story that I hear from Furnish, and later from a number of those who fought the Thirtymile Fire, resonates throughout the summer of 2001. It is a story of a tragic fiasco, one that recalls past firefighting disasters but also breaks new ground for its near-absurdity. Four young people should not have died; no one should have died. But the outcome of the Thirtymile Fire proves to be symptomatic of serious problems in the nation's firefighting effort. At Thirtymile, the work-hard-have-fun mentality that was so prevalent at Fire Guard School a few weeks earlier would prove disastrous. So, too, would the inexperience of many of the firefighters battling the blaze.

And, of course, the ponderosa pine plays a role. The Chewuch Valley, where the Thirtymile Fire had burned a week before I had lunch with Furnish, once was likely a near-classic ponderosa forest. But by July of 2001 few fires have burned there for many decades.

The valley floor is thickly carpeted with trees and brush, a perfect place for a big fire. Ponderosa pine still grow there, but in addition Douglas-fir, lodgepole pine, and subalpine fir have made an appearance. Lodgepole pine is particularly prone to "stand-replacing" fires—burns that by natural design wipe out nearly everything in place and start with a clean slate. Subalpine fir, meanwhile, is notorious among fire-behavior experts for its tendency to throw off embers that can start spot fires well in front of the main fire. Moreover, no major fires have burned through the Chewuch since the 1930s, with nearly all fires in the area since then capped at around 10 acres.

That volatile mix of foliage had combined with the blazing heat and low humidity of early July to turn the Thirtymile into a roaring blaze. The signs are there that morning as the crews work to contain the fire. But by midafternoon, with those clues largely ignored, Northwest Regular Crew No. 6 can do little to correct their mistakes.

As one crew roars up the road to help with a small spot fire, Kampen's crew suddenly finds itself pelted with embers. The fire's plume is soaring thousands of feet in the air, hurling bits of burned trees upward until gravity finally overcomes the lift of the hot air. And it has jumped the road, burning in brush and trees on the west side of the narrow gravel track. Kampen grabs his radio. "Ellreese, I'm getting spotting across the road," he shouts. Daniels can see the same. Kampen radios again: "Ellreese, we're getting out now!" Kampen's crew scrambles into a van and roars down the road as flames lick across it. Some crew members hold their hard hats to their faces to shield themselves from the heat.

A bare 400 yards north of Kampen's retreating van, Daniels and his crew make their own bid for an escape. "Double time!" Daniels hollers to his crew as they sprint for the van. Ten crew members pile into it, and with Daniels at the wheel it begins speeding out. Not everyone can fit inside, so Tom Craven, Rebecca Welch, Beau Clark, and Jason Emhoff jog along the side of the road. The van pulls ahead of the running firefighters as it rounds a corner, and Daniels slams on the brakes in disbelief. Just 100 feet or so in front of them, a wall of orange flame some 20 feet tall blocks their path. The fire has sprung its trap.

Daniels frantically turns the van around on the narrow road, backward, then forward, each time cranking the wheel around a little more for what to some in the van feel is an eternity. Rutman, pressed against a window, watches aghast as the fast-moving flames bear down on the van. He wonders if they will catch the vehicle before it turns around. But Daniels gets the truck turned and speeds north, away from the fire. He comes to the four jogging firefighters and orders them inside. They pile into the van in a jumble of arms and legs and packs and helmets. Those who had seen the firewall tell them about what is ahead. "This sucks," Jessica Johnson mutters to Welch.

The van speeds back upstream, past the spot fire that drew the crew away from their escape route. Daniels had driven up the road earlier on a scouting trip. Now he talks via radio with Gabe Jasso, who is flying overhead as a fire lookout, about possible sites to stop. He drives past three candidates, then settles on a fourth that is about a mile from the original fire. There, the van rounds a gentle bend in the road and comes to a halt. On the east side of the road— the right side to the approaching van—the Chewuch River has cut an old channel adjacent to the road, separated from the main river by a sandbar. On the west side the canyon climbs steeply upward through a jumble of boulders and cliffs, cresting out some 3,300 feet above the road.

The firefighters get out of the van. Downstream, they see a feathery cloud of smoke rising above the trees. But this place looks safe, with only a few scattered trees, a big boulder field, and the reassuring presence of water.

On the other side of the rising pillar of smoke, Marshall Brown, Pete Kampen, and their crew members watch in horror as the Thirtymile Fire erupts into its full fury. Within minutes a column of dirty brown smoke has punched 10,000 feet into the sky, and flames shoot perhaps 150 feet above the treetops just a stone's throw from their parked vehicles. It is 5 P.M. Back in the little town of Winthrop, some 25 miles away, some people hear a loud, booming roar from the direction of the fire. They also see the smoke column. Curiously, it has split into two parts, like the horns of a steer, as it curls up into the stratosphere.

Rutman lights a cigarette and stands on the road, uncertain about what to do. Daniels talks occasionally by radio with Gabe Jasso, then tells everyone to stay calm. A few minutes later, Rutman takes out a small paper journal he'd purchased, and begins writing in it: "Blackened pine and fir needles are falling on our heads," he scribbles, in a shaky hand. Dreis asks Daniels if he should get his shelter out. "If it will make you feel better," Daniels tells him. Dreis pats the canvas pouch that holds his shelter, but leaves it on his belt. Still, he begins to look around for a good place to deploy his silvery little tent.

The spot where the crew had stopped looks good to them, too, with water nearby and large rocky areas where it looks as if a fire might not burn. The Thirtymile Fire is burning mainly on the valley's east side, opposite where the crew has stopped. With luck, crew boss Daniels hopes, the fire will keep burning on that side of the valley, looping around his team's position rather than running over it.

In any event, with few options at the time it looks like a good spot to Daniels, and Gabe Jasso, flying in an aerial spotter plane overhead, concurs. The crew is out of the van now, and firefighters mill around on the road, with some clambering up into a boulder-strewn area next to the road, on its west side. Rutman snaps a picture with a disposable camera he had in his pack. Through the viewfinder, he sees Thom Taylor smoking a cigarette. Karen FitzPatrick grins as she holds a camera up to snap a photo of herself and the smoke. Another member of the Yakima bunch, 21-year-old Jason Emhoff, walks away from a knot of people, his hands bare. It is 5 P.M. By then the insignificant "mop-up" fire to which the crew had been assigned has grown from three or four acres, to 50, to 500, and it is expanding at an almost exponential rate. Every foot of blazing fire front that the fire adds puts it within that much more dry fuel that its hot breath quickly ignites, and which then goes searching for other dried grass or brush or pine boughs it can enlist to the cause.

Suddenly, a white pickup zooms down the road from the north and crunches to a halt on the dry gravel. Paula and Bruce Hagemeyer, wearing shorts and T-shirts, get out of their truck and stand around for a few minutes, not quite sure what to say to the firefighters. Karen FitzPatrick—always a gregarious young woman—walks over to talk with them. Someone else asks them where the road went. "It's a dead end," comes the answer. Some of the firefighters—Nick Dreis, for instance, and Daniels—already know that. But others do not, and assume they've stopped where they have simply because it is a safe place. Some begin to panic. Rebecca Welch now is terrified. To calm herself, she walks up into the boulders at the base of a long, rocky slope that extends far above the firefighters. There, FitzPatrick has gone to sit after talking with the Hagemeyers, joining Jessica Johnson, Jason Emhoff, and Devin Weaver. Welch also seeks reassurance from Craven. "What should we be doing?" she asks. "Should we get our shelters out?"

"Relax, Rebecca," Craven tells her. "Nothing is going to happen."

Firefighters on the road into Chewuch River canyon await the arrival of the Thirtymile Fire, the smoke from which is highlighted by the sun. Karen FitzPatrick, on the lower-right taking a self-portrait, was among the four who did not survive the fire. (MATTHEW RUTMAN)

Despite an air of foreboding, some of the firefighters even seem to be enjoying themselves. "This is the greatest thing!" FitzPatrick yells to Welch. But Welch is mentally rehearsing the drill for deploying her fire shelter, even though no one has suggested it as a possibility. So too is Dreis, a woods-savvy young man who enjoyed the whole range of outdoor activities available in the idyllic mountain environment of his hometown of Leavenworth. He doesn't like the looks of the boulder field above the road—he notices pine needles and woody debris between the boulders, and doubts his fire shelter can form a good seal against hot gasses over the uneven surface. A damp sandbar looks promising. But it is close to a thick stand of trees, and he knows from his fire classes that it is unwise to place a damp towel over your face in a fire, as the steam it would give off holds more heat than dry air. So he worries that the sandbar might literally poach him to death, if it came to that. "No," he says to himself. "The road is the place to be." The crew has been at the stopping point for about 20 minutes now, and despite hopes the fire will bypass them, it's clearly visible down the road to the south. The firefighters can hear it burning, and they see a tower of smoke that blots out the sun.

Rutman continues to write in a notepad. It distracts him from the growing feeling of danger, and he thinks it will make interesting reading later. "The roar of the fire is getting louder, louder," he writes. "The column twisting, several fires joined, it sounds like a tidal wave is coming our way. The sun is a bloody red, the smoke dark and high." Welch asks someone for the time, hoping it is late enough in the day for the temperature to cool, and the fire to subside as it does. But it is only around five, and the temperature remains well over 90.

After the fire crew flees up the road, the blaze begins to grow even more rapidly, cresting the ridge on the eastern side of the Chewuch

and moving upstream in a solid wall of flame. A column of superheated air rises above the fire, sucking in air from adjoining areas to
replace it and driving winds of more than 70 miles per hour. The fire
needs a bit less than an hour to move from its starting point to
where the 14 firefighters and two civilians await it.

At exactly 5:24 P.M., it reaches them.

At first, Welch thinks it is raining. Moments before, she had
moved away from the group of firefighters sitting on rocks just above
the parked van, and she now is on the road. There, she feels something suddenly pelting her hard hat. But instead of rain, it is a
shower of glowing embers that is pouring down on her and the other
firefighters. Daniels, alarmed, shouts for the firefighters to pull out
their fire shelters and use them like an umbrella to ward off the embers, which now have changed from charred fragments to bright orange firebrands. He still thinks that the fire will pass around their
position, leaving them largely untouched. But the flames are clearly
visible across the river, perhaps 200 feet distant. Entire trees are
torching in seconds, with flames shooting 100 feet or more into the
air. Rutman takes one more picture with his disposable camera, of a
solid sheet of flame against which a few flaming trees stand profiled.
Then he grabs his fire shelter and climbs inside, falling with it on
the side of the road and pulling it over his head. Dreis does the
same. As Dreis wraps the shelter around him, he turns to face the
flames, and their hot draft opens the shelter like a parachute. *Great,*
he thinks, *that really helps.* But then, as he falls on the road, he realizes he also has trapped hot air and smoke inside the shelter. *That
was smart,* he says to himself.

For a moment, those still outside their shelters believe the blaze
will run past them on the opposite side of the river, leaving them untouched. But it is burning diagonally across the valley floor, and as
they watch the train of fire across the river, its caboose charges

around the slight bend in the road that had partially obscured the firefighters' view of the approaching flames, falling upon them with a roar like a 747 and a shocking blast of hot wind. Some firefighters think they hear an order to deploy, but others aren't certain. Instead, instinct takes over and they yank the silvery cocoons from their plastic cases. The Hagemeyers, who have changed out of their shorts and T-shirts into blue jeans and long-sleeved shirts, yell frantically for help. Welch sees them, and beckons them under her shelter. The shelters are designed for one person—two in a pinch. Somehow Welch and the Hagemeyers all squeeze in. "Hold the sides of it down," she tells them. "And stay calm!" She hears Daniels on his radio, telling Jasso that the firefighters are in their shelters but that all are safe.

But Welch begins to doubt that they are. She feels the fire's heat, like the door of an oven opening, through the shelter's thin wall. Trees crackle with flame and crash to the ground, while hurricane-like winds pluck at the shelter. Welch prays—prays to die quickly, before she can feel herself burn to death. Prays for her parents and her twin sister and her brother, that they will not be devastated by her death. Prays for friends she will miss. Behind her, Paula Hagemeyer begins to hyperventilate, screaming, "I can't breathe!" She and Bruce flee the shelter. Welch, on the verge of panic herself, frantically pulls the flapping fabric back in place, realizing that without it she could die in seconds. In that second or two, the fire scorches Welch's skin through her Nomex clothing, blistering her arms and legs. Moments later, the Hagemeyers dive back inside— as awful as it is inside the shelter, things are much worse outside.

Near Welch, Dreis also huddles in his shelter. He presses his face to the hard road, trying to breathe cooler air through the dirt and gravel. He looks up at the shelter walls, and can see through tiny holes in its aluminum coating a fiery orange constellation of light. But he says to himself, *If this is my time to go, it's cool. I've trav-eled a lot—to Fiji, Australia, New Zealand, and more—and had a pretty good life.* Then he feels something moving at his feet— another firefighter. He gives a kick and yells, "Who's that?" It is Beau Clark, a member of the Naches crew. "How you doin', man?" Dreis yells. "I feel like a baked potato," comes the reply.

Rutman at first crouches inside on his knees, but that forces his head off the ground and into hot air at the top of the shelter. So he flattens out and presses his face against the earth. He hears screams from nearby, and for a moment he senses that death has entered his shelter. "You've got the wrong guy!" he yells. In his pocket he has a Leatherman tool—a sort of folding hardware store with blades, tools, and pliers—and takes that out, using it to dig a hole in the ground and breathe the cooler air he finds there.

Up the slope from the road, Thom Taylor huddles in his shelter, where he had been forced to crawl when flames cut off his effort to reach the road. For several minutes flames and wind buffet the shelter. When they diminish a little, he scrambles out from under it, sprints across the road, and dives into the river. "Get in the wa-ter!" he yells. "Get into the river." Welch, Dreis, and others hear him calling from the water, and they also seek refuge in the water, clam-bering over a burning log and dragging their shelters with them. Dreis catches his thumb in a crevice of the log, burning it, then dives into the water and rearranges the shelter over him. He notices that the surface of the water is covered with blackened pine nee-dles. Welch gives her shelter to the Hagemeyers and shares one with Rutman. The water is ice cold, and everyone in the water al-most instantly begins to go hypothermic. Welch and Rutman hug each other for warmth and talk about whatever comes to mind—a favorite book, the hazard pay they'll get. Welch suddenly feels pain on her legs and arms and realizes that the fire has burned her. The firefighters shout to one another, trying to take a head count. But with three crews mixed together, no one is certain who is there and who is not. It seems, though, that a few people aren't answering who should be.

And then the fire is gone, roaring upstream. A heavy smell of wood smoke lingers in the fire-baked air. After about fifteen minutes the firefighters creep out of the river onto the sandbar, then up to the road. The horn from the Hagemeyers' pickup truck blares loudly. Then the truck's tires begin to explode, startling the already shocked firefighters. "You got much gas in that thing?" Dreis asks the Hagemeyers. "The tank's full," Bruce tells him. Dreis looks at the truck warily. Charred trees lie around them like Pick Up sticks, including one that crashes down just a few feet away from where Dreis had been standing in the river.

At around 6 P.M., some of the Entiat Hotshots, along with Pete Kampen, reach the burn-over site. Those who had endured the burn-over gather around Kampen, who again tries to take a head count. "Where are the Naches folks?" he asks. Dreis had seen some shelters up in the boulder field, and points toward them. Kampen, along with Marshall Brown from the Hotshots, sprints toward the shelters. But heat radiating off the boulders in scorching waves drives them back. Some of the shelters flutter in the wind, and Dreis knows that no one is holding them down.

Dreis walks over to the van and gets inside. There he finds Jason Emhoff, and gives him a hug. Emhoff had also been in the boulder field. But he had forgotten to wear his gloves, and had badly burned his hands trying to hold the shelter in place. He'd hidden from the flames behind a large boulder, then run to the road and climbed into the crew van. The water looked tempting, but he knew from training as an emergency medical technician that the cold water could make treating his burns more difficult. Now he sat in the van, holding his scorched hands in front of him, their tendons exposed by the fire.

Welch is burned along her legs. Paula Hagemeyer has burned her hand. Other crew members have minor burns, and a few have sucked in smoke. As the crew gets ready to climb into the van—which, miraculously, is almost intact—Rutman hears someone ask Kampen about the people on the rocky slope. "It's too hot," Kampen replies. "We can't get to them." Rutman realizes they are dead. Tom Craven, Jessica Johnson, Karen FitzPatrick, and Devin Weaver lie inside or sprawled next to their shelters. The survivors get into the van, and with Dreis at the wheel, head down to where they'd eaten lunch a few hours before. Dreis is desperate to be out of there, driving so fast that some crew members plead with him to slow down. He ignores them.

The next hours are a blur of pain and tears and relief. Emhoff is flown to Seattle's Harborview Medical Center, where one hand is eventually stitched inside his abdomen in a radical effort to ensure that fat tissue will form around the exposed muscles and tendons. More firefighters come up the road, and the Thirtymile survivors sense eyes are being averted from them. Few people talk with them, or offer any help changing into dry clothes. Kampen gathers the crew and tells them to write down all they can remember about the event, something investigators will find invaluable with memories so fresh. Some crew members cry; others stand or sit quietly next to one another. After four hours the Okanogan County police and coroner arrive, and late that night the crew is driven into Winthrop and put up at a local Best Western hotel. Some deli trays of food arrive, and a few of them try to pick at the sliced meat and cheese. Welch finds a telephone and calls her father. "Hey, Rebecca, what's up?" he asks, surprised at the late-night call. "Dad . . . ," she answers, and begins to sob.

A few hours later, just before dawn, cars begin to pull up outside of a small group of homes in Yakima. At about 3:45, one stops in front of the home of John and Kathie FitzPatrick. Dave Leitch, deputy chief for the West Valley Fire Department in Yakima, and George Marcott, the fire management officer for the Naches Ranger District, walk up to the door and ring the doorbell. When Kathie answers, the two men apologize for the intrusion and ask if they can talk to both FitzPatricks. As John and Kathie get dressed, Kathie says to her husband: "You know why they're here." John nods; he had seen television news earlier about four missing firefighters. And Kathie has been trying to call Karen on her cell phone all afternoon and into the evening, with no answer. The couple goes downstairs, and in a dimly lighted kitchen hear the news about their daughter, the daughter who in her silk pajamas once jumped over the fence with a garden hose to fight a fire the local fire department couldn't reach. Similar scenes are played out in the homes of Ken and Barbara Weaver, of Jody Gray, Jessica's mother, and of Evelyn Craven, who had an infant son.

The following Tuesday, July 24, the family members of the four dead firefighters, now partners in grief, walk down the center aisle of Yakima's Sun Dome, a convention and exhibition hall, and take their seats as hundreds of firefighters file in behind them for a memorial service. The funerals have already been held, and now it is the firefighters' turn to say goodbye. Before the ceremony, the families and scores of fire engines had weaved through downtown Yakima in a six-mile-long parade made up of more than 300 firefighting vehicles, driving slowly through streets thinly lined with well-wishers. Outside the humpbacked Sun Dome, teams of firefighters line up in the bright midday sun, then walk quietly into the vast building to take their place in rows of folding chairs on the dome floor. I see Rutman in a line of firefighters and recognize him from Guard School. But I don't yet know he has been in the blow-over, and almost walk over to slap him on the arm and see how he is. Fortunately, someone else I know distracts me, and when I turn around his crew is gone.

The next two hours are both moving and maudlin. On a stage at the building's far end stand four large portraits of the dead firefighters, boots, helmet, and Pulaski neatly arranged beneath each. There is the requisite rendition of "Amazing Grace" on bagpipes, along with a far more eloquent rendition of "Guide Me, O Thou Great Jehovah," a Welsh hymn.

"Open now the crystal fountain,
Whence the healing stream doth flow;
Let the fire and cloudy pillar
Lead me all my journey through."

A Forest Service color guard, nattily attired in flat-brimmed hats and dark-olive uniforms, performs a slow, elaborate close-order drill with chrome-plated Pulaskis. Two cabinet members, Agriculture Secretary Ann Veneman and Interior Secretary Gale Norton, attend, along with Dale Bosworth, then chief of the Forest Service. The governor of Washington, Gary Locke, gives a speech that repeatedly emphasizes that the four were "heroes," neglecting the fact that three of them, at least, were no more than kids looking for a fun summer job when they signed up to fight fires. The fourth was just trying to make a buck for his wife and baby, who sit near the front row of the building in a pool of anguish that laps around the families of the four and is palpable 15 rows up, where I sit in the darkened corners of the Sun Dome.

While many of the firefighter-at-rest encomiums ring false, as if the four had charged willingly into the teeth of this onrushing beast, it is a firefighter who also hits the one perfectly pitched note. Dave Leitch, chief of the West Valley Fire District in the Yakima Valley, had been Jessica Johnson's boss when she had volunteered in his department, had worked with Craven, and had taught firefighting classes for Weaver and Johnson weeks before their assignment to the Thirtymile Fire. He'd also had the task of telling the FitzPatricks about the fate of their daughter on that awful night. In contrast to the polished politicians who spoke, Leitch, a mustached man with thinning blond hair, is obviously unaccustomed to speaking before a crowd of 3,000. But his words need no buffing. "We are an extended family, all with the last name 'firefighter,'" he says, in a rushed, soft voice. "We have four new lookouts watching out for us."

No one in the firefighters' family has an easy time of it, as Locke steps down from the stage to kneel before each family and say whatever he can. But it is particularly painful for the FitzPatricks. A mere month before, they had watched Karen walk the same stage, receiving her high school diploma. Now, from Locke, they receive a folded American flag. Months later, it still sits in their living room, amid pictures of Karen and mementoes from her short summer as a firefighter.

By then the Thirtymile Fire has been declared "contained." Its final tally in addition to four dead: 9,300 acres burned, $4,634,900 spent, no structures lost. Almost all of its damage had occurred on that one day, July 10. It largely halted its headlong rush that night, and a few days later the first of a series of rainstorms pelted it with water. By the day of the memorial, most of the firefighters who had been at Thirtymile are en route to other fires.

Jim Furnish, meanwhile, has begun to assemble the report on the tragedy's cause. He is deeply troubled by the accident. Four lives have been lost, of course, four employees of the Forest Service in which he's loyally spent his career. But something about how the four died gets to him. He doesn't like what he's learned in interviews with firefighters and after touring the site—the fact that the entire crew allowed itself to be outflanked by the fire; the lack of preparation for the blow-over, with firefighters struggling to unfurl fire shelters even as a mass of flame curled around the rocky corner and slammed down on them; the way the team apparently broke up along home-crew lines, resulting in the Naches crew taking the worst hit from the fire while the others survived, simply, it seemed, because they'd decided to sit together rather than stand among strangers. "We try to train people to walk away from a fire that poses a threat," he says to me that day we have lunch, as we walk back to my car. "But it can be hard to get people to do that. How do you really train someone to respect danger?"

And there is something else. Within hours of the fire, purple ribbons had begun to pop up on firefighters' shirts, and particularly on the uniforms of office-based Forest Service employees in Twisp and Winthrop. They are a variation on the yellow ribbon—that badge of victimhood that has become so entwined in our culture's view of tragedy and loss. Furnish has of course seen the ribbons—they are unavoidable—and does not seem to approve of their message. "It's an interesting didactic," he says, choosing his words carefully. "It's great that we can pull together at a time like this, but we need to make a commitment: No more purple ribbons."

Chapter 6

▲ ▲ ▲ ▲

Fire Lab

Thirtymile, of course, is not the first tragedy to hit the ranks of wildland firefighters. Over the years hundreds of firefighters have died while battling forest and range fires—244 just since 1986. Most perish from auto or aircraft accidents around a fire, or from heart attacks or other health problems exacerbated by the effort and stress. But many die an awful death that writer Norman Maclean described as like dying three times. "First," Maclean wrote, "considerably ahead of the fire, you reach the verge of death in your boots and your legs; next, as you fail, you sink back in the region of strange gases and red and blue darts where there is no oxygen and here you die in your lungs; then you sink into the main fire that consumes, and if you are a good Catholic about all that remains of you is your cross."

Maclean typed that line sometime during the 1980s, while working on his book *Young Men and Fire.* The book, a meditation on aging, fire, life and death, has as its core the tragic tale of a fire that to this day resonates through the firefighting ranks: Mann Gulch.

The year was 1949, a time when the Forest Service was rapidly ramping up its firefighting capabilities. Foremost in its plans for a new, fire-free West was its pride and joy: the smokejumping corps. This pioneering force had begun to emerge a decade earlier, in 1939. That October, the Parachute Jumping Experiment got its start in the town of Winthrop, Washington, still the site of a smokejumping base. Three brothers—Frank, Virgil, and Chester Derry—were among the first six guinea pigs for the experiments, which were bankrolled in part by the chief contractor for the tests, the Eagle Parachute Company. Frank Derry, Eagle's representative in Los Angeles, dragooned his brothers into the fire-jumping test (the word "smokejumper" wasn't coined until later) with the lure of money. "He promised me $500 if I'd make the jumps with him," Virgil told an interviewer years later. "That looked awfully good, because I was making $150 to $200 a month driving a laundry truck, and there wasn't any excitement in that."

In 1940 the Forest Service committed more money to the nascent program and hired 13 men to form the first official smokejumper crews. Some had taken part in the Parachute Jumping Experiment; for others, their training session consisted not only of their first parachute jumps but of their first flights in an airplane. There was an interested observer: a U.S. Army major named William Lee. Within a few years Lee took the techniques he saw the Forest Service perfect and put them to use as he established an airborne fighting corps for the U.S. Army, which was to have its combat debut in the predawn hours of June 6, 1944, dropping behind the Normandy beaches in the great D day assault on Nazi Germany.

That summer of 1940, six smokejumpers were based at Winthrop and seven were located at Moose Creek Ranger Station in Idaho. On July 12 two smokejumpers from Moose Creek made the project's first operational fire jump, on a fire in the Nez Percé National

Forest of Idaho. Eight more fires were jumped in northwestern states before winter put an end to the 1940 fire season. But the test was deemed a success. They had, it was believed, saved $30,000 when compared to slower-moving, ground-based forces.

Ten years later more than 200 smokejumpers were based in Missoula, Montana; McCall, Idaho; and Cave Junction, Oregon. Many were World War II vets, tough cookies and slow to scare. They flew in war-surplus C-47s, or in some cases prewar Ford Tri-Motors. Their success rate was fabulous—a single "stick" of a dozen smokejumpers nearly always had a fire out by the day after a landing. The crews were confident, if not cocky. But they also were surprisingly ignorant as to the true nature of their adversary. Fires those days tended to be small, a few acres in size, and easily caught with the Pulaskis and shovels the smokejumpers took with them through the C-47's door.

On August 4, 1949, a blazingly hot day in central Montana, a lightning storm swept over a stretch of terrain between the Great Plains and the Rocky Mountains. This is an area known as the Gates of the Mountains, where steep gullies and draws climb up from the Missouri River. Lewis and Clark passed up the Missouri here in April of 1805.

Several of the fires set by the lightning were put out that night. But on the morning of the fifth, another was spotted, burning along a wooded ridge between Mann Gulch and Meriwether Canyon. The fire was called in shortly before noon, and by 4 P.M. a DC-3 carrying 15 smokejumpers from Missoula circled overhead. The jumpers fluttered to earth in four groups. On the ground, they met up with a ranger who had hiked up from the guard station at the foot of Meriwether Canyon, a popular stop for boating tourists who wanted to see where Lewis and Clark had once camped on their famous journey.

At the time the fire was about 90 acres in size, burning briskly along a ridge just south of the drop zone, and a little above them as the 16 hiked down Mann Gulch toward the Missouri River. The crew's foreman, Wagner Dodge, wanted to reach the safety of the river, hook below the fire, and start digging a fireline in an area that was not burning too fiercely. It was a hot day, probably above 100 degrees in the gulch, the winds shifting and erratic. Still, most of those in the crew figured they'd have the fire encircled the next day, and would be on their way back to Missoula for a cold beer.

At about 5:30, less than two hours after the smokejumpers had landed, Dodge saw trouble: The fire had leapt from the ridge down into the gulch some 200 yards in front of the crew, and black smoke now was billowing over a small ridge between his team and the Missouri River. Dodge gave the order to reverse direction, and the firefighters turned and headed back up the gulch. They were relatively fresh, aside from the ranger who had joined the group, but it was steep going over rough, rocky terrain. The fire, now burning uphill at a ferocious pace through dry, waist-high cheatgrass and thickets of ponderosa pine and Douglas-fir, gained rapidly on the fleeing crew. At 5:43, Dodge gave the order to the crew to drop their packs and heavy tools. Minutes later the onrushing fire had closed to less than 50 yards from the now-desperate crew, which was clawing its way up slopes so steep that one smokejumper was later found to have stumbled and broken his leg. Dodge stopped, pulled out a book of paper matches, and set a fire at his feet. He tried to get the other crew members to stay with him, but one was heard to say, "To hell with that," and they continued fleeing. After a few seconds, Dodge stepped into the circle of blackened grass left by the fire he had set, lay facedown in the hot ashes, and waited for the main fire to pass overhead.

He was to live. So would two others, Robert Sallee and Walter

Rumsey, tough young men and good friends, who scrambled up the hillside to a barrier of rimrock, found a crevice to shimmy through, and staggered over the hilltop onto a broad slope of rock scree as the fire snapped at their heels and burned down either side of their stony refuge. Two others, Joseph Sylvia and William Hellman, survived the fire but were terribly burned and died the next day in a Missoula hospital. The others lay scattered along the upper reaches of Mann Gulch, each caught by a fire they could not possibly outrun.

The Mann Gulch fire shocked the smokejumping and firefighting community. But some good came of it—over the years, new safety regulations that grew out of the Mann Gulch fire tried to formalize how firefighters should behave in the face of a fire. These became the "standard fire orders," the 10 guidelines I learned in Fire Guard School.

Another monument to those dead, of sorts, is the Fire Sciences Lab in Missoula, where I spent considerable time in 2001. In the wake of the Mann Gulch disaster, Forest Service fire managers realized that their knowledge of what took place in a wildfire and what could lead 13 of the firefighting world's aces to be run down like rabbits by a fox was woefully deficient. One of those keenly interested in better understanding the Mann Gulch Fire was Harry Gisborne, universally regarded as the father of fire science. Gisborne was born in 1893 into a Vermont lumber family and took an interest in forestry. He graduated from the University of Michigan's School of Forestry in 1917—the Midwest back then was the center of the national timber industry—and by 1922 had been assigned to one of the Forest Service's first experimental forests, the Priest River Experimental Forest in Idaho. Fire fascinated Gisborne from the start, and he set about learning all he could about it. An inveterate tinkerer, Gisborne developed or used a wide array of then cutting-edge equipment, items such as the Asman aspiration psychrometer (for measuring relative humidity), a visibility meter, the anemohygrograph (which measured moisture levels in wood and the surrounding air), the double tripod heliograph (for sending messages with Morse code through mirrors reflecting the sun), and the blinkometer, an electrical gadget that used current to measure how much moisture was in a log. By the 1930s he had developed the first reasonably accurate fire danger readings, and his penchant for rushing to new fires to study their behavior and the conditions that caused them was renowned.

The Mann Gulch Fire horrified Gisborne but also solidified his determination to learn ways to prevent its repeat. Then 56, Gisborne was suffering from a heart condition, but persisted in hiking the terrain where Wag Dodge had set his backfire, and Walter Rumsey and Robert Sallee had made their mad dash to safety, where the others had perished. On November 9, 1949, he was hiking across the Mann site when he stopped to rest. "I made it good," he told his hiking companion. "My legs might ache a little tomorrow, though." With that, he closed his eyes and died of a heart attack.

A painted portrait of Gisborne, depicting an intense, sharp-featured man with deep-set eyes, a neatly trimmed mustache, and graying hair combed back from a wide forehead, graces the landing on a flight of stairs at the Fire Sciences Lab. It's fitting that it does; Gisborne's influential legacy was instrumental in building the lab, completed in 1968. Its two-story main wing held offices and laboratories for the ranks of new fire scientists working there. But its crown jewel was its 88-foot-tall burn tower, where researchers sheltered behind thick glass windows could safely set and study fires. The tower also was equipped with two wind tunnels, used to measure the speed at which fire burns under different airflow conditions. For the first time, forest fire researchers could place their subject under a figurative microscope and study fires that nearly matched their wild cousins.

In key ways the lab made good on its implied commitment to Gisborne and the 13 who died in Mann Gulch. During the 1970s, lab researcher Richard Rothermel carefully studied the fatal fire. He concluded that the Missouri River at the foot of Mann Gulch was prone to stiff southerly winds, winds that perhaps were blowing up to 40 miles per hour as Dodge's crew hiked downhill. The gulch in turn scooped up these winds, which accelerated in the narrow canyon and were further sucked uphill by hot air rising off the sun-baked ridgetops. Once the fire jumped off the ridge into the bottom of the gulch, probably when embers and burning debris were blown off the ridgetop, the firefighters were doomed. Indeed, with the wind at its back and dry fuel at its feet, the fire needed less than 15 minutes to make up the 200-yard gap between the men and the fire when they turned around and began their fateful race. With the wind in its favor, the fire may not even have needed to catch the smokejumpers. It may simply have lofted embers that fell in front of and around the men, enveloping them with flame.

As for Dodge's fire, Rothermel combined witness accounts from 1949 with a more modern understanding of how fire works. Sallee, who paused to look behind him before fleeing through the rimrock, remembers seeing Dodge's fire burn uphill in the direction of the rimrock into which he and Rumsey fled—at right angles to the path of the main fire. But how? Rothermel speculated that the convection column from the main fire—a pillar of hot smoke and gas—actually blocked the wind, while also creating updrafts that would have pulled Dodge's fire upward. His conclusion: It was unlikely that Dodge's fire was the one that killed the fire crew. A fire blow-up fed by dry grass and wood, a hot afternoon wind, and a fire-friendly slope were almost certainly the culprits.

Rothermel's study of Mann Gulch stands as one of the fire lab's most compelling achievements, a blend of science that also approached Greek tragedy in its clear-eyed depiction of firefighters running a race up that steep, burning hillside that they could not possibly win. But it's also an example of a bygone era—one where calculations were made with slide rules and scribbled formulae, or derived from thermometers stuck into piles of burning pine needles in the lab's 88-foot-tall burn chamber, its pride and joy when it first opened.

Today, researchers have pretty much exhausted the knowledge that can be taken from those methods. Now the burn chamber's 1960s-era control chamber, with its banks of dials and knobs, sits unused. The chambers themselves are used only occasionally, and then largely to test batches of fire retardant for consistency. Computer models often can help depict a fire's path across a landscape, but they too are limited when it comes to big, hot, wildland fires. The models will, for instance, allow a researcher to change wind conditions, but only wind conditions that would exist if no fire were burning. The models can't account for the winds created by the fire itself.

But better models require better data, and forest fires are not willing research subjects. It's all but impossible to get an accurate picture of the exact fuel a fire is burning, its moisture level and distribution across the ground and up into the canopy. Moreover, an advancing forest fire is not a safe place to work. "You're in harm's way if you try to plant something in front of a fire," says Don Latham. "So almost all the data gathering has to be done remotely, either with aircraft or satellites. And those can be pretty crude tools at this time." Latham, an amiable, somewhat rotund man of 54, is leader of the fire lab's fire-behavior team. His forte: what makes a fire tick.

One obvious solution: set a fire in a place where fuel loads, topography, and weather would just about guarantee one would break out. But that poses its own, perhaps obvious, problems. In 1997, however, Latham and his fellow fire-behavior researchers had an opportunity to literally light their own crown fire in a remote portion of Canada's Northwest Territories, near the town of Fort Providence. There, in what was called the International Crown Fire Modeling Experiment, Canadian and U.S. researchers set up nine five-acre plots of black spruce and jack pine, tree species not too dissimilar from the lodgepole pine that causes severe fires in the United States. Canadian scientists came in before the Montana crews, carefully measuring and weighing the fuels so that they knew exactly how much burnable stuff was there—"getting down on their hands and knees to put a ruler into the duff," Latham puts it. Then Latham and other fire lab scientists, along with their Canadian counterparts, wired the sites like a computer geek's bedroom, with heat sensors, high-speed movie cameras, video cameras, infrared imagers, smoke sampling devices, and even some small structures.

Then it was show time. To start the fires, crews drove around the sites with a flamethrower mounted on the back of a pickup truck— a pyromaniac's dream if ever there was one. The results were astonishing. One tract immolated in just minutes. In all, the heat exceeded by 100 times the warmth you'd feel on a sunbaked tropical beach. Video taken from inside the burns shows an eerie glow as the fire grows in intensity. Then what looks like glowing grasshoppers bound across the screen—a wave of hot embers thrown off by the torching trees. These in turn set new, small fires, the smoke from which is at first blown away from, then sucked back into, the approaching fire front. In one burn, firefighters' protective Nomex clothing and silvery fire shelters were placed in the flames' path. They were vaporized.

Latham and his coworkers returned to the Northwest Territories in 1998 and 1999, and will spend years digesting the wealth of data taken from the tests. But Latham says they've already shed new light on fire scientists' understanding of these big, hot fires. He's particularly intrigued by the winds directly in front of a fire. At first, they flow away from the approaching fire. But as the fire dies down, the winds stagnate, and fuels begin to emit water vapor and flammable gases. Then, as the winds pick up again and flow toward the fire, the heated fuels erupt into flame. "That's a strange wind front that we still haven't gotten a good analysis of," Latham says to me.

Data from the Northwest Territories will go far in helping researchers improve existing computer-driven models such as FAR-SITE, a program created by fire lab computer expert Mark Finney that takes into account a site's topography, fuels, and weather to show how a fire is apt to move across the countryside. Combined with the growing speed and lower prices of computers, it also will help Latham and others develop fire-specific models that show more precisely how small changes in a fire might affect its behavior. Bret Butler, a specialist in fire dynamics, uses data from the Canadian burns to help him understand the requirements for a "safety zone," where firefighters are told to go if a fire threatens to overrun them. At present, a safety zone's parameters are almost entirely subjective—basically, firefighters are told to search for as large an area as possible where rocky, moist, or burned-over ground will prevent the fire from overrunning them. But Butler has found that even a slight change in the distance a firefighter is from a fire can greatly affect his or her chance of survival. A firefighter 1,100 feet from a tall fire front may live, for instance, while one only 100 feet closer might die. "It's a very nonlinear process," Butler, a mechanical engineer by training, tells me. "A small change in the distance can change the radiant energy transfer by four or five times." Using computer models, Butler has studied many of the fatal fire incidents of the past 50 years, showing how mere feet can make a difference between life and death.

The lab also plays an increasingly prominent role in helping to shape forest and fire policy, or at least put decent data in the hands of those who do. One of the lab's most prominent researchers is Kevin Ryan, with whom I'd toured nearby tree stands earlier in the season. Ryan's specialty is determining just how much fire a tree can take before it dies. That's often obvious, of course—a tree stripped of its needles and charred from base to top is a goner. A tree that may have lost a lower limb or two to a fire, and had the bark near the ground blackened a little, likely will survive. But in between there is an incredible range of uncertainty. The basic life cycle of a tree is that the roots send moisture and nutrients up the trunk in exchange for carbohydrates sent down from the solar factories that are the needles. After a fire, a tree may be so badly damaged that only part of that cycle can occur. The roots, for instance, may be able to send water up the trunk. But the upper branches can't complete the transaction by sending nutrients down to the roots. "In time, the roots finally get tired of this deal and give up," Ryan says. "At that point the tree dies." But a lingering death may last years.

Now Ryan can give a quick test to a tree that may look as if it will survive a fire and tell whether that's the case or whether it's doomed. He does so by measuring an enzyme in the cambium—the thin layer of moist, fleshy material that serves as the tree's arterial system and the place where growth originates. Cells on the inner side of the cambium, an area called the xylem, divide toward the trunk, producing the tree's rings and causing it to grow. Those on the outside layer, the phloem, produce cells that divide toward the tree's surface, creating its protective layer. It's an incredibly thin layer, only five to 10 cells thick, and is the part of the tree most vulnerable to

Fire researcher Kevin Ryan.

heat from a fire. Even a tree that appears green and healthy may be dying if the cambium has been upset. "If a particular enzyme in that layer is not present," Ryan tells me, "I can declare that tree dead."

Ryan is working to correlate that telltale enzyme with factors such as a fire's temperature, the degree of charring on the bark, and how long and hotly a fire smolders in the duff—the layer of decaying needles and woody debris that lies around the base of a tree. In a healthy forest, duff acts like mulch in a gardener's flower bed, holding moisture and protecting the tree roots from seasonal extremes of heat or cold. But in a forest where fire has been absent for too long, the duff layer grows unnaturally thick. When a fire does pass through, it creeps into the duff like fire in an underground coal seam, burning quietly for hours or even days. The tree's roots are slowly toasted and die.

In part, Ryan's research may mediate the roaring argument between environmentalists on one side, and the timber industry and some elements inside the Forest Service on the other. Today, for instance, salvage logging is notoriously inaccurate in terms of whether it actually "salvages" fire-killed trees or merely pirates perfectly good trees under the guise of salvage. Ryan is fairly old-school on this issue; he believes no amount of tree-hugging disguises the fact that the United States remains the world's leading consumer of wood fiber for home construction and paper production. (Any talk of a "paperless" office was long ago buried beneath the crush of paper from photocopiers and laser printers as people used computers to generate more paper copies, not fewer. And then there's the continuing boom in packaging in a consumption-based society.) He also thinks it imprudent to so thoroughly restrict logging in the United States that it is driven elsewhere; even as timber harvesting ground to a halt in the national forests, for instance, it skyrocketed in

British Columbia, a province with a nearly Third World approach to forestry regulation—that is, almost none.

Ryan's belief is that good scientific data will show the way to an acceptable compromise. By more accurately identifying which trees left behind by a fire will certainly die, and which will not, he believes it might be possible to develop a salvage-logging approach that will yield some lumber and paper pulp while not removing healthy trees or taking so many trees, even burned and dying ones, that the forest is irrevocably changed. "Some elements in the environmental community are afraid that what we're really trying to do is by hook or crook figure out a way to log the good old way," he tells me, as we drive back to the lab after visiting a team of student researchers practicing their techniques for a summer they will spend studying tree canopy density. "What I hope we can do is develop good data that describes what a forest is, and a good process that shows how it works. Then we can put all that on the table and try to find a common ground where we can agree on trade-offs."

Not all the work on fire and its effects takes place at the Missoula lab, of course. Nearby Montana State University has a big fire-science program, as do the University of Arizona and Northern Arizona University. The National Fire Plan poured millions of dollars into research, providing a huge boost to a commission called the Joint Fire Science Program that had been formed in 1997. With its budget doubled from about $8 million a year to $16 million and growing, the Joint Fire Science Program has financed studies from Puerto Rico to Alaska—everything from studies of soil erosion after a fire to smoke management in prescribed burns to measuring how well the public understands how forests and fires interact.

Some of that money helps a smokejumper I become acquainted with over the summer earn his doctorate. Carl Sielestad, a lithe 33-year-old with black hair and intense, close-set eyes, is exploring the

fast-growing field of remote sensing. In his case, the goal is to figure out what's actually in a forest without the prohibitively labor-
intensive effort of crawling through tens of millions of acres of
forest and counting trees. Instead, Sielestad flies over the forest, using lasers to "read" the ground beneath. The reflection, it turns out,
dovetails nicely with how much burnable stuff is on the ground. A
"smooth" reflection means there's not much; a "rough" one indicates
a lot of material that could catch fire. It's an imperfect process at
this point; an aircraft must be equipped with specialized and expensive equipment, and the laser produces so much data that it's almost unmanageable. But if policy makers are going to talk about the
buildup of fuels in forests, and fire managers are to make decisions
about how to fight a fire based on what's apt to burn, then it's a good
start toward providing that information. It's stuff that Harry Gisborne, who loved his scientific gadgets, surely would have liked.

Science also is finding its way into the field, where it's perhaps
most needed. During one of my July visits to the Winthrop area to
look into the Thirtymile Fire and its terrible aftermath, I stop at
a Forest Service office at the base of the road that leads to the
Chewuch River canyon. Working out of the basement office, peering at a computer screen, is a big, friendly guy with dark curly hair
named Bob Tobin. Tobin is a meteorologist—a fire meteorologist.
Any fire large enough to have a fire management team assigned to it,
as happened at the Thirtymile after its big, fatal run, also has someone on hand to watch the weather. No one had been specifically
handling that job the morning of July 11—the Thirtymile didn't war-
rant such attention early that day. Whether that might have helped
is a question receiving some attention; the *Seattle Times* newspaper, for instance, has just run an article suggesting that a weather
front had moved through the Chewuch area midafternoon on the
eleventh, fanning the flames into a firestorm. If so, a good weather

forecast might have alerted crews to the danger. But it also seems that the July 11 blow-up simply was a product of what everyone there knew: It was hot and dry, and there was plenty of fuel for a growing fire to grab.

Weather plays a key factor—often having more influence than anything else on how or whether a fire burns, and usually the single biggest contributing factor to fire-related accidents. Tobin's job is to constantly check forecasts for the western and northwestern United States, looking for dry cold fronts that might bring sudden shifts in wind, thunderstorms that could start new fires, or hot, high-pressure centers that can desiccate the fine fuels that get most fires rolling. Morning and evening, he briefs fire managers on the forecast.

During my visit, there are no worries. It has rained intermittently for three days, largely dousing the Thirtymile Fire and putting crews still on the line into mop-up mode. Tobin and I chat for a while, then he calls up an image on his 21-inch PC screen. It shows the location of water vapor about 20,000 feet or so up in the atmosphere. From central California up to British Columbia, wispy trails of gray show on the map, punctuated by swirls that look as if a child has poked a straw into the sky and stirred. They are storm centers—nodes where the moisture streaming south from the Gulf of Alaska coalesces around a low-pressure vortex, usually dumping rain beneath it. "That's amazing," Tobin says as his finger traces over the vortexes. "You'd hardly ever see this many storm centers, even in December." The rain, in fact, has cooled most fire activity in the West, after the first half of July looked as if it was really going to launch the season.

We walk outside to a small outbuilding. Behind it, Tobin has set up what looks like a satellite dish I'd use to pick up 15 football games on a Sunday afternoon. Instead, Tobin collects the latest images taken from weather satellites orbiting hundreds of miles overhead. In this office he also has a fast Internet connection for checking regional National Weather Service sites. But if he were in a more remote location, with electricity from generators or the local power grid but no T1 line, he could use the dish to collect packets of weather information sent from the National Weather Service to a GOES (Geostationary Operational Environmental Satellite), positioned 22,300 miles above the earth, then to the ground-based dish antennas. On a fire, Tobin also can collect information on local weather conditions—wind, temperature, humidity—from robotlike RAWS (Remote Automated Weather Stations) that can be positioned around fires by ground crews. The little solar-powered units beam data via radio to Tobin or other fire meteorologists, who then toss it into the forecast mix along with the national data they collect.

Such a device might have saved the doomed Mann Gulch firefighters, who walked into a nascent firestorm they could not foresee. But at Thirtymile the firefighters had good weather forecasts, thorough briefings, and the benefit of aerial spotters. Something else, it was becoming clear, had been missing: judgment.

Chapter 7

▲ ▲ ▲ ▲

No Place
Like Home

About a week after I visited Bob Tobin and his meteorological toys, the low-pressure area he'd been tracking dissolves. In its place comes a far more typical midsummer pattern. a big high pressure ridge that extends from Nevada well up into Montana and Idaho. The forests, dampened for a few weeks in the middle of July, begin to dry out and heat up. On July 22 a fire starts near Jackson, Wyoming, that catches national attention. Dubbed the Green Knoll Fire after the forested foothill on which it was burning, it is a violent, hot fire that seems to have potential to turn into something spectacular. "I've never seen a fire this aggressive," Incident Commander Joe Carvelho tells reporters in Jackson.

On the other hand, it's possible that Carvelho feels obligated to hype the fire a little. Green Knoll certainly puts on a good show, torching big stands of ponderosa pines and sending smoke over the tourist-packed Jackson downtown, where turquoise jewelry, cowboy art, and ice cream shops cram together like sardines along streets of faux-Western architecture. Yet by late July the Green Knoll burns only 4,000 acres. Still, fire managers treat it like a hammerhead shark in a municipal swimming pool. Within days of its start— exactly how it gets going is never learned—the Green Knoll blaze is the number-one firefighting priority nationally, meaning that Car- velho can order up just about any resources he wants. And like any good federal employee with lots of taxpayer-financed toys at his dis- posal, he does just that. By July 26, in fact, the Green Knoll fire is the target of more firefighting power than fire managers on the biggest blazes the previous summer had been able to muster. On that day the fire is fought by 36 20-person ground crews, a dozen fixed-wing aircraft dropping fire retardant, another dozen helicop- ters using dip buckets to dump water on hot spots, nine bulldozers, 30 wildland fire engines, and another score or so "regular" fire en- gines from Jackson and Teton County.

The ground component of this effort alone is impressive, with nearly 1,000 people chasing a fire that still hasn't reached 4,000 acres. But it's the air show that really is spectacular. One-fourth of the nation's entire fleet of wildland retardant tankers zoom into Jackson Hole Airport—fat C-130s, lumbering PB4Y2s, sleek PV2 Neptunes. They fly almost nonstop from dawn to dusk, unloading 6,000-gallon tanks full of red-tinted fire retardant within a few hun- dred yards of television crews and newspaper photographers. In be- tween bomber runs, heavy helicopters such as the dragonflylike Sky Crane ferry bucketloads of water to dump on hot spots emerging in front of the advance fire. Within a week of its start the Green Knoll Fire has rung up a tab of $4 million, and its final cost of nearly $11 million makes it one of the more expensive fires per acre in recent years—$2,500 an acre.

Why so much attention showered on Green Knoll? Simple: It threatens several subdivisions filled with million-dollar homes, among them houses owned by actor Harrison Ford and Gerry Spence, the swashbuckling attorney best known for his buckskin jackets and for winning cases for clients as varied as Imelda Marcos and white separatist Randy Weaver. (Vice President Dick Cheney's home is in the area, and although it is often mentioned in press reports it is not in danger.) At one point the fire comes to within a quarter mile of the Indian Paintbrush subdivision, a collection of lavish, picturesque large homes, many of them second residences for people who visit Jackson for the skiing, fly-fishing, and close-up views of the Grand Teton mountains, a range that while not large has about the most scenic impact per square mile of any collection of peaks in the United States.

Wildland firefighting is aimed at putting out forest fires. But few things have as much impact on how a fire is handled as a house, or, in the denatured parlance of firefighting, a "structure." Fifty years ago it was relatively rare for a forest fire to take out a house. Now only fires burning in the most remote wilderness areas tend to leave homes unthreatened, and even that isn't a sure thing. Should winds or ready availability of fuels start pushing a fire out of the wilderness and toward forested lands where there might be a few cabins, then tactics will change.

The West's forests, mountains, and streams are an irresistible magnet for urban dwellers, thousands of whom have been able to move permanently to remote areas—connected to jobs via the Internet—or who have built second homes in places such as Jackson; or Bozeman, Montana; or Logan, Utah. Dave Theobald, a professor at Colorado State University who studies land-use changes, says that the population in the Rocky Mountain states of Colorado, Utah, Wyoming, and Montana jumped from 10 million to 12.2 million during the 1990s. That's an increase of more than 20 percent during a decade in which the population of many eastern states stayed level or even fell. And most of these newcomers eschewed the cities for the country, buying homes along mountainsides and forested ravines in search of views, seclusion, and quiet.

In nearly all cases, the sound of the wind singing through the tops of ponderosa pines is a plus. I have acquaintances who recently purchased a home in the impossibly remote Oregon town of Troy, located in terrain that closely resembles the rugged, wooded country of most of the intermountain West. "It's right up against the Umatilla National Forest," they tell me. And it is. But the Umatilla is one of the most fire-friendly forests in the state, and if it ever goes the home is apt to go as well. It's a story repeated thousands of times. Everywhere I go during the summer of 2001, I see houses large and small scattered over hillsides that were inhabited only by deer and squirrels probably 30 years ago. And it isn't only isolated cabins—as the Green Knoll Fire at Jackson demonstrated, even well-developed subdivisions of fairly densely packed homes can be at risk. That's because a forest fire doesn't have to reach a house to torch it. A fire pushed by a wind front, as so often they are, tosses embers and hot ashes hundreds of feet ahead of itself—sometimes farther. Alighting on shake roofs, dry pine trees snuggled up against a house, or piles of firewood stacked near a back door, these embers find ready fuel for turning a house into a conflagration even though the main body of the fire is a quarter-mile away. In other cases, those same embers may blow into roof vents, settling in hot attics and smoldering for hours before igniting.

The vulnerability of houses to wildland fire was shown graphically in October 1991, when wind-driven fires swept down on hills packed with homes overlooking Oakland, California. In the catastrophe that followed, 25 people died and 3,000 homes burned.

Everything that could go wrong, did: Firefighters couldn't find enough hydrants; homeowners had packed dense vegetation around their homes; road access was terrible.

No comparable catastrophe has struck more remote parts of the West, but many think the potential is great. In 1994, for instance, two big fires burning near Leavenworth, Washington—where the ill-starred Thirtymile firefighters met early that morning—nearly took out the entire town. Scores of other western towns similarly abut forests that are in peril from big fires.

Leavenworth, in fact, was threatened again in 2001, a few weeks after the Green Knoll Fire. I'd rolled into town after driving up from Utah, past fires in Nevada, northern California, and central Oregon. The Icicle Complex fires had erupted on August 10 after a thunderstorm lanced the dry forest with thunderbolts. Consisting of two main fires and several smaller ones, the complex was burning about six miles southwest of Leavenworth, in the steep Icicle Canyon. Among the homes threatened were a dozen or so that had been rebuilt after they were destroyed in the 1994 fires.

The following year, 1995, the Forest Service modified its policy on home protection. For years, fire managers had been trained to watch out first for firefighter safety, then protect property such as homes, and finally protect natural resources—the trees, in other words. Beginning in 1995, however, managers were supposed to place trees on an equal footing with structures. In other words, homes would no longer get the preferential treatment they long had enjoyed.

At least, that was the policy. As the Green Knoll Fire showed, homes still got plenty of attention. The same held true in Leavenworth, something that Mike Asher, a member of the incident command team and a specialist in home protection, readily admitted. "There's no question that having homes in the path of a fire changes the way we work," he says to me when we meet at the fire base on a Saturday morning. "It changes our tactics completely." Firefighters trained to dig line often are given very different assignments, arranging sprinklers around houses, sometimes wrapping them in protective foil or soaking them with solutions of chemically thickened water that wets out the roofing for hours rather than minutes, or removing firewood and shrubs that a homeowner left too close to a house.

Fire managers don't like detailing crews for that kind of work. But the pressure to do so is enormous. News reports of fires near homes invariably make the homes the focus of the stories, setting up a sporting-event contest between fire crews and the fire as the crews try to "save" the homes. At Leavenworth, as at Jackson, a fire that would hardly have warranted mention had it burned in the wilderness area a few hours' drive away was depicted as a desperate struggle, one that ignored the fact that homeowners in Icicle Canyon and Indian Paintbrush and other threatened subdivisions had willingly built homes near a flammable forest, then exacerbated the threat by sometimes loading their homes' roofs with two tons of kindling in the form of cedar shakes. Asher spends considerable time each year trying to educate homeowners about the risks posed by fire, but finds it an uphill struggle. "We'll host meetings on the subject, but attendance is pretty thin," he says to me. "Sometimes I'll come across a house where the owner has made an obvious effort to create a defensible space, but right next to it will be eight or 10 homes where the owners obviously don't care."

And where there are news reports, there are politicians. The entire vocabulary that surrounds wildland fire—that we're "battling" a fire, that firefighters are "attacking" it, that the fire is "advancing"— sets fire up as an implacable, evil foe that is bent on destruction. That black-and-white imagery plays perfectly into the hands of grandstanding members of Congress or state governors. "Fires are a place where politicians just like to be seen," one fire manager tells me. And because homeowners are voters, making an effort to protect property usually is what politicians first and foremost expect of a fire crew. It doesn't help that many remote homes are expensive vacation destinations for wealthy, well-connected residents of Los Angeles, Denver, or New York, meaning they know whom to call and what it takes to make something happen.

Still, the real or perceived threat wildland fires pose to homes has become the centerpiece of large swaths of fire policy. Clinton's 2000 National Fire Plan, for instance, dedicated $240 million in 2001 to help communities at potential risk from fire. The objective: educate homeowners about what they could do around houses or a community to create what Asher termed that "defensible space," an area where a fire would not be able to leap from tree crown to tree crown, but would be forced to burn across the ground where a fireline or other firefighting tactics might bring it to a halt. The money also helped bankroll work on constructing firebreaks on public property.

Early in the 2001 season I'd seen at least some evidence that the money was having an impact—although the terror caused by the fires of 2000 probably was more influential in shaping behavior. While visiting forests in Montana with Kevin Ryan and Mick Harrington from the Fire Sciences Lab, we'd passed subdivisions in the foothills north of Missoula where the local residents had been frantically beavering away to remove underbrush and scrub trees. The stuff was piled along the road, awaiting pickup in trucks financed by National Fire Plan money. "This area was just a disaster waiting to happen," Ryan said to me as we passed the homes. "But they've been working on it, and they're making progress." Then we passed the home of someone who hadn't gotten the message. It had dry pine needles stacked high on a roof, and a load of firewood next to a garage. "Look at all the needles there," Ryan said, shaking his head as we drove past. "This guy is gonna cause a fire to take out his neighbor's house."

It's understandable why people have long been reluctant to clear the land around their homes. Living near the forest is nice, but living *in* a forest is even nicer. And homeowners know that trees have benefits—trees near a home keep it warmer in the winter and cooler in the summer, both worthwhile objectives in states such as Montana where the temperature can drop to zero for days on end in January, and peg at 100 for days on end in July. That in part explains why homeowners here likely had not taken out hatchets and chain saws until they'd spent the summer of 2000 under a pall of smoke from scores of fires burning a few dozen miles south of them in the Bitterroot National Forest.

But there also were signs that the 1995 policy change was percolating down to ground level. After all, big fires had burned near Missoula in 1988, including an arson-set blaze that had blackened a big draw we drove through that day. The difference: Forest Service officials here had told people not to count on heroic efforts should a fire break out. In other words, they were on their own.

In some cases, entire towns are trying to turn themselves into defensible space. Roslyn, Washington—a small onetime coal-mining town of about 1,000 people that had a few years of fame as the setting for the television show *Northern Exposure*—has used National Fire Plan money in a demonstration project aimed at showing the feasibility of protecting large areas. Roslyn is one of an estimated 11,000 western towns where a big fire might pose a risk; it edges up against the Wenatchee National Forest, where big stands of ponderosa pine trees have become far less fire-resistant than they were when the little town was established in 1886. Now, though, about $340,000 has been spent trimming trees and brush in a circle cov-

ering about 80 acres total. As in Missoula, a big chunk of the motivation for doing the work comes from gentle hints that a town that
hasn't taken steps to protect itself shouldn't count on an army of
firefighters to save their bacon when a crown fire starts marching
down the valley, pushed by the gusty east winds that buffet Roslyn
much of the peak fire season. "You can educate with a stick or you
can educate with a carrot," says George Flanigan, a state fire commander who helped supervise the project. "Right now we're educat-
ing with a carrot."

Still, while Roslyn makes for a good talking point, it's not clear
how feasible such work would be on a large scale. If every town like
Roslyn got the same treatment, for instance, the bill would near $4
billion—10 times as much as has been set aside annually for such
work under National Fire Plan funding. And it's not a one-time deal;
a few wet winters and springs would result in a healthy crop of burnable material once it dries out, and within 10 years there'd also be a
substantial number of young 10-foot trees, just the size that gives a
fire plenty of fuel once it climbs out of the grass.

There's even a question of whether this sort of fireproofing Marshall Plan is necessary. It's true that wildfires burn homes each year.
But is it the epidemic depicted by the press (which, in August, is
desperate for anything that looks, smells, or acts like news)? In recent years one of the most destructive fires to "property" was the
Valley Complex, a giant, 200,000-acre-plus fire that burned in Montana in August 2000 and that scared the bejeebers out of the people
whose homes I drove by near Missoula. Yet the final tally in terms of
"structures" lost, while an impressive-sounding 227, included many
woodsheds. About 70 homes ultimately were lost. Not trivial, but
not much when compared to the national tally of run-of-the-mill,
cigarette-in-bed–type fires. In 2000 alone, 368,000 home fires were
reported in the United States, causing 3,420 deaths, 16,975 in-

juries, and $5.5 billion in direct property losses. House fires are the deadliest disasters in the nation, killing more Americans each year than all natural disasters combined. Yet few of those fires are reported much outside the city in which they take place, while news reports may breathlessly tell of two or three "structures" lost in a wildland fire, when what was lost actually comprised a garage and maybe someone's workshop.

With that in mind, some critics of forest policy I spoke with advocate a much more hard-line approach: You live in a fire-prone area, you assume the risk and responsibility for your property, defensible or not. Under one proposal, homeowners would be paid cash in return for signing an agreement that they will expect no heroics if a wildfire creeps their way. The idea is that it's cheaper to fork over $50,000 or so up front and be done with it than take the risk that homeowners and politicians will start screaming for $1-million-a-day firefighting efforts. Robert Nelson, an economist with the University of Maryland who contends that firefighting exemplifies just about every land-use mistake ever made by the Forest Service, suggests giving the agency the authority to pay homeowners the replacement cost of a burned home plus even 50 percent. That might still be cheaper than dispatching scores of firefighters to wrap homes in something akin to aluminum foil, set up sprinkler systems, and remove brush and small trees the homeowner should have taken out months before.

But the odds that such a plan ever would succeed are not good. Homes aren't merely physical objects. They're filled with emotion, with memories. The notion that firefighters would walk away from rows of homes in all but the direst circumstances would not sit well with the American public, no matter how persuasive the argument might be that such is the best course. It's true that fire managers are making progress instilling a sense that "bad" homeowners shouldn't expect help if they don't take steps to render their homes more fire-resistant.

Certainly, no one at the Green Knoll Fire can make a case that their home was abandoned. The fire came so close to the Indian Paintbrush and Crescent H subdivisions that embers were tossed amid the homes, but teams of firefighters quickly pounced on any small spot fires that broke out, while entire homes were encased in fire-resistant coatings such as "green slime," a sort of chemically thickened water, and shed any sparks that struck them. Nor were any homes lost in Leavenworth. Close calls, but nothing more.

Chapter 8

▲ ▲ ▲ ▲

Yellowstone

For Steve Frye, commander of the Northern Rockies National Incident Management Team, the summer of 2001 has been a relief compared with 2000. By mid-July, in fact, his team hasn't even been called up. That is unusual—most summers Frye and the others have responded to at least one fire by that point, sometimes two. But the same weather that had precipitated the Green Knoll Fire— warm and dry, with occasional thunderstorms—soon sparks another blaze. This one is not far north of Green Knoll, in Yellowstone National Park. Early on the morning of July 31, Frye's phone rings. He is off to Yellowstone.

On August 2 I follow, booking a flight into Idaho Falls and driving north and east to the fabled national park. After entering through the impossibly touristy town of West Yellowstone, packed to the rafters with T-shirt and Western art shops, I pass many of the places that are cemented in America's wild-country lore: Old Faithful, Fountain Paint Pot, Fishing Bridge. In between, I also pass vast swaths of young lodgepole pine trees, most only 20 or 25 feet tall, their bases stuck like spears between the sun-silvered carcasses of thousands of their forebears. Those bleached logs are the detritus of huge fires that swept through the park in 1988. Those fires were some of the most severe in the United States in the past 100 years and have had a tremendous impact on how fires are viewed.

Since then just about any fire burning in Yellowstone has been big news. That was certainly what drew me there—a chance to see how the National Park Service was handling its fire policy in the wake of continued scrutiny of the 1988 fire and its aftermath. In particular, I was interested in one aspect of those big fires: Yellowstone's elevation to poster-child status for a growing number of environmentalists and others who say that the park now stands as an example of fire's benefits, and that western forests might be better off if similar huge fires swept over much of the landscape.

Anyone who has not been to Yellowstone would be hard-pressed to imagine the immensity of the place. Established in 1872, four years before Custer's Last Stand, its creation was an amazing act of self-awareness on the part of a nation not yet a century old and still mired in bitterness over the Civil War. Even today the national park system in the United States is unlike anything else in the world—a conscious effort to set aside the landscape that makes the country unique, in many cases long before development poses any severe threat. Yellowstone, established when the West was largely unpopulated, is for that reason among the largest national parks, with more than 2 million acres. On road maps it covers the entire northwestern corner of Wyoming, slopping over into Idaho and Montana. By comparison, Mount Rainier National Park, by most standards a big park, covers a paltry 230,000 acres, or one-tenth the size of Yellowstone. At freeway speeds it would take an hour to traverse Yellowstone; at the slower posted speeds, and with stops and slowdowns to plain gawk, it takes four times that long. That scale is one of the park's most attractive qualities. Unlike Rainier and many other national parks, Yellowstone isn't centered on a single object (Old Faithful, for all its prominence, is a minor attraction within the park). Rather, its focus is the preservation of a landscape relatively unchanged for perhaps 140 years, a look at what much of the West once resembled.

Not that you can always see much of that through the throngs of tourists, their cars blocking the road when a herd of buffalo or American elk approach, their plaid-shorted bodies blocking the view of said buffalo or elk as they approach the huge creatures as if the park were some kind of vast petting zoo. The behavior of people in the typical American national park is appalling—unlike anything seen in the national forests, or anywhere else on the western land-scape. Much of that, I think, is due to the exceedingly regimented atmosphere in most parks. The terrain is crowded with signs advising visitors to stop for this attraction or watch out for that animal. There are scenic vistas with information booths, and regular vehicle turnouts for viewing a steaming fumarole or a vista of the Yellow-stone River. And, of course, the lodges—great shingled piles that in Yellowstone loom out of the terrain like battleships in the sea, at Old Faithful, Mammoth Hot Springs, Yellowstone Lake. The effect they create is jarring. You run the very real risk of being stampeded by buffalo or charged by a grizzly bear in the afternoon, then that evening recover from the experience over a gin and tonic and a very fine tenderloin steak in one of the elegant lodge restaurants. That philosophy of wild-but-comfortable perhaps made sense when visitors traveled for days by train and Model T to get there. Today, in an age of recreational vehicles the size of the *Queen Mary* and as well appointed, it seems faintly ridiculous. My own conviction is that the greatest threat faced by our national parks is the National Park Service, which is as much a development and highway construction agency as a natural-history one.

Certainly, though, neither Frye nor the Arthur Fire team is finding much time for gin and tenderloins. Nor are they finding much comfort. The fire camp is wedged into a parking lot behind park maintenance buildings overlooking Yellowstone Lake. The management team's tents are crowded along several dirt roads. Behind them stand the mess tent and shower trucks. The tents of the 500 or so firefighters on the scene are scattered among several thickets of lodgepoles.

By the time I get there, the fire has burned nearly 8,000 acres, working its way through stands of lodgepole pine and alpine fir as winds drive it eastward. The park's east entrance is closed, for fear the fire might jump down the ridge and overrun the east entrance road, or burn down to the east entrance itself and torch Yellowstone's facilities there. Along with a public information officer for the fire management team, I drive east to the fire. An afternoon thunderstorm is clearing as we traverse the road, empty of vehicles owing to the east gate's closure. Finally, we round a corner and come into a long valley that descends from the park's vast, volcanic plateau down to the surrounding foothills. A thin haze of smoke fills the valley, and firefighters' vehicles and crew buses are scattered along the road. Helicopters flit up and down the valley like giant insects, swollen canvas buckets of water slung beneath their bellies.

That night, at 8 P.M., the incident command team holds its evening briefing in a large tent. Electric lightbulbs cast a harsh light across metal seats where the team members crowd in. One of the first to speak is Ron Hvizdak, a tall, lean, 47-year-old Montanan who is the team's fire-behavior analyst, or "F-ban." His job: figure out what the fire might do next, perhaps before the fire gets around to even thinking of it. "The fire played its card yesterday," he says, arranging a map of the fire perimeter on a briefing board. "It made a big run along the ridges, but now it will have to back downhill if it wants to go very far." Meaning: For the fire to progress, it will need to throw burning cones and other stuff downslope from the fire front. Many fires do this, but they tend to burn much more slowly this way than when racing along a ridgetop with the wind behind it, or climbing uphill.

Reports from the fire meteorologist and ground operations chief follow. One problem facing ground crews: grizzly bears. Several have been spotted near firelines, apparently foraging on carcasses of bighorn sheep that have died in the area. So helicopters have flown bear traps into the backcountry, with the goal of capturing the bears and ferrying them to a more-remote section of the park. Paul Linse, the air operations supervisor, also had a problem that day: A civilian sightseeing aircraft blundered into airspace packed with helicopters and retardant tankers. "That guy was out in la-la land," he says. "The FAA is going to be having a little talk with him."

Then it's Frye's turn to talk. He doesn't say much, first joking about the bison herd that wandered through the firefighters' tent complex the night before. "We had a good day today, but this fire still worries me," he adds. "Let's work hard to make sure we get more line around it tomorrow." A few more words and the meeting wraps up. The tired team members soon head for small meetings to plan the next day's work on the fire. Then it's to bed for what they hope will be a better night's sleep than the bison afforded them the previous evening.

It isn't. I set up my own tent in the campground near Fishing Bridge, perhaps a mile from the fire base. At 11 a parade of thunderstorms passes overhead, illuminating the surrounding camps in split-second blasts of stunningly bright light, followed a half-second later by a deep, crackling roar. And rain.

The rain, at least, cools the fire. In the morning the blaze sends up thin wisps of smoke that fill the eastern road valley under the morning temperature inversion, a common phenomenon in the West's mountain terrain in which a lid of cool, relatively dense air forms over the peaks each night, trapping a fire's smoke under it until either the morning sun dissolves the inversion or the fire's energy punches through it. "That rain last night will give us about 24 hours, but that's all. It's still dry out there." So says Hvizdak, fire-behavior analyst, the next morning. I'm going to tour the fire with him.

Hvizdak parks his green Dodge Ram pickup, and we shoulder packs and hand tools and plunge off the road down a steep embankment to a flat, grassy meadow some 300 feet below the road. Hvizdak has been an "F-ban" for 16 years. When not scouting fire, he works with fire in the Kootenai National Forest in Montana. There, as a fire management officer, he works on developing firefighting plans for the forest and manages programs aimed at reducing heavy fuel loads.

Within a fire management team, fire-behavior analyst is one of the most visible positions. Along with the fire meteorologist, Hvizdak gets the lion's share of time at the morning and evening briefings, reviewing the fire's progress, where it might be apt to make a run, and what the fuel conditions are like. During the day he patrols the perimeter of the fire, literally watching it to see what it's up to, and getting a firsthand look at the forests and fuels it might encounter if the weather doesn't give firefighters a break or if the flames jump a fireline. It's an exhausting schedule. Hvizdak typically clambers out of his tent (Frye insists his team "sleeps in the dirt" in tents and sleeping bags, same as the firefighters) well before 6 A.M. to review maps and infrared images taken from aircraft during the night that show the fire's perimeter. The morning briefing usually takes place at 7:30, then Hvizdak grabs a quick breakfast in the mess tent before tossing a sack lunch in his pack and heading for the fire. He's back in camp for the evening briefing, then meetings with other members of the fire team, and finally bed well after 11.

One benefit: plenty of fresh air and exercise. After we leave his truck on the road, Hvizdak strides easily ahead of me through the wet grass of the meadow, while I start to gasp a little owing to the unaccustomed elevation. About 1,000 feet up the slope, in a thick stand of lodgepole pine, we encounter the fire. There is little drama in the moment, as the Arthur Fire is showing its calm face after having been cooled by the night's rains. Plus, fires typically have a tougher time going downhill than uphill. They can do it, creeping steadily downslope, but to do so they must hug the ground, finding fuel right on the deck that the base of its flames can grab and burn. Sometimes, a bigger fire will become a little more aggressive, tossing burning pinecones and other debris downslope, spreading by literally throwing matches in front of itself.

But the Arthur Fire is creeping, crackling noisily in the quiet air, its flames only a few inches tall at its edge, maybe a foot or two where it has gotten hold of a downed tree or old stump. Hvizdak kicks a smoking stump with his tall, tapered-heel White Smoke-jumper boot. "We spend a lot of money fighting these things, and sometimes I wonder why," he says, as I puff behind him. "With all the old lodgepole pine and subalpine fir here, plus the wind-downed fuel, a big fire here is almost inevitable."

Hvizdak's notion is relatively new. For much of the twentieth century, firefighting policy in Yellowstone was absolutely mainstream. Its fires were almost always suppressed by firefighting crews before they got to be more than an acre or so in size. That wasn't necessarily an enormous task; Yellowstone is exceedingly high (most of it is more than 7,000 feet above sea level), so winter snows are late to leave. Moreover, it shares with Arizona and New Mexico a predilection for monsoonlike summer thunderstorms that sail up from the Gulf of California and southern Pacific around Baja, bringing with them drenching rains beginning in late July, a time when the fire season is really hitting its stride in drier parts of Montana and Idaho. By the late 1980s, climate and fire suppression had kept Yellowstone free of large fires for well over two centuries. The National Park Service, in its paternal approach to parks, had been lulled into thinking that big fires posed no risk, and in 1972 had instituted a policy of largely letting fires burn. That actually was an enlightened decision, one taken decades before most land-use agencies such as the Forest Service tried to shift their firefighting emphasis. But it also was one that had not been given a severe test.

The summer of 1988 provided that test. After a dry winter and warm spring that brought only one-third the normal levels of snow and rain, the stands of old, mature trees that crowded Yellowstone were bone dry, with moisture levels even in the heavy timber hovering around 10 percent, far drier than normal. Still, when lightning storms began to spark fires in late June, park officials weren't particularly worried. The fires would burn for a few weeks, they figured, then summer thunderstorms would douse them. The thunderstorms, however, didn't come, and on July 22 a firefighting effort was ramped up. Still, there wasn't a lot to worry about, as fires had by then blackened only about 50,000 acres, a small fraction of the park.

Firefighting continued through August, with some success—the Fan Fire in the park's northwest corner was caught and suppressed. But other fires on the park continued to burn, while wave after wave of dry thunderstorms lighted new ones. Then came "Black Sunday"—August 20. A dry cold front passed over the park that morning, causing the winds to shift and accelerate, with steady winds of 30 to 40 miles per hour and gusts approaching 70. Firefighters scrambled for their lives as the dozens of fires burning in the park exploded. More than 160,000 acres burned in that one day, sending a dense pillar of smoke 30,000 feet into the air. The Storm Creek Fire, in the northeast corner of the park, made a 10-mile run that day. The Hellroaring Fire, to the north, nearly matched that, advancing through heavy timber at a mile-per-hour clip all through that terrible day.

The fires continued to burn for weeks after that. On September 6 a firestorm roared down on Old Faithful, destroying 16 cabins but missing the Old Faithful Inn. Fires appeared on the ridgetops over Mammoth Hot Springs, and near Gardiner at the park's north entrance. But four days after Old Faithful was scorched, the first fall snows began to drift down. Finally, nature solved a problem that 25,000 firefighters, 665 miles of firelines, and 1.4 million gallons of fire retardant could not.

The aftermath of the fire was nearly as hot as the fires themselves. The park's "natural burn" policy transmogrified into headlines as "Let It Burn." The lack of respect that phrase seemed to show toward a national icon found an echo in alleged remarks made by fire ecologist Ron Despain. "Burn, baby, burn," he was quoted as saying, a remark prompted by the belief of Despain and other ecologists that the Yellowstone fires were not a disaster but a sign that the park was behaving like a "real" ecosystem. But politicians were furious with park officials. Both Wyoming senators—Alan Simpson and Malcolm Wallop—demanded the head of national park superintendent William Mott, while Yellowstone Park superintendent Robert Barbee was characterized as riding "a dead policy into hell." A headline in the Chicago *Tribune* summed up a common attitude: "Arrogance and Neglect Create Legacies of Unspeakable Loss," it read.

Thirteen years later, though, the fires of 1988 seem like the best thing to have happened to Yellowstone. As I drive through the park to the Arthur Fire, past areas burned in 1988, it is obvious that Yellowstone's forests are thriving. That impression is reinforced a few weeks after the Arthur Fire, when I return to the park to talk with Roy Renkin, the Park Service's fire guru in Yellowstone. Renkin, a stocky, mustached man in his mid-forties, strikes me as like a Philly cheese steak sandwich in a French café. A Pittsburgh native, he's retained an East Coast "Hi-how-are-ya!" way of speaking that is utterly at odds with the determinedly western drawl found in most places in the fire world. Renkin has been in Yellowstone since 1987, studying the effect of fire on the park's elaborate ecosystem and trying to understand how fire can be made to coexist with the park visitor's desire that Yellowstone remain much the way they might have seen it in a 1960s Walt Disney nature film.

Even for someone as fire-savvy as Renkin, the 1988 fires were a shock. "One thing I learned is that I didn't know nearly as much as I thought I did," he tells me as we chat in his book-stuffed office at Mammoth Hot Springs, the park headquarters. "I never would have believed that a fire could just burn until it ran out of fuel, as we saw here that year." But the fires also convinced him of the incredibly important role that flames play in the park. "Back then, it seemed like things had really been damaged," he says. "But look around now—it's coming back beautifully."

We get in his truck to do just that, driving through some of the huge areas where fire burned that summer. The scope of the blazes remains astonishing. Some 1,240 square miles of the park burned— a third of its size. One fire alone, the North Fork Fire, accounted for two-thirds of that total. Maps that Renkin has helped draw show the fire history of the park in colored squares. The map is utterly dominated by the yellow checkerboard pattern that marks the 1988 fires. But fire isn't just a part of the ecosystem at Yellowstone; it may be the absolutely essential part. "Fire is an omnipresent force here,"

Elk in Yellowstone National Park graze among trees that burned during the 1988 fire, later falling to the ground. New lodgepole pine can be seen sprouting on the hillside.

Renkin says as we bounce along past herds of bison. "It has been with us for a long time—we just hadn't really noticed it until 1988."

The lodgepole pine shows how well the park is adapted for fire, even huge, destructive fires. The lodgepole is a somewhat spindly tree that takes its name from a slender, straight trunk that Native Americans used to support their lodges. It's second only to ponderosa pine as a tree that is at home across much of the West. Lodgepole, however, prefer higher elevations than the ponderosa, above 6,000 feet. Here they often grow in thick, uniform carpets, creating an extremely dense woodland quite unlike the open, park-like setting of a classic ponderosa pine forest. And lodgepoles are fast growers, usually reaching full maturity in only 80 years, well before ponderosa pine, Douglas-fir, and other western tree species that can easily live for 500 years or more.

Also unlike the ponderosa, the lodgepole is not designed to withstand fire. Rather, a lodgepole forest grows with the genetically imprinted intent to self-destruct—to burn to the ground every 100 to 200 years. Mature lodgepole forests are too crowded for sun-hungry seedlings to flourish, and the old trees are prone to bug infestations. Spruce and subalpine fir crowd beneath them, creating a perfect layer of fuel. When a fire comes, it's a big one—not the low-intensity burn of a classic ponderosa pine forest. Yet the bed of ashes that is left after a fire is, for the lodgepole, a rebirth. Most cones of a lodgepole are "serotinous," a term meaning "late-developing." In effect, they lie dormant until fire-activated. The blast of hot air from a passing fire melts a waxy substance inside the cones, releasing the seeds so they can germinate on the mineral-soil seedbed that fire cleans of organic matter that could cause the sensitive seeds to mold. For the lodgepole pine, the 1988 fires were just the ticket, ensuring they'd dominate the landscape there for decades more. Ron Despain once counted 1 million lodgepole seedlings on an acre of land burned by the 1988 fires. In many areas, 30,000 young trees per acre now stand.

And lodgepoles weren't alone in benefiting from the fires. By the mid-1980s, for instance, the three-toed woodpecker, a black-headed bird with a white belly and white flecks across its wings, was on the verge of disappearing from Yellowstone, crowded out by hardier birds. But the fires created one giant happy hunting ground for this little bird, which prefers to nest in cavities of dead trees—now stunningly abundant—and found a lavish menu in the insects and grubs that began to reduce the burned trees to piles of woody duff.

It's true that the fires hurt some wildlife species. Moose, elk, and pine martens, which prefer mature forests because of the shelter they afford, were less happy in the new, more open Yellowstone that appeared in the wake of the fires. Many birds that require mature, living trees for nesting also fared poorly. But many birds in addition to the three-toed woodpecker thrived—agile tree swallows and the charming, azure-hued mountain bluebird among them. Ground squirrels and voles are back, happy in the lower ground cover that allows these small animals to hide yet peek out. And the sheer numbers of elk and buffalo along the roads—and the dozens of unseen wolves that prey on them—indicate that any harm done to their habitat was not long-term.

Fire benefits other species as well. Quaking aspen, the lovely deciduous tree whose leaves speckle the park with gold in the autumn and whose white trunks are immortalized in Ansel Adams's photographs, relies on fire to eliminate competition. It's not fireproof itself, nor are its seeds jump-started by fire. But its roots are deep and widespread, and groves of aspen expand by sending out suckers—small shoots—from its roots. It had been in serious decline in Yellowstone since the 1950s, but the 1988 fires opened up big chunks of terrain where it could thrive, while not damaging the aspen's deep roots.

Moreover, the fires that burned 13 years ago will help ensure that there is no such repeat for many years to come. The Arthur Fire itself was hemmed in by burned-over terrain from 1988, areas where a big crown fire can't get a start. "Fires that hit a burned area show completely different fire behavior," Renkin tells me. "They usually drop right down out of the trees, maybe spotting out in the burned area but not carrying through it. Because of the '88 fires, I will not live so long as to see something like that again. But the lessons from that fire are like classic Led Zeppelin—they'll be around forever."

In short, Yellowstone is hardly the "smoke-blackened ruin" that the *Wall Street Journal* portrayed shortly after the fires burned through the park. On the contrary, the park likely has not been so vibrant and "natural" since it was declared a national park. For Yellowstone, the fires were less a sign of some serious problem than an emphatic declaration that the landscape would behave as it always has behaved, tourists' vacation schedules notwithstanding.

With all these impressive benefits, it's not surprising that Yellowstone has emerged as Exhibit A in arguments against vigorous firefighting. Writing the year before the Arthur Fire, natural-history journalist Ted Williams made just that point in an article written for *Audubon* magazine. The 1988 fires' "only real environmental damage," he wrote, "was caused by human intervention." And in a way, he's absolutely right. There's little question that firefighting has serious environmental implications. The use of backfires—fires set in the path of a fire to deprive it of fuel—is a common practice in forest firefighting, and often effective. But in some cases it also does little more than increase the area a fire damages. A team of firefighters hacking line with Pulaskis may leave a trench that will remain visible for many years, perhaps causing even more severe damage if fall rain and runoff from spring snowmelt find the old trench an attractive path downhill, eroding the mountainside as it goes. Worse, a bulldozer cutting a big firebreak in effect digs a road where none existed. Not only will the visual record of it remain for decades, perhaps amplified by erosion and an invading armada of all-terrain vehicles, but invasive weeds such as cheatgrass and leafy spurge can use the disturbed soil as a launching pad for invading a forested area once free of them. And while most people think of "weeds" as lawn annoyances such as dandelions or crabgrass, in the West's forests they're a creeping catastrophe, changing habitat for wildlife and altering the fire behavior across millions of acres.

Then there's the reddish fire-retardant "slurry" dropped on advancing fires from aircraft. This fire retardant— an ammonia-based chemical compound that slows the spread of fire even after it dries—sometimes contains sodium ferrocyanide as an anticorrosion agent that prevents it from eating through the aircraft holding tanks. If the retardant is untouched by fire, ultraviolet radiation from the sun breaks down the ferrocyanide into ordinary cyanide, a highly toxic substance. Small fish and tadpoles, laboratory tests have shown, are easily killed by this poison, and its lethality can linger for days if the retardant is on a sunny slope. Moreover, the national forests often are the watershed for urban water supplies, and while the end concentrations of cyanide are not typically harmful, I doubt that few people watching dramatic footage of aerial retardant bombers associate the pretty pink plume cascading from the plane's underside with trace amounts of a dangerous poison in their tap water.

These days, most fires end with a "rehab" phase in which teams are assigned to cover the tracks of firefighters as much as possible. The Forest Service also details so-called BAER (Burned Area Emergency Rehabilitation) teams to help reseed or water-bar (place diversion logs) both on burned terrain and where firelines have been cut. Some of these efforts yield impressive results; Renkin and I stop near a bulldozer track cut during the 1988 fires that would not be remotely visible had he not pointed it out to me. But the sheer scale of the job makes it a labor of Sisyphus. Even a relatively modest fire such as Arthur, at 2,800 acres, has a perimeter of perhaps 30 miles, much of it in remote sections of the park and all of it marked by a fireline. Big fires may have a perimeter totaling hundreds of miles, making the idea of reconstruction an impossible task.

In Yellowstone, the National Park Service seems acutely afflicted. In its effort to allow the park to function as a natural landscape, the Service allows many Yellowstone fires to burn—keeping an eye on them should they threaten park infrastructure or park visitors but otherwise leaving them unmolested. In the weeks after the Arthur Fire, for instance, a half-dozen fires burn in the park, none of which is deemed enough of a risk to merit a major firefighting effort.

The Arthur Fire, in contrast, earns the full treatment—800 personnel, a crack management team, 14 helicopters, two fixed-wing aircraft. Possibly, it could have overrun the east side road, or threatened the ticket booths at the east entrance, where heavy traffic from Cody, Wyoming, enters the park. The fire might also have jumped park lines—fires, after all, are not hemmed in by jurisdictional lines—and entered the Shoshone National Forest, where different and more aggressive firefighting rules are in effect. So the park calls in the dogs.

Steve Frye is acutely aware of Yellowstone's special place in fire lore. "Back in 1988, we didn't see any fire behavior here different than we'd seen anywhere else in the West," he tells me over (really bad) coffee in the mess tent one afternoon, recalling his own work on the 1988 fires. "But it was in Yellowstone, and that made a huge difference." Not much has changed, he realizes. "The fact there is a large fire burning in this park, with a large management team managing the fire, generates a lot of interest."

But the park's response to the Arthur Fire, Frye insists, is absolutely appropriate. "It's a by-the-numbers operation," he tells me. "The Park Service did exactly the right thing in the way they handled this fire. They work to make the most appropriate response for each fire, and in this case the appropriate response was to provide for the protection of firefighters and the public, protect structures that were downrange of the fire, and put this fire out. That's exactly what we've done."

Well, really, it was the wet thunderstorms that put the fire out, but I didn't argue.

There's another way to tally the Arthur Fire: More than 800 firefighters and $6.1 million went into saving a tollbooth, a road, and a few outbuildings dozens of miles from the nearest large town. Years from now, despite restoration efforts, backcountry hikers to the Arthur Fire likely will find downed trees, the remains of hastily built log footbridges, and muddy trails where fire crews hacked line out of a forest that hadn't seen significant changes since before mountain man Jim Bridger visited the area in the 1830s, taking with him bizarre stories of waterfalls that shot upward, and of petrified birds and trees.

Certainly, with Hvizdak I never sense any looming danger, although of course a quiet fire can rapidly turn into a vicious one. At around 1, after hiking along the perimeter of the fire, occasionally poking into beds of hot ashes and assessing what the fire was up to, we stop for lunch. It's a gorgeous midsummer afternoon, around 80, and we're in one of the most beautiful spots in North America. A little haze from the fire, but nothing unpleasant. Hvizdak takes a bite from his ham sandwich and looks around. "This fire actually has done a lot of good," he says. "This is an area that really needed it."

From a few hundred yards away, we hear the shouts between members of a Hotshot team. They've just built a log bridge across a nearby stream, and we hear a chain saw fire up. Downhill from where I'm sitting, I see a path cut by firefighters across the grassy meadow at the base of the hill. This in a park where a ranger will write you a ticket for dropping a gum wrapper in the parking lot.

Chapter 9

▲ ▲ ▲ ▲

Hotshots

Among those firefighters beating paths through the pristine backcountry of Yellowstone National Park are the Logan Hotshots, a crew based in the northern Utah town of Logan. The next morning, after a night in the Bridge Bay campground that was this time mercifully free of midnight thunderstorms, I met up with the "Logans" as they stood around their two big transport vehicles just off the road to the east entrance, a half-dozen miles from the park's boundary and the road to Cody.

Hotshots are the backbone of the West's firefighting corps. They might spend weeks on a fire, digging fireline 14 hours a day and "spiking out" in remote camps where they're supplied by helicopter with military-issue MREs (Meals Ready to Eat) and water. The work can be brutally hard, and Hotshots train like football players, working out all winter and showing up at their home bases in May for several weeks of physical training as well as instruction or review in a host of firefighting techniques and equipment. Even smoke-

Members of the Logan Interagency Hotshot crew, one of the fire world's elite units, dig fireline in Yellowstone National Park.

jumpers, usually seen as the most elite wildland firefighters out there, are quick to give Hotshot crews their admiration. "If there's a fire that's getting out of hand, there's not a smokejumper around who won't take a couple of Hotshot crews over two planeloads of smokejumpers," McCall, Idaho–based smokejumper Carl Sielestad tells me. "The production you get out of them is just incredible."

Once the season starts, it's typically nonstop work for the 90 Hotshot teams based across the West from New Mexico to Alaska, the latter the home of the picturesquely named Midnight Sun team. But the home bases are more for administrative purposes than anything else. From late May until September the Hotshot crews are on the move constantly, caravaning from fire to fire in buses or crew trucks. A team may work as many as a dozen fires in a season, driving all night from its base, working the firelines for up to 14 days, taking a mandatory two days' rest, then hitting the road to another fire to start the routine over again.

The Logan crew have been at the Arthur Fire for five days when I meet them. Starting with a fire near Salt Lake City in May, the team had put thousands of miles on their two GMC crew transporters—12-seat passenger boxes mounted on a truck chassis. Before scrambling to the Arthur Fire, the Logans have spent a few days resting up at their home base in Logan, in Wasatch-Cache National Forest, headquartered in Salt Lake City. Logan itself is in the Cache Valley, 4,500 feet up in the picturesquely rugged Wasatch and Bear River mountain ranges. It's an incredibly beautiful area, with hiking, fishing, mountain biking, and dozens of other activities. But the Logans uniformly hate time in base—loafing around town doesn't earn any money, and a Hotshot stands to make $18,000 or more in a good season.

The Logans' supervisor is Scott Bushman, an amiable 46-year-old career Forest Service employee with thinning blond hair and tired-

A firefighter in northern California sets a backfire in an effort to deprive an advancing fire of fuel.

looking hazel eyes, the latter a product of the long summer and short nights. The crew looks sleepy too, as they stand around their trucks in the hazy morning sun, dragging tools from the trucks and awaiting the day's plan. Many faces still have grime from the previous days' work, and the olive Nomex pants and yellow Nomex shirts are caked with soot. They're a rugged-looking bunch, trim and wiry, mostly young men but with a scattering of women, their low-slung packs hanging over their backsides, fusees (flares used to light back fires) jutting out of each side. In one of those vignettes that I continually find almost comically ironic, Bushman lights a cigarette before gesturing toward the mountain across a valley that cuts beneath the road and reviewing the day's assignment. "We're going to pick up about where we left off yesterday and keep cutting line along this slope," he says, waving the butt in his hand. "If this thing starts to crank, then the plan is to back off and let the heavies [helicopters] and retardant bombers take care of it. But if we can hold on to it, then tomorrow it might cool off some and we can gain more ground."

A few questions pop up, as the crew members shuffle their feet from side to side, some with Stihl chain saws encased in canvas blade guards slung over their shoulders like automatic weapons. Bushman assigns a lookout to stay on the road, where the entire slope can be surveyed, and we march down east on the asphalt to a trail marked in orange tape that cuts down the slope and across the valley. It's not an official park trail, but rather one cut by previous firefighting crews.

Bushman and I veer away from the main crew to scout a safety zone and figure out where the Logans were apt to tie in with the next crew on the line. We hear distant shouts as the firefighters call to one another, and the occasional rasp of a chain saw. The fire is hidden from view, but the smell of wood smoke is strong in the cool air. After clambering for 15 minutes up the steep slope, grabbing exposed roots and tree branches, we reach a large, rocky open area between the tall stands of lodgepole pine and Douglas-fir. Bushman gasps for air; cigarettes aside, we're at 7,000 feet, and I'm also barely acclimating to the elevation after two days there. He looks around the clearing. "Whaddya think?" he asks me. "Will this work as a safety zone?" Hard for me to say. Back in a classroom, or at a briefing, the idea of a safety zone seems perfectly clear. But out here on the ground, where you can't see more than 50 yards because of the trees, you pretty much take what you can find. Nature doesn't conveniently drop a rocky, wood-free chunk of ground within an easy hike of the assignment area.

Still, this one looks pretty good. If the fire blows down this way, a crew would likely find itself strafed by burning pinecones and branches bouncing down the mountain. But there isn't much woody debris here, and bare rock juts out in many places. Bushman, for one, certainly takes the idea of a good safety zone seriously here. "This fire worries me," he says. "Unlike a lot of people here, I've seen what this place can do." Bushman was among those who ultimately couldn't do much more than watch as a third of the park burned in 1988.

We work our way up the slope, marking the route to the safety zone with fluorescent orange marker tape, and in about 45 minutes we hear the Logans approaching. Actually, what we hear is the loud rasp of a chain saw, followed by that distinctive snap and crack of a big tree starting to lean. Then a slow *whoosh!* and a thunderous impact as a massive Douglas-fir hits the forest floor. "What the hell was *that?*" Bushman asks of no one in particular.

A few minutes later we spot the Logan crew. Anyone who thinks firefighting is glamorous work would be disabused of that notion within minutes of first watching Hotshots at work. "It's like above-

A bulldozer path cut to block a fire's path. Critics of firefighting charge that the act of battling a fire can do as much damage as the fire itself.

ground coal mining" was how one fire manager described the activity to me earlier in the summer. *More like ditch digging* was always my reaction. The Hotshots are moving laterally along the steep, uneven slope, putting to practice the techniques I'd learned six weeks earlier in fire school. Out front are two young women swinging Pulaskis. They chop at the hard ground, scraping vegetation up and cutting through shrubs and roots. Behind them follows the rest of the crew. Some use shovels, others Pulaskis, still others combi tools to widen the narrow ditch begun by the team leaders. It takes about a minute for the entire team to pass a single spot. By then, what had been a forest floor thickly littered with needles and shrubs and crisscrossed with tree roots had become a neat, 24-inch-wide ditch, cupped gently at the bottom to catch any burning debris that might roll downhill from the fire above.

Hotshots, like smokejumpers, are largely a product of the 1930s-era determination on the part of the the Forest Service to stamp out forest fires once and for all. The Logans can trace their roots to a team of 40 firefighters that was assembled in southern Oregon in 1938. Chosen for "physical prowess . . . and hardened by work," as one report put it, and trained as a self-contained firefighting team, the 40 were taught to work on their own, without extra support, for up to three days. Their field kit was surprisingly modern, with lightweight goose-down sleeping bags and dehydrated food, along with rice, anchovy paste, and other delicacies. Each crew member's food, clothing, and tools were carried in a Trapper Nelson pack, a canvas-and-wood pack devised by an eponymous Alaskan trapper in the 1920s and commonly used into the 1960s. The 40 men were kept close to camp so they could be dispatched within an hour of getting a fire call. And they had plenty, working eight large fires from July through September. On station, the crew's half-dozen ax men led the way, clearing small trees and brush (chain saws existed then, but were huge, wheel-mounted monsters). Then came 10 men with Pu-laskis, followed by men swinging hoes and digging with shovels.

The 40-man crew cut fireline for about a third of the cost that the Forest Service had come to expect. Plus, once in the field they required little supervision, in stark contrast to the teams of bar bums that often constituted fire teams at that time. But the crew also proved too large to manage effectively, and transportation was a particular headache. The next year, 1940, a 20-man crew was put together in Oregon's Willamette National Forest. Dubbed the "Willamette Flying 20," the crew quickly became the model for the later Hotshots—a very fit, well-trained crew that was assigned to the toughest part of a fire and given the task of getting a line in front of the fire in one shift. On July 8 of that year, for instance, the Flying 20 crew left the road at 7 P.M. to tackle a 165-acre fire burning 11 miles into the woods. They hiked eight miles that night, carrying tools and 35-pound packs, then arose at 3 A.M. to fix a quick breakfast. The crew worked until 3 in the afternoon, cutting line and backburning between the line and the fire, then hustled to another section of the fire to help a crew that had lost control of its portion of the line. There were no trails, and the terrain was so rugged that some of the civilian crews drafted into duty gave up and walked out before coming close to the fire.

World War II put a crimp in forming new firefighting crews, aside from teams formed to watch for incendiary-laden balloons the Japanese drifted across the Pacific in the hope of setting large fires. But four years after the war's end, the first four Hotshot crews were assembled. The new teams quickly proved their worth, and were instrumental in the Forest Service's seemingly admirable work during the 1950s and 1960s of largely eradicating fire from the western landscape. The program expanded to some 90 teams scattered across the West but often based in small towns such as Entiat (Washington), Warm Springs (Oregon), and Greybull (Wyoming). At Entiat, while I was undergoing fire training in classrooms at the local high school, an instructor who had grown up there walked the halls during class breaks, pointing out past Hotshots from the group portraits hanging on the walls.

Hotshots build their esprit around their ability to work fiendishly hard for days on end and endure summers spent within a few feet of their teammates, either in camp, in the chow line, or on the fireline. Hotshot crews can be spotted from miles away—most fire crews, and even smokejumpers, hike in sort of scattershot fashion along a trail. Hotshots don't hike anywhere. They *march,* neatly spaced three feet apart, maintaining a steady pace of about two miles an hour whether on flat land, hiking up a steep hillside, or descending a rocky slope. Certainly, the Logan crew shows what a good Hotshot outfit can accomplish. By early afternoon they've carved nearly a half mile of fireline out of the steep hillside, working steadily and largely in silence except for the occasional calls of "Bump one!" or "Bump two!" that indicate the first line-cutters are doing so well that those in back can skip a few Pulaski swings and tighten up the line.

But the Logans also are a little more laid-back than some other Hotshot crews I've dealt with, crews that sometimes act more like Army Rangers than a bunch of kids on a summer job. And that's mostly what the Logans are. One example: Jeff Lathen, the lead sawyer for the Logan Hotshots. Lathen has his butt chewed a little by Bushman over the aggressive logging, but the tree had posed a potential threat to the crew. Its base was smoldering and charred, making it hard to say how likely it was to stand. Falling trees, in fact, are one of the biggest hazards posed to firefighters. Charred snags in particular are dangerous, as they're apt to fall silently and without warning, clobbering an unsuspecting firefighter. The proliferation of dead trees in the forests, in fact, has led many fire managers to abandon the once-popular practice of fighting fires at night, when cooler temperatures and higher humidity make a fire tractable. But darkness also makes it much more difficult to spot dangerous snags.

Still, Lathen's impish grin reveals that he also is a 22-year-old with a chain saw who enjoys the chance to take down something big. Within a Hotshot crew, the sawyers (most teams have two) are at the top of the little pyramid, with the most skilled—and dangerous—work. "As a sawyer, every situation is a little bit different, and you have to be thinking all the time," says Lathen, a tall, lean young man with a Fu Manchu mustache. "The danger comes with the job. It's one of the things that keep you on your toes. Once you become lackadaisical, it's time to give up the saw." It may not be reassuring to some to know that Lathen will eventually give up the saw for a career in dentistry. For now, whacking trees pays for rent and a pickup truck while studying metallurgical engineering on a scholarship at the University of Idaho.

As the day progresses, the mountain air warms and dries. Dust kicked up underfoot travels a little higher; thin sticks crack a little more loudly. Aicha Hull, a young woman from Idaho whose cherubic appearance is entirely at odds with her firefighting career, which already includes rappelling out of helicopters onto fires, gets out the team's hygrometer, a gadget that looks like a thermometer on a chain and is used to check relative humidity. Hull puts a little clean water in one of two tubes in the device, then spins it like a top. As the water evaporates it cools one of two thermometers in the tube, and the gap in the temperatures can be used to calculate humidity—the bigger the gap, the greater the rate of evaporation, meaning lower humidity. "Twenty," Hull announces. "And the temperature is 82." Although it's not real hot, the humidity is low enough to give any fire some push if the wind increases. And the fire is indeed showing some signs of shaking off its rain-induced lethargy. We hear calls over the radio for helicopters to cool hot spots, and can see an occasional puff of smoke overhead through the thick canopy of trees.

But things stay quiet on our little part of the fire. By midafternoon, in fact, a steely-eyed crew that had glared at me early in the morning while I was introduced in my sparkling clean Nomex dissolves into something of a recess-time gang of school kids, jostling and kidding one another and occasionally coming close to starting an all-out water war with the long hoses that are hooked to a Mark III pump stationed in a stream 400 yards away. It is a wholly understandable breakdown; the Logan Hotshots have dug their line for the day, and now are engaged in mopping up their sector. And mopping up is dirty, dull work as the firefighters attempt to ferret out every warm spot they can, cooling them with either dirt or water. At such a time, a forest fire seems like a very tame, easily controlled thing.

Which is, of course, a complete illusion. For smokejumpers, the touchstone of tragedy always will be the infamous Mann Gulch Fire. For Hotshots, the words that resonate with a mix of wistfulness and anger are these: Storm King Mountain. It's fairly recent history, so many know the rough outlines. On July 2, 1994, a string of lightning storms crossed Colorado, setting dozens of fires. One was about seven miles west of Glenwood Springs, a town of 7,500 people. Initially, it was reported as the "South Canyon Fire," even though it actually was burning near the base of Storm King Mountain, a broad-shouldered peak close to 9,000 feet. Like much of the West that year, Storm King was gripped by drought. The Gambel oaks, ceanothus, and manzanita that covered its flanks were dry as dust. Still, for two days the Storm King fire burned unmolested. Finally, on July 4, an engine crew arrived at around 5:30 P.M. to size things up. From Interstate 70, just southeast of the fire, the blaze could be seen about 2,000 feet upslope. But it wasn't doing much, almost choking on its own smoke in the calm, hot air. Besides, it was on rough, steep terrain, and the engine crew decided to hold off tackling the fire until a full workday was available.

The next morning, a seven-person crew from the Bureau of Land Management hiked two and a half hours to reach the fire. By then it had reached about 20 acres—still small. It was a hot, dry day, hitting 90 by midafternoon, with relative humidity in the low teens. But the winds remained calm, and although the fire torched individual stands of trees, it didn't make any big runs. Air tankers dropping retardant supported the small BLM crew working on the fire until they retreated to sharpen chain saws and rest. From below the fire, the BLM team watched as eight smokejumpers from Missoula dropped near the fire at around 7 P.M. A short time later, the smokejumpers radioed out that the fire had jumped the BLM fireline. The smokejumpers began a second line, working into the night—once a common strategy, as cooler temperatures and higher humidity persuade most fires to "sit down" on the ground rather than climbing into treetops. But at midnight the smokejumpers abandoned the fight, chased from the scene by rocks rolling down from above and the difficulty of working the precipitous terrain in the dark.

A few hours later, as dawn broke on July 6, the BLM firefighters and smokejumpers headed back into the fray, scrambling up the steep, brushy, trail-less slope to the fire and working to reinforce a fireline on its west flank. By midmorning, temperatures had again hit 90. Moreover, the wind was beginning to gust. The firefighters knew that a cold front was expected to hit at around 3. Meteorologists, in fact, had posted a "red flag" warning, meaning they expected the winds to become so strong—40 miles per hour or more—that the fire might pose a threat. The firefighters were worried about the front, but felt it was hours off. Some even mentioned the possibility that rain would accompany it. Meanwhile, they were relieved to see reinforcements arrive. First, another contingent of smokejumpers dropped in. Then, at around noon, a Hotshot team from Prineville, Oregon, arrived. This was a typically Hotshot crack team, and they seemed unfazed by the stiff hike in, striding toward the fire in their usual tight Hotshot formation. Fifty-two firefighters now were working the South Canyon Fire.

At about 3, a band of clouds preceded the cold front. The front had originated over Idaho the previous day, and although it was devoid of rain its clockwise rotation packed winds of more than 40 miles per hour. These winds soon began sweeping over the fire, breathing life into what had been a pokey, smoky blaze. These new winds also hit breezes already blowing upcanyon as the hot afternoon sun warmed ridgetops, sending hot air aloft and vacuuming cooler air from below. The collision of these two airflows in turn caused wind "shear," small cyclones that began to dance around the base of fire at around 3:30. One spot fire had made a particularly fatal move—blazing to life downhill from the main fire, below the firefighters scattered across the steep, rocky slope and directly into the whirlwind created by the colliding wind patterns.

Within minutes, every firefighter on the hill was in a race for his or her life. Smokejumper Tony Petrilli was perhaps the first to understand the gravity of the situation. At a few minutes before 4, he had taken one of the few photographs to document the tragedy as it unfolded, shooting a picture that showed the tiny figure of another smokejumper, Dale Longanecker, walking through a stand of scrub oak, nearly shrouded by smoke, as orange flames could be seen shooting through a stand of juniper trees right behind him. Then Petrilli saw the new fire, radioing out that the fire had spotted into the drainage, before joining other smokejumpers in a scramble uphill.

The new fire hit a bowl-like depression in the terrain, where it found dried grasses and shrubs that had flourished there because of moisture the bowl trapped in late spring. From there the stiffening winds blew it into dense stands of Gambel oak, trees that stood only about 10 feet high but that obscured the view of the fire from retreating firefighters while giving the blaze fresh fuel. At this time the new spot fire may also have joined the main fire, by now burning more fiercely as the winds increased to 40 or 45 miles per hour—so strong that it blew sand and grit into the cockpit of a helicopter flying high overhead. Still, lulled by the fact that danger was not all that visible, the well-trained firefighters staged an orderly retreat toward what they thought were their "safe zones"—the first helicopter landing area that had been cleared two days before. BLM firefighter Brad Haugh watched as a line of Hotshots came into view below him as they cleared one of the many corduroy sub-ridges that etched the surface of the hillside; as they had when they arrived, they marched in neat order, looking for all the world like a grimy yellow caterpillar inching across the slope.

As Haugh watched the crew approach, he heard a sound that reminded him of the tornadoes he'd seen while growing up in Ohio— a dull roar, overlaid with a high-pitched keening sound. At the same time a pillar of smoke, tinted orange from the flames that propelled it upward, began to rise from behind the marching Hotshots. "Drop your gear," Haugh yelled. "Get the hell out of here!"

For a few moments, nothing happened. Across the hillside, firefighters stood as if rooted, watching the fire explode. For some, those few seconds spent watching meant the difference between life and death. For all, the next minutes were a madness of flame, confusion, and grief. Four teams of firefighters were scattered across the steeply pitched hillside, all directly in the path of the flames now racing uphill, lashed on by the winds and moving easily upward from one volatile Gambel oak to the next. One team, the Hotshots, had been trying to make it to the first helicopter landing zone, then reversed themselves and headed toward the second chopper pad. Other firefighters desperately tried to clamber uphill as spot fires erupted around them and canisters of fuel dropped by chain saw teams exploded. Still others tumbled over the top of the ridge, mere feet ahead of flames that seemed to explode from the trees, then ran madly down a boulder-strewn gully toward I-70 and safety.

The fire, meanwhile, doubled in size virtually every minute, gobbling vast chunks of terrain as it rolled uphill like a giant wave. Forest Service researchers later, building on Richard Rothermel's work on the Mann Gulch blaze, estimated that the fire was moving through brush and grass at about three feet per second—two miles per hour, or the rate of a moderate walk. But in the Gambel oak it picked up speed as it climbed into the treetops and leaped from tree to tree in the higher winds. There it may have traveled as fast as six miles per hour. That was plenty fast enough to catch the Hotshots and smoke-jumpers, already tired from a hard day's work and moving across rocky, brush terrain that in places plunged at a 55 percent grade—as steep as a tough ski run in one of the nearby resorts. Strong hikers, unencumbered by panic and fatigue, would have a hard time merely walking rapidly, let alone running.

In places the fire began to catch the fleeing firefighters. Smoke-jumper Eric Hipke was knocked flat by a seeming explosion of fire directly behind him. Somehow he regained his feet, clambering up the last 80 feet of steep terrain before cresting a ridge. He had lost his helmet, and shielded his ears and neck with his hands as he stumbled downslope. He ran into Haugh and another firefighter, smokejumper Kevin Erickson, and the three plunged on, fearful that at any moment another fireball would appear. Twenty minutes later, they reached the safety of I-70. Another group found a patch of trees that had been partly burned over. They unfurled their silver fire shelters and climbed inside. Like Haugh's group, they too would live.

But 14 firefighters would not. Mere minutes after Haugh shouted his warning, a fire that may have been traveling three times as fast as their adrenaline-fueled dash to safety overtook nine members of the Prineville Hotshot crew and three smokejumpers. The suddenness of the fire's approach, combined with poor visibility from blowing smoke and the thick vegetation, apparently prevented this group from understanding the full gravity of their plight. They died virtually in neat marching formation. Few even had time to reach for their fire shelters, suggesting that the fire's arrival was a nearly complete surprise. Not far away, on the other side of the fire's U-shaped leading edge, two heli-attack firefighters—Type 1 firefighters who rappel from helicopters into a fire area—also sought to escape the 200-foot wall of flame surging behind them. The two, Robert Browning and Richard Tyler, climbed into a steep rock gully, perhaps hoping it would provide some shelter, then dropped their packs and madly attempted to deploy their fire shelters. They died before they could even climb inside, probably after inhaling superheated air that turned their lungs into soggy ash with just a few breaths.

The Storm King Fire shocked the wildland firefighting community as much as Mann Gulch had. Blame for the disaster was ascribed to the suddenness of the winds, and a fire that defied any firefighters' experience with the speed and savagery with which it evolved from a hot but manageable fire into a blaze capable of literally running down 14 tough-as-rocks firefighters. The fuels also were prime for disaster—dry, with just the right mix of fine, grassy material that burned extremely quickly and slightly heavier oaks and junipers that gave the fire staying power to go with its sprinter's legs.

Gambel oak in particular is a dangerous tree—one that almost refuses to burn unless extremely dry, at which point it burns like gasoline. And there was the terrain along the canyon, with its gullies and draws that acted like chimneys, sucking the fire upward as heat-driven winds accelerated in the narrow defiles.

But Storm King also exposed serious problems in how fires—and particularly this fire—were attacked. The day's weather forecast was remarkably accurate, with the cold front passing over the fire area within minutes of when meteorologists said it would earlier in the day. Nonetheless, firefighters made no effort to clear out of the area in advance of the wind front, nor were any fire managers keeping a close eye on the advance of the front and the firefighters' position. On the fireline itself, little attention was paid to the risks posed by the terrain, such as the way the thick foliage and ridged terrain often blocked firefighters' view of the fire. A few firefighters working the South Canyon Fire noticed topographic features such as two narrow gullies, later dubbed the "double draws." These proved critical, as they apparently funneled the fire up toward some of the escaping firefighters. But in the face of the morning's relatively quiescent blaze, little attention was paid to the potential danger posed by the two draws.

Recriminations were quick and bitter. In particular, critics of fire managers' actions that day compared the Storm King Fire to the Mann Gulch blaze 45 years earlier. The similarities were striking: As at Mann Gulch, the Storm King Fire had suddenly blown up as a spot fire erupted below and downwind from firefighters, overtaking them as they tried to escape up the hill, their only possible route. But by 1994 a second Mann Gulch was thought impossible. In 1949 the smokejumpers had gone into the fire all but blind, with little information about the potential weather or what the fire might do. At Storm King, the firefighters were well informed about the approaching cold front, well equipped with radios, well trained about how fires behaved. And yet the catastrophe had unfolded like a Greek tragedy, with a script everyone seemed to know but no one could change. Most tragic of all, the Storm King Fire was doing little damage, burning through fast-growing tree species that have no commercial value and marginal scenic value, and that grow back quickly after a fire. It was as if 14 urban firefighters had been sent into a burning but empty warehouse. A good show, but pointless.

Back in the Fridley Fire base, dinner that night is barbecued ribs, one of the specialties served up by Big Sky Catering. Then it's time for bed in the Logans' corner of the crowded Arthur Fire camp—a small cluster of tents in a stand of lodgepole pine trees next to a gravel parking lot. By 9, most are in bed, getting as much sleep as possible before the 6 A.M. reveille. It was actually a short day for the Logans. Hotshots routinely spend 12 hours or more on the lines, then it's back to the camp for a quick dinner, maybe a shower, and bed—a sleeping bag in a tent pitched in a county fairground, a rancher's pasture, or, in the case of the Arthur Fire, a park service parking area.

In one way, it's a seemingly healthful lifestyle: plenty of time outdoors, more exercise in a day than most Americans get in a year, a balanced (if a bit starchy) diet all but force-fed them, little or no alcohol or drugs due to strict and only rarely broken prohibitions on drinking or drugs in camps. The peer pressure to enforce the latter is severe; a firefighter caught with beer or grass is sent home—along with the rest of the crew, which must then await another fire rotation before it can go back out and make more money. So violations are not nonexistent—while I was at a fire in Montana a crew got shipped back—but they are rare.

A summer at the spa, however, firefighting is not. Despite the best efforts of fire camp managers to keep camps clean and in order and

Firefighters line up for their evening meal at a fire in Oregon. Feeding and equipping a thousand or more firefighters requires an enormous and expensive supply system.

well equipped with showers (something that still amazes firefighters over the age of 40), hygiene is appalling. Under ordinary circumstances, no doubt Hotshots and other firefighters would take advantage of the trailer showers in camp. But most are too exhausted from a day on the fireline to spend another 30 to 45 minutes standing in line outside the shower house. Most eat and dive into bed. So Hotshots kid each other about going for a week or more without a shower, wearing the same clothes day in and day out, faces and hands crusted with grime and sweat. And while drugs and alcohol are sharply limited, smoking and tobacco-chewing is rampant—particularly chewing, which I'd estimate is practiced by more than one-third of the firefighters with whom I spent time.

Smokejumpers have it substantially easier—one reason many Hotshots aspire to airborne work. Compared to the vagabond ground-based Hotshots, who basically spend the entire summer on the road except for short two-day rest periods at their base, the smokejumpers have a "home," and the firehouse atmosphere there encourages lifetime friendships. McCall, Idaho, where I spent time in June watching rookie smokejumpers train, is particularly attractive—a hard-nosed logging town when the base was established, now it is a resort town in a beautiful setting, awash in young women sunning themselves on the beach or water-skiing. That, the firehouse camaraderie of the base, and the appealing rhythm of training, packing parachutes, sewing packs, and jumping, create a palpable sense of joy among smokejumpers. If anything, smokejumping is too attractive for the good of its practitioners. The career ladder is short and not particularly high-reaching; after several years, a jumper may make a transition into training and administration, but otherwise it's another year, another batch of fires, year after year.

Smokejumpers also face an uncertain future. They still argue that they play a vital role as fast-responding "initial attack" forces, the first teams to reach a fire in the hopes of corralling it while it's still small. "We can deliver more people quickly than any unit," Neal Davis, a lean, avuncular man who is the base manager at McCall and who started working there as a smokejumper in 1969, said to me while I visited his base. "Even if there's a rush someplace and local firefighters start running out of resources, we can send 15 or 20 firefighters from here, and another 15 or 20 from Missoula, and we can catch that fire." True, but fire managers today have a far wider range of resources on which they can call, including ground-based initial attack teams that are stationed through the West and that can usually be on the scene of a fire within an hour or two. Moreover, since the 1930s, helicopters have become a common sight on fires, dropping small teams of "heli-attack" firefighters in addition to loads of water—and doing so with even more precision and flexibility than can smokejumpers dropped from a DC-3. Today more than 300 heli-attack helicopters fly, scores more than the eight or 10 smoke-jumping ships in use. Helicopters can fly in winds of more than 30 miles per hour; smokejumpers can't jump if they're higher than 15. And helicopters have far more flexibility in how they're based. A wide spot in the road and a gas truck makes up a helicopter base; smokejumpers need an airstrip.

Lastly, smokejumping bases are flat-out expensive. The budget for the McCall base is $1.3 million a year—which sounds cheap until one factors in that it doesn't include the cost of flying and maintaining the three aircraft based there. Once a load of smokejumpers head for a fire, in fact, they're part of that fire's budget, not their base's. And while it's not a gold-plated operation (anyone who saw the semisqualid housing many smokejumpers live in could appreciate that), plenty of money is thrown around. On one occasion, for instance, I saw a single smokejumper shipped off to help "boost" a firefighting contingent in another state. Getting that smokejumper there involved flying him to Boise on a government aircraft, then by commercial airlines to his final destination. And back. Nor is it uncommon for small teams of smokejumpers to make showy jumps essentially within sight of a freeway. The rationale is that an aircraft gets there faster than ground crews, but it's not quite what the original smokejumper experimenters had in mind.

Still, smokejumpers have successfully, and at least partly deliberately, cemented themselves into the public's imagination as *the* essential wildfire-fighting unit. It's doubtful, in fact, that many casual readers of fire news in the *Seattle Times* or *Washington Post* would know what constitutes a "Hotshot," or how a Type 1 crew differs from a Type 2 outfit, or what "initial attack" means. But "smokejumper"? You bet they know. There may be only 400 of them nationwide, but years of good publicity probably ensure that smokejumpers will long be safe from any serious effort to rationalize how firefighting teams are deployed and financed.

Whether a smokejumper, Hotshot, heli-attack firefighter, or Type 2 crew member, the work is hard and physically wearing. Quite apart from the risk of being killed in a blow-over, or crippled by a falling snag, or crashing in a helicopter, the work site itself poses very real hazards to those on it. Firefighters work for days on end in a dense fog of smoke, dust, ash, and carbon monoxide, at best using a bandanna to filter out a tiny percentage of the airborne articulates before they're sucked into the lungs. Studies on wildland firefighters and the effects of smoke and ash on firefighters are mixed. But most studies compare the carbon monoxide, carbon dioxide, and tiny pieces of airborne ash from a forest fire to moderately severe urban pollution—not pleasant, but in most cases not apt to cause long-term health problems. Still, it's also clear that a not-insignificant percentage of firefighters—maybe 3 to 4 percent, according to one Forest Service study—will pretty routinely inhale hazardous levels of smoke. And unlike urban firefighters, wildland firefighters don't carry any air tanks or face masks. Some cover their mouths with a bandanna or light fabric face mask, but even that's often uncomfortable in the hot summer air.

The work takes its toll. "The stuff you breathe is really nasty," Robert Barnett, the goateed assistant supervisor for the Logan Hotshots, told me. Barnett is 40, but two years ago was struck with pleurisy (an inflammation of the membrane that encases the lungs) and pneumonia, and subsequently had a chunk of one lung surgically removed. "This work has definitely had an effect on me," he says, leaning on a combi tool as the crew works down the line. "It's what I do, that's for sure, but I'm not sure I get paid enough for this."

Still, spending even one season with a firefighting crew—or four or five seasons, as many do—is superb training for just about any profession a person might choose. To work on a Hotshot team, for instance, requires the ability to work and sleep in far closer proximity to other human beings than is required in virtually any other activity—social or business—outside of the military. It's hard physical labor, but also work that requires a good deal of decision-making, not to mention considerable understanding of forest fire behavior, meteorology, forest ecology, and geography. It also ensures that you'll never feel the need to pack more than a 20-pound duffle, just about no matter where you're going.

My day with the Logan crew is mostly that—physical labor, without much of a hint of danger. By 5 most of the crew is lounging around on the forested mountainside, waiting for a few other crew members to finish "cold-trailing" a few areas—literally, grubbing around on hands and knees searching for warm embers with the back of the hand (which is more sensitive than the palms and fingers, and quicker to detect heat sufficient to burn skin). At 6, the order comes from Bushman to move out. The Logans line up, three feet apart, tools downhill, and start to hike out. Down the steep slope, then across the flat, grassy meadow, then back up a hillside to the road and the waiting vans. They don't vary their pace, uphill or down, by so much as a step.

A few weeks later I find the Logans in northern Nevada, where they are dispatched to fight a series of brush fires blazing through the northern part of the state. Bushman and his crew are cooling their heels in a parking lot, playing softball and going for early-morning runs, while a new transmission arrives for one of their GMC crew vehicles. They also—in a bit of a comedown for a Hotshot crew—are filling in as a local "initial attack" crew, responding wherever needed as part of the local firefighting forces of crews and trucks. "We dunno when the truck part is going to be here," Bushman says to me after I sit in on a morning briefing with him and Rob Barnett. "Could be a few days."

Patience, it turns out, is another virtue learned on a Hotshot crew. They'd be there almost a week.

Chapter 10

▲ ▲ ▲ ▲

Fire Town

I return home from the Arthur Fire for a few days' break, to wash smoke-smelling Nomex clothes and clean the ash out of cameras and tape recorders. Then it's time for a road trip. Early on the morning of August 11, I point a rented maroon Dodge Intrepid south from Seattle. I am after fires.

And they are beginning to break out in profusion. The Green Knoll and Arthur Fires had been almost solo performers, without much else of significance burning in the West. Now, though, fires break out in rapid-fire succession: a cluster of blazes in central and southern Oregon, fires in eastern Washington, big sagebrush fires ripping through northern Nevada, and numerous fires burning in eastern and northern California.

During a long drive that takes me through central Oregon, through California and Nevada, and into Utah, I rarely am in a place were no fire plume is visible. In Bend, Oregon, I awake to see a cloud of smoke billowing to the south from a lightning-set fire from the previous day. Cool and damp air, along with a few loads of fire retardant, have slowed the fire, and that morning I kick a few burning logs along with a photographer from the Bend newspaper as we tour the fire with a media handler from the new fire base. Behind the fireline several hundred acres of ponderosa pine forest is utterly charred, black sticks against a black background. That evening, in the southeast corner of Oregon, the road near Paisley winds through a sea of blackened sagebrush like Moses' parting of the sea. The day before, the 3,000-acre Lakeview Fire had roared through here. At its fire base, I chat with people I'd met at earlier fires while we watch a big plume rise from the Blue Complex, a collection of fires burning 80 miles south of us in California. The next morning, in Nevada, I see three or four plumes at once, and the vast valley through which I-80 runs is hazy with smoke. Not far west, in California, flames black an interstate highway.

In Nevada I track down the Logan crew. Not much action there, but the Modoc Fire in northern California continues to heat up, so I turn my Dodge Intrepid around and head northwest.

That night I pull into little Alturas, California, a small crossroads town in the state's northeast corner. Firefighting vehicles clog the roads like a July 4 parade, and every hotel in town is booked solid—the California Department of Forestry and Fire Protection has been called to this fire, and although a fire camp is set up for federal crews, state firefighters in California book hotels if they're available, and eat in local restaurants. The next morning, the Black Bear restaurant is jammed with Nomex-clad firefighters, ordering five-egg omelets and stacks of buckwheat pancakes as if their lives depend on it. In the fire camp itself local contractors are unloading cases of bottled water and Gatorade, vacuuming out portable toilets, and running sprayer-equipped water tankers up and down the vehicle lanes and parking lot to hold dust to a minimum. Two T-shirt vendors are outside the gates, selling "Modoc Ablaze!" T-shirts.

Alturas has hit the fire jackpot.

Each summer, firefighting transforms big chunks of the West's economy. The Forest Service alone pours $1 billion or more each year into firefighting—plus what the Bureau of Land Management, the Park Service, and other agencies spend. A chunk of that, of course, goes toward paying firefighters. But at a fire that might cost $1 million or more per day to fight, firefighters don't get much more than one-tenth of that. The rest goes to a growing roster of private contractors, and almost all fire-support services are private: rolling kitchens, showers, laundry facilities, aerial retardant bombers, mail-order vendors of Nomex pants—the list is long. By some estimates, more than half the money spent on fires in recent years went to private contractors.

And into towns near where fires break out. In Alturas, moribund logging and ranching industries have been barely offset by the bird-watchers who occasionally visit the nearby Modoc National Wildlife Refuge to train their Leica binoculars on cinnamon teal, white pelicans, and pintails, or railroad buffs who come into town for a hamburger at the Black Bear restaurant and a tour of the Alturas Railroad Museum. Sales tax revenue in the little town was down more than $370,000 in 2001, even as an aging population put more and more pressure on services in Alturas and surrounding Modoc County. A 2001 proposal to build a coal gasification plant that would have dumped $44 million a year into county coffers—more than the entire budget for the city and county—ran afoul of environmental concerns, delaying it and perhaps killing it.

So it is a big deal when several fires break out near the town. Within days a large fire camp sprouts on the county fairgrounds, netting $4,000 a day for local government (the fire camp also covered any increase in police costs for patrols or traffic control). Merchants and hotel owners also see a big bump in revenue.

A fire camp isn't a complete bonanza. The crews don't carry much cash, and in any event are out all day fighting fires, then do little more than eat and sleep. Alcohol is forbidden in camps (although of course some sneaks in), so that path to profits is largely barred. And aside from the profligate California crews, most meals are taken in the camp too, sometimes with food trucked from big wholesale suppliers many miles away as the local Shop'n Save isn't apt to have chicken breast in sufficient quantities to feed 1,200 people. But taken as a whole, having a fire nearby is a pretty good deal. Even in a largely federal fire with private contractors from hundreds of miles away swarming into town, local merchants who can supply items such as bottled water in big quantities make out like bandits. And there's always the chance that fire crews will need some "boosting" from local recruits. Which explains, at least in part, why arson is a persistent plague in western forests. It's usually some local unemployed knuckleheads who think they'll make a mint joining a fire crew that do the damage, as was the case in 1992 around Hayfork, California, where an arson ring composed of unemployed local mill hands and city water tanker contractors set a rash of fires that summer.

No one would suggest that the fire contractors are responsible for the blazes now so common in the West. But all freely admit that they have a vested interest in big fires—the bigger and more numerous, in fact, the better. That and the ready availability of fire-related resources make it easy for federal officials to pursue a big-iron approach to firefighting. It creates a potentially powerful interest group should any federal agency decide to take a lower-cost, lower-key approach to managing wildfire. And it drains money that could go to long-range programs aimed at preventing fires or reducing their severity, not extinguishing them. Each year the Forest Service and other agencies budget for fire, but a big fire year rapidly eats through that fund—in 2001, the Forest Service spent a quarter of a billion dollars more than budgeted. That cash has to come from someplace, and often it's taken from the budgets of national forests that had intended to use the money for trail maintenance, forest restoration, or other programs. Meanwhile, the money spent on fire suppression often does exactly what it's supposed to do—not so much stop big fires as prevent small fires from getting big, fires no one ever sees on the evening news. But that simply adds to the load of fuels in forests, making a big blaze inevitable.

In a way, the Forest Service's push to fight fires fills the same role its logging management once did. The agency got its start more than 100 years ago, a time when huge tracts of western forests had been liquidated and "reforestation" wasn't even a word. Loggers working for huge companies gobbled up much of the West as the federal government tried to encourage development. Loggers moved mercilessly through a forest, leaving behind a wrecked landscape of denuded hillsides and debris-clogged streams.

Large portions of the remaining woodlands—most of it in remote, mountainous areas that the loggers hadn't bothered to enter—formed the nucleus of the nascent national forest system. Although these new national forests were designed as tools of conservation, they also were quickly freighted with social responsibilities. Gifford Pinchot, the forester who helped create much of the early national forest system, had been forced to study forestry in Europe in 1889 because no such programs existed in American universities. There, he learned much about forestry—but of a very different kind than perhaps was most appropriate for the United States. European forestry had for centuries been based on the notion that forests were community property, a concept that dated back as far as 1111, when a communal forest was established near the village of Fiemme in the Italian Alps.

When he returned to the United States, Pinchot quickly sought to give American forests a European flavor. "The greatest good for the greatest number in the long run" became his guiding principle. An appealing concept, it also set the Forest Service down the unfortunate path of viewing forests as a tool for social and economic progress. That put it on a collision course with post–World War II anticommunism, which pried the agency from its "socialist" roots and drove it deeply into the arms of private, capitalistic industry, leading to accelerated harvests and the search for a "scientific" forest that came to view natural forests as decaying and decadent. Nonetheless, the agency retained a belief that forests could serve as agents of change. Throughout the West, particularly during the housing boom of the 1940s and 1950s, the Forest Service sought to exploit its timberlands as a job-creation tool for rural communities. This found its purest expression in Alaska, where two paper mills built in the 1950s were granted exclusive 50-year contracts for cutting trees in the Tongass National Forest. These contracts, awarded almost solely for the purpose of creating jobs, were held as sacrosanct until well into the 1990s, even though by some measures the federal government received only a dime on the dollar for each Tongass tree that was harvested. But similar measures were taken through the West, with many rural towns' economies becoming closely entwined with the national forests that often surrounded them. Dozens of western lumber mills could saw only big, old-growth trees—trees available only on federal lands. As was the case in the Tongass, those public forests often were treated simply as timber-supply sources for privately owned mills.

Not that any of it did much good. Timber is a classic extractive industry, with large profits for a few and just enough good-paying jobs to make a nearby sawmill or working forest an attractive proposition. But Thomas Power, an economist at the University of Montana who has long studied the western economy, believes that for much of the West the timber industry was more of an economic brake than an engine. It always was a wildly volatile industry, tied closely to the American housing market, which in turn was tossed like a cork in a hurricane by interest rates, recessions on the distant American coasts (where, of course, most homebuyers lived), and growing automation that by the 1980s had slashed thousands of jobs even as lumber demand hit record highs. Rather than ensuring economic stability, Power says, tying a community to a mill ensured economic instability.

Moreover, cutting logs and sawing them into lumber made certain that a timber-based town remained mired in economic mediocrity. Mills and logging jobs, although wildly dangerous (logging has long been the most hazardous occupation in the country), provided reasonably good pay for white males with high school educations— or less. So a pattern established itself in most logging towns as its workers fell into seductively well-paying jobs that required little education or ingenuity, ensuring that no innovative, entrepreneur class developed that might scratch its collective head and find a better way to make a buck. The very nature of a local timber industry, which by stripping the surrounding country of trees ensured its eventual demise, discouraged outside investment because the town was eating up its chief resource. So once a mill town, always a mill town. The result, Power notes, was that while timber-dependent communities survived, none prospered. Even during boom times, logging towns such as Forks, Washington, and Darby, Montana, were economic backwaters.

This way of life was not without value. People living in towns such as Forks and Darby were bound together by a common way of life and their own remoteness, making them tough, proud, independent, and respectful of tradition. But that also made them mistrustful of outsiders and resistant to change, both of which they faced during the 1980s and 1990s as a growing outcry over logging's destructiveness to not only forests but watersheds, wildlife, and salmon led the Forest Service, with great reluctance, to all but stop timber harvesting in the national forests. Among conservative circles logging became a bellwether issue, a useful proxy to beat over the head bugbears such as Bill Clinton (whose 1993 "timber summit" was an earnest but ultimately failed effort to make peace between greens and loggers), the Sierra Club, and the heavy hand of government in general. Typical of the continuing rhetoric from the right were these remarks from Jane Swift, the Republican governor of Montana, in a speech to a state logging group in 2001: "As the former Clinton-Gore administration has closed our roads, reduced our grazing allotments, stopped our oil and gas exploration, crippled our timber-dependent communities, and threatened recreation-dependent businesses as well, the financial security of our families has fallen to nearly dead last in the nation."

Great rhetoric—but in many ways false. It's true that logging cutbacks hurt many small western towns, and loggers who once made decent middle-class wages were forced to take lesser jobs in service industries, or move to cities. But increased mechanization had started that process well before environmentalists began to win a series of court cases in the 1980s and 1990s that dramatically changed how forests were managed. Contrary to Swift's assertion, it often was only when logging began to wane that real economic growth occurred in such diverse areas as western Montana, southern Oregon, and northern Idaho. The engine: quality of life, much of it built on the remaining un–clear-cut forests. Small high-tech companies, well-off retirees, even value-added timber concerns such as the string of log-cabin builders located along Highway 93 between Missoula and Darby, all helped drive the greatest economic boom the rural West had known in a century. Then there is tourism. Fly-fishing guides, rafting outfitters, backpacking companies—all began to contribute significant amounts to the western economy in a wry play on the notion of a "knowledge worker," knowledge, in this case, meaning how to negotiate a river rapid or cast a fly line. Power notes that by the late 1990s, eight of 10 national forests in Montana generated three times as much income from tourism and recreation as they did cutting down trees and turning big pieces of wood into little pieces of wood. Typical of the new West's new economic order are companies such as North Fork Anglers, founded by fishing guide Tim Wade in Cody, Wyoming, in 1984. Today the shop employs 15 retail employees and guides, and hosts as many as 400 fishers a year who pay $300 (for two) a day for the privilege of wetting a line, and who also fill Cody's hotel rooms and restaurants and add to the coffers of airlines such as United and Delta. Moreover, Wade's company is theoretically permanent. It is not destroying the rivers its guides use to demonstrate casting techniques, in contrast to loggers who gradually decimate the very thing that keeps them employed.

But the ghost of the old logging industry lives on in today's firefighting economy, aided by a big push to privatize as much of the firefighting effort as possible. The impetus to take firefighting out of federal hands got its start with the Reagan administration during the 1980s, picked up steam under Bill Clinton, and continues to grow rapidly. Today, companies that profit from fire are found throughout the West, tucked away in corners of Montana, Washington, Idaho, California, and Wyoming. Of course, that's also wherever there are trees, and with the logging industry a shadow of its former self, the fire industry has emerged as a parallel economy, rapidly gaining the same influence that logging once had, employing many of the same people, and now sometimes making the same arguments in favor of fire suppression that once were made in favor of logging.

Today, the capital of the West's fire economy is Missoula, a city of about 50,000 set on a flat plain formed by an ancient lake bed, now cut through by the Clark Fork River. The courthouse where Norman Maclean, author of *Young Men and Fire,* set several scenes for his memoir *A River Runs Through It,* remains, and downtown Missoula is a picturesque place where sturdy brick and terra-cotta turn-of-the-century architecture provides a muscular framework for its neat grid of streets. Alas, as is the case in so many American cities the Missoula downtown now has a *doppelgänger,* a row of malls along Reserve Street with that predictable mix of Home Depots, TGI Fridays, Barnes & Nobles, Targets, and Old Navy stores.

Missoula was built on logging and mining. Both have just about vanished, but fire has helped fill some of the gaps. At the Missoula airport a flotilla of eight two-engine retardant bombers owned by Neptune Aviation flies across the West each summer. A few hundred yards west of Neptune, past the low-slung airport terminal, the tall, boxy profile of a parachute loft marks the home of the Missoula smokejumping base, where 50 or 60 smokejumpers work. Next to it is what some regard as the intellectual center of the West's firefighting world, the Fire Sciences Lab.

Fire research, in fact, has become a blazing hot field. Across town at the University of Montana, fire science classes fill the School of Forestry's schedule, and professors such as Hayley Hesseln (economics), Ron Wakimoto (fire science), and Lloyd Queen (remote sensing—basically measuring forests and fires from the air) are known throughout the fire world. They in turn attract plenty of students, lured both by the available grant money for postgraduate research and the chance to make a name for themselves fairly quickly in a field that was on the fringes until just a few years ago. "It seems like just about everything we do here is directed at fire," Hesseln, a petite brown-haired woman in her thirties, told me when I visited her in her office. Hesseln, for instance, has seen a particular growth in the study of fire's impact on the West's sociology. Her own projects, one of which was financed by the fast-growing Joint Fire Sciences Program, a grant-making organization based at the National Interagency Fire Center in Boise, include studies of how fires affect recreation and whether people prefer controlled burns or mechanical thinning for reducing fuel loads in forests.

Some of the research smacks of touchy-feely stuff, but Hesseln says that plenty of decisions are being made with little evidence they're the right course. "The Forest Service just has pathetic data collection," she says. "They'll go out and do a controlled burn, and just send some kids out to do it. They don't keep track of what it actually costs, what good it did, how they handled the public—any of that stuff."

But Missoula also supports the grittier aspects of firefighting, not the least of which are the scores of University of Montana students who spend their summer fighting fires—so many that the school has been known to delay the start of fall classes during severe fire years. Out past the airport, for instance, an old logging-supply company called Peterson Machinery is trying to reinvent itself as the maker of a giant machine called the Proteus Fire Master. Sort of a firefighting tank, the Proteus chugs around on six deeply lugged tires that stand nearly as tall as a man. Perched in an enclosed cockpit some 15 feet off the ground, its operator can manipulate a huge claw jutting out from the machine to grab and move burning snags and logs. A pneumatically driven chain saw built into the grappler can cut through debris if need be, while a hose that's also built into the machine's proboscis can squirt water or fire retardant loaded into a 3,000-gallon tank dragged behind the tractor. And a small bulldozer blade jutting out front of the Fire Master cuts fireline.

Over the summer, the Proteus became something of a figure of fun, its driver and two-person supporting crew dressed in spiffy matching Nomex jumpsuits and helmets and looking a little bit like extras in a James Bond movie. Then there was the Fire Master itself, which seemed likely to cause as much damage as it prevented. "I'm not sure you can justify this thing," said one Forest Service guy to me, as we watched the Fire Master get ready to do its day's work. "Maybe where the terrain is just perfect, but otherwise it might do as much damage as it prevents." Then there is the cost—about $6,000 a day for the machine and its crew.

That isn't necessarily too much money; in theory, the Proteus could do the work of a crew of firefighters equipped with pumps, a bulldozer, even a log skidder. And in action, the Proteus certainly is an impressive device. Its big, wide tires spread out the load so it generally tears up the landscape less than bulldozers—especially when turning, as 'dozers turn by spinning the treads at different rates, ripping the ground beneath them to shreds. While I watched it work one afternoon the Proteus covered nearly a mile of ground in about an hour, extinguishing spot fires with its hose and breaking up several piles of dry, about-to-burn slash with its grappler. That same amount of work might have taken a 20-person crew most of a day. But I also saw a tendency to use the Proteus simply because it was available, not because it filled some special role. And its actual time on a fire seemed limited—mostly I see it going to a fire, getting ready to fight a fire, or heading back from the fire.

Missoula also is the home base for several longtime fire-support operations. One of the most welcome in a fire camp: Big Sky Catering, run by two brothers, Steve and Hal Nelson. Food is perhaps the

The Proteus Fire Master works at a fire in Montana.

highlight of any firefighter's day. For one thing, it's fuel for young men and women who burn calories like a big forest fire burns pine needles. For another, it's entertainment. A fire camp is not set up with its occupants' amusement in mind. No TV, no videos, not even any newspapers except for the few local papers that find their way to the media tent, and the clippings about the fire posted on a communal bulletin board. There's no alcohol, no video games. Instead, aside from showers, food is about the biggest diversion there is.

In early August, I caught up with Steve Nelson at the Virginia Complex in eastern Washington, a collection of two or three fires that for a few days was number one on the nation's priority list before fizzling out under a summer rainstorm. The Nelsons have been in the fire-catering business since 1986. They had a little restaurant experience, and had an acquaintance who had been making good money as a contract caterer for the Forest Service fire crews. So the Nelsons bought a refrigerator truck and a mobile kitchen, wrote up a bid, and went into business. Now they're ready to roll on four hours' notice, dispatching three big tractor-trailer rigs to a fire with a rolling kitchen, a refrigerator truck, and an assembly trailer where thousands of sack lunches come together. A crew of 15 or so goes along, a force usually supplemented by local workers.

The evening I visit with Steve the menu calls for roast turkey, mashed potatoes, dressing, and vegetables. While each caterer has a little license to be creative, the basics are spelled out in excruciating detail ("the fruit shall be one apple [minimum size 100 count] or one orange [minimum size 88 count] or other fresh fruit of comparable size") in a 157-page contract issued by the National Interagency Fire Center's contracting office. And the caterers are watched carefully to ensure that the guidelines are followed. At each fire base, someone from the logistics tent is apt to spot-check the food for portion size, if not taste. Meals are counted as well to ensure that a caterer is not padding the tally, as they're paid by the head—about $41 per person per day for three meals, a little more for groups smaller than 200. At that rate, the money adds up quickly—on a fire with 1,500 firefighters and support personnel, a common size for a fire camp these days, the Nelsons' operation will take in more than $60,000 a day, which in a busy summer might tally close to $4 million for the two kitchens Big Sky operates. "We're definitely in it for the money," Steve Nelson tells me unapologetically.

Not for the fun, certainly. For the Nelson brothers, the summer is a nerve-racking time spent wondering where the next call will take them and how they'll get in supplies once on-site. The night before my visit, for instance, Steve Nelson had just come in with a crew and had to set up to feed 1,000 firefighters—several hundred more than he anticipated as firefighting crews rolled in rapidly due to the fire's sudden high priority. Steak was on the menu, but he didn't have enough on hand. In a miracle somewhat akin to that of the loaves and fishes, a supplier's steak-packed refrigerator truck came by halfway through dinner. A chain gang was quickly set up and the steaks migrated from the truck to the grill to firefighters' plates. "That was a close one," Nelson said to me in a bit of understatement.

The Nelsons run a tight operation, which is obvious just from walking around. The trucks and kitchens are spotless, the crews hardworking and well-paid (a cook might make as much as the Hotshots he serves). The night I was there, while crews started to line up for dinner outside one of the big silver trailers, a neat striped tent was set up just outside, where bowls of lettuce and fruit salads, blue cheese and French dressing, fresh peach pies and cookies awaited crews as they came through with their plates of turkey. At the tables, the famished firefighters did more eating than talking. "This is pretty good," one newly arrived firefighter from Georgia said as he worked through a plate heaped high with food. "It's a real morale booster to have a good meal after you've been working all day." I had a plate myself. And it wasn't bad—for turkey that strongly resembled the pressed meat found in most grocery-store delis, and potatoes made from dried flakes. One downside: Light cuisine it's not. For the rest of the evening, I felt as if I'd swallowed a large brick.

Not all support businesses are in the fire camp. In an industrial park in Spokane, Washington, for instance I visited the factory that makes the White Smokejumper boot. It's the boot that to firefighters is as Nike is to runners, and the Smokejumper's distinctive, tall, wedge-shaped heel is everywhere in fire camps. In the White's factory, some 100 employees turn out 18,000 pairs of new boots each year, plus rebuilding 9,000 more (theoretically, a White's Smokejumper can last almost forever). The company makes all sorts of work and hunting boots, but fire-related footwear accounts for close to 75 percent of its sales of Smokejumpers, its best-selling boot, says Gary March, the company's vice president. And the boom in the fire industry has meant White's has plenty of customers. "We're at full capacity all year," March told me. "We'll get a call from a dealer who will tell us, 'We need 200 pairs of Smokejumpers,' but we just can't do much more to fill the order. We haven't been able to fully stock our own store for two years."

The White's factory is a whirring buzz of big Pfaff industrial sewing machines and leather cutters, as workers turn piles of oil-tanned leather into boots. It's a throwback process in an automated world, none more so than behind a big set of plate-glass windows, where customers of White's retail store can watch the company's handful of elite boot makers perform the final assembly on a boot. Shane York, a 28-year-old boot maker, has been with the company for 10 years, two years as a boot builder. His job is to take the partially assembled boot uppers and stitch them to the midsole of the boot, using a hand-formed "last" in the shape of a human foot to form the boot. It's tough, demanding work, requiring the precision of a surgeon with the brute strength needed to push thick waxed nylon threads through tough cowhide more than a quarter-inch thick. In a good shift, York can finish seven pairs of boots. But that will bump up to 10 pairs or so within another year as his skill increases. He's paid by the boot, and might earn $40,000 a year.

One of the more comical aspects of the fire economy is the ubiquitous presence of a T-shirt vendor outside of every fire camp I see. Just outside the entry to a fire camp in Montana in mid-August, I meet Elaine Sellars, who's open for business. The trunk of her Thunderbird is stuffed with T-shirts, fresh off the silkscreen press, bearing the name "Fridley Fire," along with a photograph of the fire in which, it is said, if you look carefully you can see the face of Satan. I don't, but it is getting dark.

Sellars owns a T-shirt shop in Greybull, Wyoming—Wyoming Classics—which she founded in 1991 in a circa-1908 brick building across from what long was the town's Rexall drugstore. In 1997, during a spate of fires in Montana and Wyoming, she noticed that tourist business dropped considerably, and with it T-shirt sales. "Even if the fires weren't near us, we'd notice the impact," Sellars, a chatty women in her early fifties, tells me. "People would just stay away." So Sellars applied the lemons-to-lemonade rule and printed up some shirts for the firefighters streaming toward nearby blazes. Now sales of fire T-shirts generate about $10,000 a year—nearly half Wyoming Classics's summer business.

Sellars's designs are among the best—for the Arthur Fire in Yellowstone, for instance, she designed a stylized knight's helmet ("King Arthur") against a flaming background. But Sellars relies on more than design ingenuity, over the years cultivating moles in the firefighting world who tip her off when a fire looks as if it might grow to "project" status, meaning it will require a long-term team and a fire base. "Sometimes I get calls from guys in helicopters flying over a new fire," she confesses. "If they give me information that lets me get T-shirts made first, they get free stuff."

Certainly, hawking T-shirts compares favorably with what might be the most dangerous job in the fire world: aviation. One staggeringly hot afternoon in Nevada I watch a huge, slab-sided PB4Y2 lumber toward its refueling spot on the runway outside of Battle Mountain, its nose bobbing as the pilot hits the brakes. Out of a hatch pops a stocky man who'd pass for a truck driver in his slightly sweaty T-shirt, jeans, baseball cap, day's growth of beard. It's Milt Stollak, the 48-year-old pilot. I walk out onto the sun-baked runway to talk with him. "This is the oldest aerial tanker in the industry," Stollak tells me. "It was built between 1944 and 1946. It's a tough airplane to fly. It's very heavy, and there aren't any hydraulic assists on the controls. But it's a good ol' airplane."

The PB4Y2 came into existence late in World War II as a Navy version of the B-24, the twin-tailed bomber flown by George Mc-Govern and made famous in Stephen Ambrose's book *The Wild Blue*. B-24s had flown with Navy colors for several years during the war as antisubmarine and long-range patrol bombers, and performed well. But the Navy wanted its own model, so the B-24's maker, California-based Consolidated, added seven feet to the fuselage, changed the armament, and replaced the distinctive two-rudder tail of the B-24 with a tall single rudder, giving what never was an elegant-looking aircraft an even more ungainly appearance due to its disproportionate height. Still, the Navy loved the PB4Y2, as it called its version of the B-24. It could fly seemingly forever (nearly 3,000 miles—or from Seattle to New York) on a single load of fuel, carried more than five tons of bombs, and was studded with machine guns.

For "warbird" buffs, forest fires also were long a place where it was possible to watch fleets of aircraft familiar to just about every combat theater in World War II still doing their thing, albeit with retardant instead of 500-pound bombs. Slim A-26 Invaders, high-winged Catalinas, big four-engine B-17s, the former naval torpedo bombers known as Avengers—all were long familiar sights around fires. In the 1990 movie *Always,* for instance, the firefighting pilot character portrayed by Richard Dreyfuss met his doom in a fiery crash of his A-26—a two-engine bomber that first flew in 1942—despite the efforts by his best friend (played by John Goodman) to douse the flames with retardant from Goodman's PBY Catalina, a lumbering seaplane that was flown by aircrews who spotted the elusive German battleship *Bismarck* in 1940.

Stollak has been flying aerial tankers for 10 years with Hawkins & Powers, a Wyoming-based company that is one of the key players in aerial firefighting. The big ex-bomber he muscles through the air now can carry 2,400 gallons of aerial retardant, an orange-dyed chemical slurry mixed in huge vats next to the runway that coats trees in a fire's path and slows its pace. Over a fire, Stollak talks by radio with controllers on the ground or in spotter planes, confirming the location for the retardant drop. Then he puts the craft into a shallow dive, eventually skimming as few as 100 feet over the treetops or sagebrush—this in an aircraft designed for level, high-altitude bombing from 25,000 feet. But today there are no Norden bombsights; the pilot drops based on his eyeballs and experience, toggling a switch on the steering column that activates a series of pumps and valves in the belly of the plane that can eject the entire load in just a few seconds, or dribble it out to cover an area the size of several football fields.

Stollak walks into the converted mobile home that's the Battle Ground airport's flight center, and walks back out with a Gatorade. It'll be a 14-hour day for him, with eight hours of that spent in the air. A few minutes later he hops back into the un-air-conditioned cockpit and pushes the switches that bring the four radial engines back to life. They drag the craft down the runway, then into the air in an ungainly climb that looks nothing like the athletic leap made by a modern 737. Stollak guides the PB4Y2 in a long, lazy turn, then heads in the direction of a large smoke plume to the north. There are many hazardous jobs in firefighting, but his may be among the riskiest: flying antique equipment into some of the most mountainous terrain in the West, through skies filled with smoke, debris, and other aircraft. For that, he'll earn about $35,000 to $40,000 during a season. And there's no hazardous-duty pay—it's *all* hazardous duty. Two weeks after I talked with Stollak, two retardant bombers flown by the California Department of Fire and Forest Protection collided over a fire, killing both pilots.

Two months after meeting Stollak, I sat in the cockpit of that PB4Y2 at the home base of Hawkins & Powers, the company for which Stollak works and that maintains a fleet of four PB4Y2s, plus a dozen other vintage aircraft that the company flies on firefighting missions across the West. Founded in 1969 by two tough aviation veterans, Dan Hawkins and Gene Powers, the company has been one of the leading aerial firefighting operations ever since. During the summer of 2001, for instance, 11 Hawkins & Powers aircraft logged 2,400 hours of flight time dropping retardant and water.

Along with Gene Powers's grandson, a soft-spoken young man named Ryan Powers who had spent the summer copiloting a stubby four-engine C-130 transport converted for fire use, I clambered over, under, and into a half-dozen of the aircraft the company bases in Greybull, Wyoming, a quiet ranching and oil town about 160 miles due east of Yellowstone Park. The town today is best known for Hawkins & Powers, a big bentonite (a powdery, claylike substance that goes into toothpaste and cat litter, among other things) mine just outside of town, and the annual Chainsaw Carving Competition, held in July. It's also where Elaine Sellars's T-shirt shop is located.

Following Ryan's lead, I climbed up a thin aluminum ladder, stepped carefully across the riveted skin of the old bomber, and dropped down a hatch that at one time was filled by a gun turret with two .50-caliber machine guns. The interior is remarkably stock: the control panel little changed since the airplane rolled off an assembly line in 1944, olive-green paint peeling in places between the old analog dials showing oil pressure, airspeed, and a host of other functions. But behind me, instead of a bomb bay, the surprisingly roomy fuselage held the plumbing and tanks for the retardant.

A dozen other firefighting aircraft sat scattered across the tarmac in front of the big Hawkins & Powers hangar. Among them: the C-130 that Ryan copilots, a transport craft with jetlike turbine engines instead of the PB4Y2's old-style radial-cylinder engines, a design that Lindbergh would have been familiar with. Compared to the cramped side-by-side seats of the PB4Y2, the C-130's flight deck seems big enough for a staff meeting, and its wide windshield offers a far more sweeping view of the world than that from the old World War II bomber. But a little more modern isn't necessarily better. The three C-130s flown by Hawkins & Powers were among the first such aircraft off the assembly line in the mid-1950s, a time when aeronautical engineers were working with new alloys and designs. As a result, the C-130s aren't holding up as well as the older PB4Y2s, which were built with perfected "old" technology rather than untested "new" technology. The C-130s, in fact, are plagued with wing cracks, which, although repairable, you don't really want in an aircraft.

But it's not easy keeping any of these aircraft in flying trim, given the arduous summers when a single aircraft might make 15 or more trips to a fire. In a capacious hangar, Hawkins & Powers mechanics spend the off-season, from October until May, rebuilding just about every aircraft in the inventory. During my visit, a second PB4Y2 was resting on huge jacks, most of its engines dismounted for overhaul. One was on a work stand in a corner of the hangar, where a mechanic installed new spark plugs. Originally, this engine—a Wright-Cyclone R-2600 with 14 cylinders each and the ability to generate 1,700 horsepower—was mounted on two-engine B-25s, the aircraft made famous in the Doolittle Raid. But they offer a bit more horsepower than the engines originally used on the PB4Y2, and bolt directly to the firewall without the need for any custom work.

And while it's true there isn't a tool shop in downtown Greybull that specializes in 60-year-old aircraft parts, items such as the six-inch spark plugs Shawn Jones is screwing into the finned pistons in the one-ton engine aren't all that difficult to come by, even though each aircraft requires 56. "The Internet," says Jones's boss, Jim Hederman. "We find all sorts of things there. Where the Internet places get them, I don't know." The AC-Delco spark plugs are factory fresh and still in their box. But the typography and faded cardboard of the boxes suggests they initially were made during the 1950s. That's also when the manual on the engines was printed. Hederman flips through it. "There's no way we could keep these engines going without this thing," he says. A few minutes later, Jones starts fastening a four-foot wrench to the drive shaft of the engine to start a process any home auto mechanic who worked on cars built before about 1980 remembers: cranking the shaft so each cylinder hits top dead center in the piston, and adjusting the timing to ensure that each plug fires at the right time.

Ironically, given the age of the PB4Y2 and the fact that they may well outlast the newer C-130s as firefighting bombers, the airplanes themselves were not built for the long haul. Consolidated, the man-

ufacturer, figured they were good for 500 hours of flight time—long
enough for training flights, 20 or 25 missions, and for the war to end
or the craft to get shot down. So there wasn't much provision made
for ease of repair, aside from the ability to bolt and unbolt the engines quickly should one take a bullet. And now, with as many as
10,000 flying hours on them, plenty of maintenance is required.
Under one of the thick wings, mechanic Jerry Moran struggles to
reach a portion of the wing near where the landing gear folds under
an engine. There, he is trying to repair a crack that had appeared in
the wing's laminated aluminum skin. The PB4Y2's "Davis wing,"
named for its designer, was revolutionary in the early 1940s, giving
the airplane enormous range. But they also had proven fragile, sometimes snapping off at the root when struck by enemy fire. "A wing
repair is a big job," Moran says. "This one might take as long as a
month." Moran has been in Greybull for a year, after working for the
BFGoodrich commercial airliner maintenance facility in Everett,
Washington, near Boeing's mammoth 747 factory. "I came here to
get out of the rat race," he tells me as he peers up into the gaping
hole in the wing. "That, and I love antiques."

Duane Powers, a son of the Hawkins & Powers cofounder, says
that the romance of flying vintage aircraft, plus the unusual nature
of the work, is a big draw. "I've flown all of these myself," he says, his
arm carving a sweep that takes in the aircraft lined up below his
second-story office window in a building near the hangar and runway. But it's also a tough business in which to survive. Maintaining
the vintage aircraft flown by aerial firefighting companies is labori-
ous, despite the Internet and a global web of surplus parts suppliers.
And if parts aren't a problem, finding mechanics qualified to maintain the sometimes 40-year-old engines can be. A plan to make surplus military aircraft available to aerial firefighting companies has
been languishing for five years, although there is some talk now that

mothballed 737 jetliners might work, given their payload capacity, reliability, and maneuverability.

To complicate things, the National Guard has come to play an increasingly prominent role in aerial firefighting, deploying squadrons of C-130 transports, newer versions of the old C-130s Hawkins & Powers flies, that can be converted to retardant bombers with a plug-in hose and tank assembly that slides into the craft's cavernous cargo hold. A month before I met with Hawkins, in fact, I'd watched three National Guard C-130s from North Carolina fly into the Boise airport with much fanfare, after Oregon governor John Kitzhaber and Washington governor Gary Locke had appealed to the National Guard for help fighting a big outbreak of fires. It was a spit-and-polish group, with a ramrod-straight general in charge and dozens of scurrying troops. The display drew a covey of newspaper and TV reporters to the Boise airfield; if the military was being called in, then the situation surely was serious.

Weeks later, Powers fumed. "We had aircraft available—but nobody called us," he said. "The National Guard sent out three aircraft, one of which didn't even fly as an aerial tanker—it was just a support plane. And they must have had 50 support personnel with them, eating catered lunches. We send out a mechanic and a pilot and they live in cheap hotels and grab a sandwich if they have time." Dispatching a PB4Y2 or a C-130 to a fire isn't cheap—they run about $8,000 a day when flying on a fire—but Powers says that's a bargain compared to what a National Guard crew costs. Trouble is, the National Guard aircraft and crews are often "free" to the Forest Service if the Guard units consider the work a training operation. And they don't require a standby contract, as the private carriers require. The taxpayer still foots the bill, and it's probably much higher than for a private contractor. But to the fire budget, the National Guard looks like a bargain.

Nonetheless, recent years have been good to the aerial firefighting industry. Firefighting command teams love to bring aerial resources—when conditions are right, they can be extremely effective, and can attack fires directly rather than the usual ground practice of digging firelines well in front of a large fire and waiting for the fire to trip over itself when it hits bare ground. Hawkins & Powers employs some 50 pilots, and they're typically busy from March until well into October.

The same pattern plays out across the West, where private contractors find a way to grab a bigger and bigger piece of the firefighting pie. In Oregon and Washington, for instance, the National Wildfire Suppression Association's nearly 200 member companies each summer field as many as 8,000 privately trained and paid firefighters—numbers that are close to twice what they were in the mid-1990s. Association chair Rick Dice is a fire contractor who has run crews from his base in Springfield, Oregon, since 1976 and now hires as many as 10 20-person crews in addition to as many as 10 fire engines.

Dice downplays the money he can make. "Firefighting is just in my blood," he says. "I'm a fifth-generation firefighter." But a contractor can make big bucks in a busy year. A 20-person crew may earn a contractor $72,000 in a week. It costs money to train and equip a crew—about $700 a person each season—and crew members make around $10.25 an hour plus overtime. But that still might leave $40,000 or more that the contractor earns on one crew for one week. Multiplied out by five or 10 crews and a fire season that could run 12 weeks, and the money adds up. But Dice insists it's a bargain. "We're able to control our costs better than the government," Dice says. "We're called only when needed, and that makes it cheaper for the government."

There's no evidence, however, that the push to privatize has saved the federal government a dime. On the contrary, by any measure it costs more to fight a fire today than it did 30 years ago. During the 1980s, for instance, most fires cost around $492 per acre to combat. By the late 1990s, after adjusting for inflation, those costs had soared to $792 per acre and were climbing fast—despite growing privatization that took over large parts of the firefighting operation. All told, of the $1.7 billion spent between 1993 and 1997, about $1.2 billion went to private contractors.

It isn't that using private parties to fight fires is bad. Often, it may indeed be more cost-effective than asking the feds to maintain a fleet of aerial tankers or mobile kitchens. But the system today is bad financial juju. On one hand, tax dollars are available in unlimited quantities when fires start. On the other, you have a private firefighting machine with absolutely no interest in raising a hand and saying, "Excuse me, but maybe our tankers won't help that much today." And much of the money spent doesn't even go toward firefighting, but instead goes to keeping units on "standby." In most cases, an aerial retardant tanker and crew are paid $350,000 simply to stay available. A helicopter, $210,000. A fire engine, $85,000.

The Forest Service, the federal agency that spends the most on firefighting, has tried to reform its spendthrift ways in the recent past. During the 1970s, as fire seasons intensified and the money spent to extinguish fires yielded increasingly poor results, it attempted to substitute fire "management" as a guiding policy, as opposed to fire "suppression." But the swelling battleship of the firefighting world was reluctant to turn or slow—so long as smoke-jumpers and Hotshot crews and aerial tankers were available, field managers confronted by fire were reluctant to do anything different from what they had been trained to do: stamp out fires. So little changed. A more serious effort to change the way fire is handled came after the 1994 fire season, in which 34 firefighters were killed,

4.7 million acres burned, and suppression costs hit a then-record figure of $950 million. The Forest Service's managers feared that the skyrocketing toll from fires, both human and monetary, would prompt Congress to turn off the dollar spigot, which had always opened as wide as deemed necessary, when deemed necessary. In response, the Forest Service and the Department of the Interior (which manages the National Park Service and Bureau of Land Management) developed what was called the Federal Wildland Fire Policy Review. Signed by Dan Glickman, then the boss of the Forest Service in his role as Secretary of the Department of Agriculture, and Department of Interior Secretary Bruce Babbitt, the new policy directed fire managers to shake up their priorities in an effort to improve firefighter safety and cut suppression costs. Its most profound philosophical shift was to try to change firefighters' priorities. Previously, saving "property"—even if an outhouse—was the main objective of fire suppression, followed by human safety and resource protection. The new rules stipulated that firefighter safety would be the number-one concern, with property and resource protection trailing. The fire policy review also required federal land managers, such as the chiefs of specific national forests, to develop fire-use plans that would basically break forested areas into zones in which suppression efforts would automatically range from extensive to minimal when a fire broke out.

As this document was working its way through the federal pipeline, the Forest Service held an internal review of its tactics and policies in the face of fire. Directed by Denny Truesdale, who in 2001 was helping implement the Forest Service's portion of the National Fire Plan, the report took fire managers to task for their blind adherence to costs-be-damned firefighting. "Many people, both inside and outside the Forest Service, fail to recognize that wildfire is a normal, positive force in the ecosystem," Truesdale wrote in the report. "Often it is neither preventable nor susceptible to suppression actions. Paradoxically, every time a fire is suppressed, fuel in adjacent unburned areas continues to accumulate. Thus, successful fire suppression may increase the potential damage and cost of future fires. This cost should be considered in the process of deciding how to suppress the fire." The Truesdale report also tried to emulate National Park Service fire policies that tried to calculate the cost of fighting a fire against the cost of treating it as a prescribed fire, and perhaps having less fire to deal with in the future. In other words, the report tried to factor in the notion that firefighting actually increases the future costs of fire by adding to a forest's fuel loads.

The reports had minimal impact. Costs continued to rise, only a handful of national forest managers had completed fire plans by 2001, and as Thirtymile showed, putting firefighters in harm's way despite threatening conditions remained standard operating procedure. By 2000 it was absolutely business as usual, with the result that yet another plan—the National Fire Plan—emerged in an effort to restore a measure of sanity to firefighting.

It could be argued that America spends $1 billion or more on fires each year and gets essentially nothing. Andy Stahl, executive director of Forest Service Employees for Environmental Ethics, puts it this way: "It may make financial sense to put out small fires that have just started in places we don't want burned—say, the grasslands around suburban Los Angeles or the backyards of Santa Fe. But the notion that we should continue to fight fires when they're 10,000 acres or 100,000 acres is ludicrous. We never put out fires of that size. Nature does. But we always fight them. We might as well drop dollar bills on them." The General Accounting Office agrees, observing in a 1999 report that "large, intense wildfires are generally impossible for firefighters to stop and are only extinguished by rainfall or when there is no more material to burn."

It's ironic, in a way. When the fire machine makes its biggest splash, when 1,000 firefighters are at work and a crack incident command team is running things and the airstrip is abuzz with Vertol helicopters and PB4Y2 retardant bombers, is also when it's the least effective—the wizard behind the curtain, nothing more. That's when it might make sense to pull back and treat a big fire as inevitable. But when such a fire breaks out, rational economic planning is tossed out the window. Firefighting simply gets too much positive feedback to stop itself, with nighttime news of firefighters marching in line toward the fire, local homeowners posting "Thanks, We Love U!" signs along the roads, politicians helicoptering into a fire camp to rally the troops. A major effort against a large fire creates an impression of action and determination in the face of a looming catastrophe. And sometimes it seems as if that is the goal— to make a big public show of "extinguishing" a fire. If it is, then the show is beginning to backfire. The Valley Complex fires in 2000, as well as just about any fire that burns for more than a few days, shows that there really isn't much that can be done once a big fire gets the wind at its back and starts to run. Throwing millions of dollars at it may make federal agencies feel like they're really something, but it's not going to accomplish a hell of a lot except run up a big bill.

Chapter 11

▲ ▲ ▲ ▲

Fridley Fire

By the time I leave Alturas the fire season has accelerated. Sixteen new large fires—100 acres or more, with the potential to grow much larger—are reported. Another dozen big fires that had been burning for a week or more still are chugging along. And initial attack crews are busy across California, Oregon, Washington, Montana, Nevada, and Idaho, hosing down or digging line around the scores of small fires that often break out each day but that never make the headlines. It is hot across much of the West, with thunderstorms moving from Arizona and New Mexico into Utah and Nevada, bringing with them the promise of fresh starts.

Across the West, more than 12,000 firefighters are at work. Dozens of aerial retardant bombers are flying, and helicopters. Fire crews need rides from one fire to another, and fire managers all feel that their particular blaze is the most threatening one around, worthy of the most support. In Boise, the National Interagency Fire Center has ramped up quickly to Level 5—its highest alert level.

Crews work around the clock at the Center, juggling requests for firefighting teams, aircraft, and equipment, ordering supplies, and trying to prioritize which fires demand attention and which might be left alone for a bit.

From Alturas, I drive to Boise to see how things are going. A few hours after arriving, I watch 34-year-old Coloradan Tyler Doggett gain some perspective he'd lacked when fighting fires as a smoke-jumper, an occupation he'd had to give up temporarily owing to a broken femur incurred during a jump earlier in the year. "I used to wonder why things didn't happen quickly when we'd be on a fire and order more resources," he says to me, as he pages through computer screens full of data on crew availability and location. "Now I know why. There's just so much going on right now, it's hard to get crews from one place to another, and there's a lot of competition for re-sources." And he needs some for a fast-growing collection of a dozen fires that is threatening Monument, Oregon, a small town in the eastern part of the state. "I've got eight Type 2 crews out of the Great Basin headed their way, but that's all that's available right now," he says. "There just aren't any Hotshot crews to spare." The Hotshot crews are what incident commanders want—they do the most work in the least amount of time, and unlike Type 2 crews need relatively little supervision.

Doggett, meanwhile, is learning a reality of the summer fire sea-son. "Every fire," he says, "is the most important fire to the people who are there. That makes the stress here just incredible. I go home at night, and my head is spinning."

NIFC, though, exists largely to make the decision about which fires matter and which don't—or, at least, those that don't matter enough at a given time to command scarce resources. Just off the edges of the hubbub, Center coordinator Neal Hitchcock is taking the fast pace in stride despite nearly two weeks of 12-hour days.

"Compared to last year, which was a marathon, this is more like a sprint," he tells me calmly. "Right now we're holding our own in some areas, falling behind in others." Each day, Hitchcock and his intelligence officers meet two or three times to assess the progress of existing fires and the potential for new ones. Earlier in August, when only a dozen or so large fires were burning, NIFC could generally deliver to fire managers the crews, aircraft, and helicopters requested. But now it's time for some fire triage—some fires will get crews, some will not. Oregon and Washington were at the top of the priority list, with the Monument Fire and blazes near Leavenworth and Omak, in Washington state, all threatening homes and buildings.

Hitchcock is keeping a close eye on weather reports. Although the western high pressure area is well-established, a large low forms in the Pacific. Fire managers have come to anticipate an "August singularity"—a band of storms that often moves across the West during the third week in August, cooling or even extinguishing fires that flourish during the hot, dry first half of August. But meteorologist Heath Hockenberg, watching forecast information on an array of computer screens in an office down the hall from Hitchcock's, isn't sure it is forming. "This is a little too diffuse," he says, pointing at a band of clouds lurking off the Pacific coast. "I think it's going to warm up again after this passes through. Maybe then we'll get the singularity."

As it turns out, the fire meteorologists working in Boise do a good job of nailing the fire forecast. Three days after my visit, a band of storms moves over the Cascade mountains of Oregon and Washington, cooling some fires that had threatened to wreak havoc. But then it warms up, and the remnants of that front, stripped of moisture, cause their own problems, particularly for a little, 200-acre fire in southern Montana that is just then showing up on fire planners' radar.

It's called the Fridley Fire, and Steve Frye's Northern Rockies National Incident Command Team has just been dispatched to handle it.

At noon on August 23, a Thursday, I pull my Dodge Intrepid off of I-84 in Bozeman, Montana, and stop downtown to grab lunch. It is a warm day, above 80, with light haze in the sky. But all around Bozeman's low-rise brick-and-stone downtown, the low hills and mountains that frame the city are clearly visible. To the east, over one stretch of hills baked tan in the summer sun, a wisp of smoke can be seen.

The Fridley Fire had started four days earlier when a fast-moving lightning storm swept across southern Montana, sparking a fire in the steep, heavily wooded Gallatin National Forest. Within 24 hours the phone rang at Frye's desk. He had just gotten back to Glacier National Park after wrapping up two weeks at Yellowstone, and was facing 370 e-mails and a pile of paperwork. Twelve hours later, he's in a plane bound for southern Montana, while the rest of his incident management team is speeding that way in their Dodge Rams and Ford Explorers.

The Fridley Fire starts lazily, torching its way through timber as if it hasn't quite decided its intentions. After three days of sparking and smoking, throwing embers in its path like a kid tossing bread crumbs to ducks, it is still a relatively compact 4,000 acres. But the fire worries Frye the moment he gets to the Paradise Valley, where a temporary fire base is established near the little crossroads town of Emigrant, about 20 miles north of the border with Wyoming and Yellowstone National Park. It is burning in a chunk of national forest that is nearly inaccessible by road and that is crisscrossed by precipitous cliffs and valleys. A tough place for fighting a hot fire, he thinks.

The same notion crosses the mind of Ron Hvizdak, the fire behavior officer for Frye's Type 1 team. Hvizdak looks at maps of the

Gallatin National Forest and doesn't like what he sees. Blanketing the hills is a thick mantle of 100-year-old lodgepole pine, interspersed with thickets of alpine fir. Hvizdak loathes alpine fir—a scrubby, high-altitude tree that tends to create fires that "spot" wildly, sending miniature firebombs out ahead of the main fire that can jump firelines and wreak havoc with firefighting plans. Lodgepole pine is no picnic to deal with either, as anyone in Yellowstone in 1988 recalls.

Worse, two days after arriving at the fire, Frye and his team of fire managers can't do much more than watch from their vantage point in a field behind a rural fire station. From there, they can look across the sloping valley and the Yellowstone River at a plume of smoke rising from near the eponymous 10,150-foot Fridley Peak. They would have preferred taking some action. But they're on the thin end of a badly overstretched supply line. Every fire crew in the West is at work, and even as Frye frets about his own fire, fire managers in Boise are more concerned about brush fires that are ripping through thousands of acres in northern Nevada, four big fires in northern California, and a blaze near Leavenworth, Washington, that still poses a threat to dozens of homes there. So on the evening of the twenty-third the Fridley team has available a mere four Type 2 crews, about 80 firefighters total, and no Hotshot crews. The Type 2 crews simply are no match for the terrain, so Frye holds them in reserve and puts them to work setting up pumps and removing brush around houses along several gravel roads that crisscross the Gallatin north of the fire.

Assigned to Frye's team as fire meteorologist is Bob Tobin, whom I'd met at the Thirtymile Fire. Tobin is a tall, loose-limbed, good-natured guy who looks a little like radio host Howard Stern, with a small silver-stud earring and long curly brown hair emphasizing the resemblance. Based in Pendleton, Oregon, Tobin has been working as a freelance "fire met" for three years. Tobin is a tech geek—he loves his satellite dish, his PCs, his ability to troll National Weather Service Internet sites for the latest forecasts and satellite pictures. "I'm an information junkie," he says. "I need everything I can collect. Nothing has a bigger effect on a fire than the weather, and it's the hardest thing to forecast."

Still, Tobin also is smart enough to know that looking at a PC screen of multicolor weather-radar images isn't always enough. He loves his data, but also makes a point to talk with the locals. Weather may start out as a 1,000-mile front over the Pacific, but a place like the Gallatin Mountains has a way of bending even the biggest storms to fit local conditions. And Tobin knows from chatting around that this valley can get incredibly windy; it forms a natural funnel that flows out of the Gardiner entrance to Yellowstone National Park and shoots straight north for 50 miles until it fans out into the more open country north of Livingston, a former rail and cattle town that now sports a Montana-chic downtown of steakhouses and bars.

About 24 hours earlier, a cold front had swept in from the Pacific, dumping rain in eastern Washington and dousing several good-sized fires there. But by the time it crossed the Idaho panhandle, the mountains had pretty well wrung it dry. And dry cold fronts are one of the main culprits in turning a quiet fire into an inferno. They invariably bring wind, and the strong counterclockwise rotation of these fronts means these winds could shift suddenly—blowing out of the southwest as the front approaches, then from the northeast as its trailing edge sweeps over a fire. Dry cold fronts have been to blame for a number of fire-related tragedies over the years—most notably the Storm King Mountain tragedy in 1994.

At the evening briefing on August 22, held in a corrugated-steel firehouse, Tobin warns Frye and his team that the next day could be dangerous. "I figure that around noon the winds are going to pick up and come from out of the south," he says, pointing to a giant print-out of the West's weather as Frye's team and people from the Forest Service and Gallatin County Sheriff's Department lounge around on folding metal chairs. Tobin gives great briefings, waving his arms, prowling back and forth in front of his audience, graphically de-scribing the clash of fronts and the interplay of high pressure and low pressure, talking about "back-door fronts" and "water-vapor trails" in a way that makes it sound like he's calling a Packers game rather than giving a weather forecast. Winds the next day might hit 40 miles per hour, Tobin says, and likely would last until well into the evening.

Then Tobin hands off to Hvizdak, who tacks up a big map of the Gallatin National Forest, the current perimeter of the fire a Ror-schach blob in the southwest quadrant. The wind, he says, is going to combine with the north-south orientation of the dry timber in this portion of the Gallatin to create the conditions for a big burn. His advice to Frye: Keep fire crews well back from the fire, and con-centrate on a line running along Trail Creek Road, a gravel road ex-tending north and west to Bozeman, traversing hilly country dotted with old hunting cabins, modest homes, and the occasional Mon-tana Ranchette that has become so popular in the state in recent years. He thumps a finger on the map, far away from the bold dot-ted line that aerial reconnaissance had shown to be the fire's perimeter the previous evening. "It could reach this point tomor-row," he says. The spot where his finger points is some six miles from the current fire perimeter.

The next day, around 2, I drive out on the main street that points east out of town and eventually merges with I-84. My plan is that when I hit Livingston, about 15 miles away, I'll drive south and find the fire base. At a stoplight, I flip up the sun visor and peer through

the windshield to see if I can still see the plume of smoke I'd noticed earlier. For a moment, I think a thunderhead is forming in the
hazy sky. Then, with a start, I realize I am looking at a boiling mass
of smoke, ridged and convoluted like a giant cauliflower, so tall I
have to lean into the Intrepid's deeply inset windshield and crane
my neck to see its top.

The Fridley Fire has blown up.

I'd seen big smoke columns before, but this is a giant. I am reminded of a May morning in 1980, when my wife-to-be Jane and I
sat in a cow pasture near Longview, Washington, forced off Interstate 5 by stalled traffic as I tried to rush back to my newspapering
job in the town of Vancouver, and watched a giant ash cloud billow
from the ruins of Mount St. Helens and darken the sky over half of
Washington State.

I speed down I-84 at Livingston, watching the smoke pillar as I
weave through traffic. In Livingston, I find the local Forest Service
office, buy a map of the area from a harried desk clerk, and get quick
directions to the fire base. There, as the wind that also is whipping
the Fridley Fire causes the management team's tan tents to snap
and billow, I find Frye standing on a sunbaked field of stubbly grass,
looking across the valley at the enormous plume, arms folded across
his chest, a black, low-crowned baseball cap keeping the sun off his
eyes. He is utterly calm. "No need to get excited," he tells me, after
talking with a reporter from the Billings newspaper. "These conditions had been predicted." Still, Frye is impressed by what he is
watching. "Even if all the crews we had on order were here, they still
wouldn't be out in front of this fire," he says. "I suspect it's one of
the most significant fires in this area in recent history—maybe in
the last 150 years. It's hard not to be awed by something like that.
But today, we'll just stay out of its way."

Tobin, who had hit the wind forecast squarely on the nose, is more animated, dashing into his weather yurt to check weather reports on his PC, then back outside to stare at the plume. He pulls out a small device that measures relative humidity, the prime indicator of how active a fire might be. "Ten percent," he mutters. "Holy sweet Jesus." Earlier, Tobin had called the Bozeman airport to see if its radar was picking up the smoke—as if it could be missed. "They've got it," he says. "They say it's hitting 40,000 feet." Even while watching such a horrifying event, the meteorologist in him can't be contained. "Wow, look at the way it punches through those lenticular clouds," he exclaims, as a flat deck of cold gray clouds, carried by the front, crashes into the mushrooming pillar like a doomed sailing ship into a reef, curling itself boomerang-fashion around the dense, warm smoke. Nearly eight vertical miles up into the troposphere, the pillar still has so much energy that it can be seen moving, growing, even with the naked eye. Around the column's base, where it emerges from the green hills, orange sheets of flame occasionally blast aside the smoke and climb above the trees. Hundred-foot lodgepole pines flare into pillars of flame three and four times the trees' height, the tops of the flames snapping off like solar flares and rising, unattached, through the air.

At around 5, I drive down to Highway 89 near the Yellowstone River for a better vantage point. From there the flames are even more prominent, lapping over the hilltops in waves, then receding behind the black smoke. Nearby, horses graze, unconcerned by the apocalyptic scene behind them. Through the smoke, with my Minolta binoculars, I see a twin-engine Neptune retardant tanker orbiting in what seems to be the heart of the fire, then dive behind a hill to unload its slurry. *That,* I think to myself, *is a tough way to make a living.*

The next morning I glue myself to Hvizdak, who is heading for the fire to get a better idea of how much terrain it covered the day before. By the previous evening, the winds had calmed and the smoke pillar had changed from a seemingly solid mass of hard-edged smoke to a wispier, but still large, plume. And winds are forecast to stay calm during the day. So Hvizdak figures it's safe to take a look. He'd spent the previous day driving roads in the fire's path, trying to guess where it might burn next and advising Frye's fire crews on where to station themselves to protect homes and ranches. Along with him is Tami Parkinson, a slender, brown-haired 29-year-old from the Clearwater National Forest who is learning the fire behavior game. We bounce along Trail Creek Road in Hvizdak's pickup, then drive south toward the fire perimeter. At an intersection the road is clogged with ranchers' pickups and horse trailers. The ranchers are mounting up on horses and ATVs and fanning into the hills to round up any cattle that hadn't been barbecued by the previous day's holocaust.

The fire had done pretty much what Hvizdak and Tobin had predicted. Between noon and around 6 P.M., when the cold front finally passed and the winds calmed, it had razed about 15,000 acres of timber, advancing nearly seven miles. The fire front was close to four miles wide, and with winds of 30 and 40 miles per hour lashing it from behind, the blaze had moved at a steady pace of nearly two miles per hour—a decent walking speed for an average human. Flame lengths at the front had easily topped 300 feet at times, while temperatures inside the inferno had exceeded 2,000 degrees.

The three of us wind our way into the hills in the Ram, stopping occasionally to open wire gates. The air has a dry, scorched smell to it. We haven't gone far, maybe a mile or two, when we start to hit small fires smoldering in stands of lodgepole pine and alpine fir. "Darned alpine fir," Hvizdak mutters. "That stuff burns spotty as hell." The small spot fires are like scouts—some burning a half mile ahead of the main fire front, set by embers blown by the wind from the main fire.

Hvizdak and Parkinson want to walk the fireline to assess the fire's behavior and its potential for another blow-up. Hvizdak drops Parkinson and me off, then drives back down the road the way we came. Parkinson and I will walk down to the truck, then leapfrog in it farther down the slope and find Hvizdak as he continues walking. It is a hot day. By 10 the temperature nears 90. I am sweating heavily in my Nomex and hard hat as Parkinson and I hike downhill through an old clear-cut.

Like many Forest Service employees, Parkinson caught the fire bug in college while attending the University of Idaho, one of many schools in the West that produces more firefighters than football players. "I liked the adrenaline rush of it," she tells me, as we pick our way over slash in the clear-cut. Proponents of logging and intensive forest management as a way to minimize fires would find some ammunition for their argument here; the blaze had burned up to the edge of the old cutting unit and stopped. Then again, fires can't burn where there isn't much fuel—and logging had certainly cleared the fuel. In some cases, though, fires seem even more prone to burn through logged areas than not. Logging typically leaves debris on the ground that dries and makes wonderful fuel. Moreover, the sunny openness of recent clearcuts encourages thick, flammable brush that easily dries out during the long sunny days of July and August.

Parkinson hadn't gone into firefighting full-time; she'd gotten her master's degree in forest resources and joined the Forest Service in 1997. In Idaho's Clearwater National Forest she works as a fuels specialist—cataloging the burnable stuff in the forests so fire managers can know what to expect should a fire erupt. She also is a fire-behavior analyst in training, sort of an inferno novitiate, hoping someday to fill the same role Hvizdak fills for Frye's team. "Fire is a growth area, jobwise," she tells me. "But a lot of young people get into the firefighting end of it and stay there. And that's a poor career path—what can you do with it when you're 40?"

Parkinson and I find the truck, and later Hvizdak, Parkinson, and I walk more of the fireline. Although there is no wind, the fire continues to advance—to "creep," as firefighters say. It's an apt description. A fire may simply work its way along the ground, burning so slowly that it's perfectly safe to walk up and kick dirt onto it. But intermittently, that low creeping burn will hit ladder fuels. In a stand of lodgepoles, I stand almost directly under a tree as the skulking blaze hits its lower branches. Fire leaps up the tree, accompanied by an evil crackling sound, as if someone were wadding up giant sheets of cellophane, then a loud *whoo-OOSH!* as resin-filled pine needles ignite like gasoline. I unlimber a camera to get a picture, and as I do, a shower of glowing embers bounces off my hard hat and rolls over my shoulders and shirtsleeves. That's how a big fire can move even on a still day; as a tree ignites, it throws out embers that fall 5 or 10 feet from the tree. These light new fires that crawl along the forest floor until they hit a new tree, which then lights with a roar, sends off a new ember shower, and the process begins anew.

As I labor to keep up with Hvizdak's ground-eating stride, I hear a mournful "ooo-OOO, ooo-OOO" from some yards away. "What the heck is that?" I ask. "A mama cow," Hvizdak says. "She's looking for her calf, who probably didn't make it out." Earlier, we'd also seen a moose stiff-legging it across the road. Whether from ash or fire it was hard to tell, but the tall animal was black from just above its belly down to its hooves. At least big animals like moose or deer, or even cows, can cover enough territory to escape a fire, if they think to do so. Thousands of animals that go to ground in a crisis—yellow pine chipmunks, golden-mantle squirrels, martens, and short-tail weasels—had no doubt perished, not to mention brown trout and rainbows that had been literally poached in the streams. Occasionally firefighters will find a squirrel or some other small animal that has been killed by a fire, frozen in midflight, its front paws reaching out for safe ground it couldn't reach. Larger animals may survive the initial burns, even becoming euphoric as humans do when they have been severely burned. But then the body goes into shock, dumping poisons into the bloodstream and losing fluid and heat through the burned skin. It may take days for a burned deer, elk, or bear to die.

The next morning, after the briefing, I hook up with Jack Kirkendall, one of two line operations chiefs on the Fridley Fire. If Steve Frye is the general of this army, and Hvizdak and Tobin its intelligence officers, then "line ops" Kirkendall is a colonel. His job is to stay close to the front lines while keeping in his head as much of the big picture as possible. He needs to make sure that firefighting teams are in the right places, that they meet their objectives for digging fireline, and that if any trouble spots flare they quickly get attention.

Kirkendall hadn't been at the Arthur Fire, so he was new to me. I'd first seen him during the evening briefing the first day I was on the fire. A fire truck had that morning been slow to respond when called to help with structure protection. Now Kirkendall made it clear he expected every crew and truck to be ready to roll as needed at 7 A.M. sharp. "If you can't meet this schedule," he'd said in a voice that was calm but left little room for a dissenting opinion, "you can go on home." Kirkendall backed up that round-in-the-chamber tone of voice with the bearing and appearance of a particularly tough Marine drill instructor: At 48 years of age, he stands about 5 feet 10 inches, with a well-muscled frame, an intense expression in his eyes, and a bristling gray mustache over a firm mouth. He'd started fighting fires in 1972, when he saw an ad for a Hotshot crew on a college bulletin board. "I figured that sounded a lot more fun than summer school, so I went down and applied," he says. "They looked at me—I weighed 15 more pounds then—and figured I could swing a Pulaski." He did, and well enough to qualify for smokejumper status two years later, jumping out of the big Missoula base until 1979. Frankly, Kirkendall scared the hell out of me. But I also figured he'd find some action.

Before we set out, Kirkendall has some camp chores. First is to get a crew of firefighters from Florida squared away so they can make a contribution. Florida may strike some as an odd place for wildland firefighters, but any resident of the state knows they're perfectly at home. Florida combines tropical fecundity with Texas-style drought, a perfect formula for huge fires in its thickets of slash pine. In 1998, 487,000 acres of Florida forest burned in the state's worst fire year in recorded history. Three people died. In June of that year, nearly 7,000 firefighters were fighting some 2,200 separate fires.

But Florida firefighting also is very different from what is found in the West. In Florida, road access usually is fairly easy. And, of course, by any standard the topography of Florida is, well, flat. In Montana, as in most of the West, fires often burn in wilderness, and a hike of even a mile may involve scrambling up a 2,000-foot ridge and down the other side. The Florida crew, while willing, was tired from the long trip to the Paradise Valley. Plus, the men lacked good maps, and hadn't arranged with the base motor pool for transportation. Kirkendall huddles with the crew chiefs as they riffle through the day's action plan. "Here's what we're going to do," he says, as he explains where they'd be and their objectives for the day. "You'll fly in by helicopter to this stretch of the fire's southeastern flank, dig fireline for the day, and with luck get airlifted out in time for supper.

Jack Kirkendall, an operations chief on a fire management team, walks through a portion of the Fridley Fire in Montana.

But be ready to hike out or stay put for the night. Things can get weird around here if the wind picks up or one of the helos breaks down."

Kirkendall walks away and rolls his eyes a little. "I thought they just needed maps," he mutters.

Next on the agenda: housekeeping in the new fire base, which is moving west of Highway 89 to accommodate promised reinforcements now that the Fridley Fire has climbed to near the top of the national priority list. After a breakfast of scrambled eggs and pancakes, Kirkendall fishes a Eureka tent out of the back of his pickup and strides out into the rangeland where he will live for the next few weeks. Here and there, gopher holes punctuate the ground. "A good place to break an ankle," he observes. Or a good home for rattlesnakes. The next day, on the fire base bulletin board, someone posts a photo of two big Western Diamondback rattlers—each a good six feet long and as big around as a softball, grappling with one another outside a burrow from which they'd emerged even as logistics crews were setting up tents for the incident command team. Loaded with two-inch fangs, Western Diamondbacks are aggressive, high-strung snakes that kill more people in the United States each year than any other poisonous reptile. And like all reptiles, they're cold-blooded and seek out heat—whether it's sun-warmed pavement or a cozy tent interior.

Living under such conditions isn't easy. It's one thing for Hotshots and other firefighters to spend the summer in a tent. They're in their twenties, for the most part, and pretty adaptable. But Kirkendall, like many people in the Type 1 management teams, is middle-aged, with a family (he's the single parent of an 11-year-old boy who stays with a grandmother when Kirkendall is off on fires) and a career. Here he is, living in a tent with a floor the size of a twin bed, sleeping five feet from a gopher hole that might house a rattlesnake the size of two baseball bats laid end-to-end and that might show a lively interest in sharing a sleeping bag.

So it's a little surprising to learn how little turnover there is among a Type 1 team such as Frye's. Kirkendall has been with it since the team formed seven years ago; same with Hvizdak, deputy commander Jeff Scussel, and several other members of the team. Part of that longevity is because of the camaraderie that develops in this sort of outfit. The team members clearly enjoy one another's company, clustering at the breakfast tables after the morning briefing, and invariably rolling down a pickup window to jaw with a counterpart they come across on a gravel road. There is the clear sense that for many people, fighting a fire is like being sent to summer camp—and getting paid for it.

But for many who work in federal land-management agencies, particularly one that's as high-profile and politicized as the U.S. Forest Service, fighting a fire is their only opportunity to actually *act*. No environmental impact statements, hearings, policy reviews, planning sessions, and reports. One can question whether that paralysis is a bad thing or not. Heaven knows, left to take action during the 1960s and into the 1980s, the Forest Service set a tone for forest management in the United States that was far more wrongheaded than right, with its judgment-free "multiple-use" policy, its determination to rid its lands of "decadent" old-growth trees, its mindless penchant for punching roads into wilderness areas. But for a guy like Kirkendall, and many others, today's state of affairs is intolerable. "On a fire, you really get to do something," he tells me, as we bump along yet another gravel road en route to a flare-up of a blaze on the Fridley Fire's eastern perimeter, a flare-up that could threaten some nearby ranches.

Certainly, working a fire is as close to unsupervised fun as anyone in a government agency is apt to find. Fighting a fire is a nonstop crisis, or at least a brewing one, and crises don't wait for some 200-page report to wind its way to D.C. and back. And damn the cost. During each briefing, for instance, a fire management team's finance officer gives a report on how much has been spent on a particular fire. That total adds up in a hurry—a big fire easily runs a tab of $1 million a day, particularly when $6,000-per-hour helicopters start Ping-Ponging back and forth from an air base to a fire. But not once, not in a single briefing, did I hear anyone suggest that maybe this fire or that fire didn't quite justify the cost, or that maybe the helicopters might stand down for a day while the much cheaper ground crews (an hour of helicopter time will keep a ground crew of 20 paid and fed for two days) try to get a leg up on the blaze.

Some of this profligacy is understandable. Forest fires are dangerous, and if something goes awry and firefighters are killed or injured, no fire manager wants it on the record that he or she had grounded helicopters or refused extra resources in the interest of saving a buck. By July, for instance, Colorado congressman Scott McInnis, a Republican, made considerable hay out of suggestions that helicopters assigned to fight the Thirtymile Fire had been delayed over worries that its bucket might dip endangered bull trout as well as water out of the Chewuch River. Maybe, just maybe, that had contributed to the four deaths, was McInnis's clear intimation. So no one wants to be accused of letting a fire go in an effort to save a buck. Or a trout.

That makes the message clear: Fire duty is a blank check. For the average National Park Service or U.S. Forest Service manager beset by tourists, tree-huggers, unemployed loggers, congressional delegations, Endangered Species Act regulations—not to mention wholesale policy changes every time a new presidential administration breezes into Washington, D.C. with a fresh ideological slant—fighting a fire is Christmas, the first day out after a 20-year sentence in a federal penitentiary, and three cherries in the slot machine all rolled into one. If the trade-off is a diet of overcooked eggs, lukewarm Gatorade, and ham sandwiches in a paper bag, sleeping in a tent next to a rattlesnake burrow, and 16-hour workdays under a sometimes blazing Montana sun, well, so it goes.

For Kirkendall, the work also means riding herd on a dozen division chiefs, each of whom is responsible for fire crews along a specific stretch of the fire, usually a fireline "division" between a half mile and a mile long. "We've had a helluva lot worse crew problems," he says, alluding to the mini-fiasco earlier in the morning. "I've been on fires where we've had 200 pieces of equipment and 3,500 firefighters. What a mess trying to sort *that* out. There are some advantages to a lean and mean organization— you get too many people, and you spend time managing that organization, not managing the incident."

Managing the incident is the task of the Type 1 Incident Command Teams that form each summer. Kirkendall's team, led by Steve Fryc, is the Northern Rockies National Incident Command Team, mustered out of Montana. Simply put, the command team is the fire's general staff. Its members concentrate on strategy, tactics, supply—all the big-picture items—so that fire crews can concentrate on digging fireline rather than where the next meal might come from. Command team members include logistics and finance managers, a safety officer, a meteorologist and fire-behavior analyst, line supervisors who manage specific sections of a fire, air operations directors, a planning chief, and a public information officer. In most cases the team arrives at a fire before the firefighters, sizing up the fire and ordering in the firefighting crews it figures will be needed to fight the blaze. And it will stay with the fire, typically, for 14 days before it's relieved by a second team (if necessary) and its members scatter back to their home bases.

For Kirkendall, part of the pleasure in the job also comes from working with Frye, whom he holds in high regard. "I've worked with a lot of ICs and Type 1 teams, and Steve is far and away the best incident commander I've seen," Kirkendall tells me. "He's supportive of us personally and professionally, and trusts our judgment. I've never had a disagreement with Steve—which is due to skill on his part, not mine.

"And he hasn't lost his enthusiasm for this business."

Frye has a knack for keeping in clear control of a team without really appearing to do so—or even appearing to work hard, for that matter. He lets his deputies handle most of the morning and evening briefings that cover the fire and the firefighting plan, rising only at the end to say a few words that usually are built around some theme such as safety, or goals, or doing the best job possible with limited resources. During the day he might be glimpsed walking along the row of yurtlike tents that serve as field offices for the command team, or driving out to near the firelines with one of his line bosses. It's a studied approach. "There's very little 'management' that needs to occur with this team," he tells me one morning over coffee in the fire camp's open-air mess tent. But he knows exactly what is going on at all times with the fire, and team members know that he's apt to ask them for an update on what's going on no matter how peripheral their task at the time might be. So they stay on their toes, not to avoid Frye's wrath—although I sense behind his measured speaking style the ability to change his tone of voice with a sound like a rifle bolt clicking into place—but rather to avoid letting him down.

Frye's drive for discipline derives in large part from his own sense that the job has grown more difficult. Like every other person who has more than five years of experience on fires, he's seen them get bigger and hotter. "There's just been a dramatic buildup in fuels," he says. "That really changes how a fire behaves." Kirkendall agrees. "Thirty years ago, we'd just drive a 'dozer around a fire and catch it," he tells me. "When I started out, a 100-acre fire was a big deal. Last year, on the Bitterroot fires, we'd call it a good day if only 10,000 acres burned. Now there are very few fires you can catch with a two-man crew. I've seen that change—it's part of my history."

True to my first impressions, Kirkendall is a tough field commander—he doesn't like excuses and doesn't like slow progress. But he is also chatty and amiable, invariably makes a detour after leaving fire base to get a latte at a minimart in nearby Emigrant, and peppers his speech with early-seventies vernacular ("Right on!"). And he lets his guard down to talk about some of the issues fire managers across the nation are agonizing over in the wake of the Thirtymile Fire. Foremost among them: leadership.

"On Type 2 crews, leadership is an issue," he says. "They just don't have enough crew bosses and squad leaders who are confident in their own ability to direct people effectively. That's what Type 1 teams pride themselves on—they can act independently in a much more aggressive manner, because they have that mix of book learning and experience. I just hope the NFP [National Fire Plan] fosters a more thorough development of the Type 2 program, so we can get some people into permanent positions and get them better-trained."

Nonetheless, it has been the vaunted Type 1 crews that have suffered some of the worst firefighting disasters—if not the worst, the 1994 Storm King tragedy. Part of that is simply because they're the best firefighters around, so draw the toughest assignments. But no one is immune to poor judgment, or a change in the weather if it's not forecast. And veteran firefighters, especially those in the elite units, contract a perhaps-understandable case of hubris. "It's not all that unusual to get into a position where you say to yourself . . .

'Hmmmm . . . this isn't quite right,'" one smokejumper had said to me earlier in the year. "You just deal with it."

After leaving camp, Kirkendall and I spot a large plume of smoke looming over the hills south of us, and radio traffic indicates that a large spot fire is starting to cook as the sun heats it. "Let's go have a look at that," Kirkendall says. We bounce up a private road, past a complex of barns and a handsome ranch home, before reaching the end of the road and three small cabins. The owner, a New York attorney, apparently had money to burn so his ranch wouldn't—he has his own fire truck and crew, as opposed to the spare garden hose that is the extra fire gear at most homes in the area. With the help of some firefighters from the base, the ranch crew has set a sprinkler array around the cabins. The fire is perhaps a half mile away, burning behind a spur ridge that drops steeply from a mountainside on the south side of the valley we'd just come up. As we watch, smoke boils up behind the spur turned from tan to dark brown, then to black. With an audible roar, orange flames push the black smoke aside to lace the sky above the ridge. Burning limbs can be seen rolling down the hill, setting off new spot fires as they do. Still, Kirkendall figures that open ground between the ridge and the cabins will hold the fire in place, so we drive back down the road.

At the ranch complex's main house, a handsome, two-story structure overlooking a trout pond, we run into the owners—Ken Wilson, his wife Linda, and their teenaged daughter. All look understandably worried. "We've had fires around here before, but never one like this," Wilson tells Kirkendall. "We hope it's going to stop up there past the cabins. But we're getting ready in case it doesn't." Kirkendall talks with the Wilsons for a few minutes, then returns to the truck. "You can't make promises," he says. "All you can do is show empathy." He prefers to talk to women in these situations. Men want action—helicopters, fire crews, retardant tankers, right goddam it *now.* "Women are a lot more receptive to what I have to say," Kirkendall says.

A few hours later we encounter what happens when male pig-headedness collides with a force of nature. Kirkendall and I drive up Pine Creek Road, at the north end of the fire and near the end of where it had made its headlong charge two days earlier. There, sitting forlornly in the parking lot of a trailhead, are a large bulldozer and two heavy-equipment trailers. The fire has run over this area, leaving in its wake a valley that looks like a black-and-white photo. No greens, only black and shades of gray, and the pencil-like profiles of lodgepole pine trees that have been stripped of their limbs and foliage by the searing blaze. It is eerily quiet around the vehicles—no birds sing, nor can a stream that normally flows through this little draw be heard.

The trucks and 'dozer are blackened—the tires burned off the truck rims, the paint peeled and blistered from the bulldozer body. The vehicles belong to a private contractor who did road work in the area the week before. When the fire threatened to make its big run two days earlier, firefighter crews had advised the contractor to move his equipment well out of the area. "Nah," he'd said. "The fire is a good five miles away. It'll never reach here." Kirkendall and I poke around the burnt-out vehicles, now as much a part of Fridley Fire camp lore as the rattlesnakes. "Guess he should have listened to us," Kirkendall says, battling a smirk.

Pine Creek had been in the path of the runaway locomotive that had been the Fridley Fire a few days before. As the fire grew, most people living in the area had evacuated or been encouraged to do so. It was a surreal day for residents. It began with a fire so distant that the smoke was barely visible. It ended with a 200-foot wall of orange flame that receded only after popping over ridgetops a 10-minute hike distant. For Helmut Pommee, it had been not only surreal but eerily evocative of an earlier time in his life. Pommee is a retired engineer, a lanky 65-year-old with a goatee, a short ponytail, and the faint remains of a German accent. His family had lived in Hamburg, Germany, during World War II, when Pommee was a small boy. On the night of July 24, 1943, British Lancaster bombers flew over the city, dropping loads of incendiary bombs. Houses burst into flames, the coal in their basements catching fire as well. The resulting firestorm created hurricane-force winds as it sucked in oxygen, suffocating thousands of residents, burning to death many thousands more. The final toll was more than 40,000 dead.

Pommee shakes his head at the recollection when I visit him one afternoon at his small, neat house a mile downhill from the Fridley Fire's path. "It's amazing how memories come back," he tells me as we sit in lawn chairs outside the front door of his neat, steel-roofed house. "My wife Linda panicked a little when flames started to come over the hill there. We had the truck packed with everything we thought we'd need."

I'd overheard Kirkendall talking with another firefighter about Pommee, and complaints he'd made that the fight against the Fridley Fire had been more talk than action. It didn't take much prompting to get the loquacious Pommee to warm to his subject. "These guys need a General Patton—Patton would know what to do," he says. "The way they operate today, with all the logistics, you need 10 guys to supply one guy on the fireline. And the biggest problem is, there aren't enough people with the balls to make a decision. Everyone is afraid to make a decision—they just drag their feet." Pommee is particularly annoyed by reports that the fire had burned for a day or more before any action at all was taken against it. "One plane with a load of retardant," he gripes. "That would have taken care of it."

But after his brief tirade, Pommee gets philosophical. "It's just nature's way of clearing house," he shrugs. "We just happen to be here when it happened. The biggest problem was we just didn't have enough snow last winter." More snow would have left moisture in the trees and brush until later in the year, perhaps slowing the fire's advance even in late August, or stalling it close to its origin.

That evening, when I return to the fire base, I figure Pommee will really get excited if he sees what is going on. More than a dozen big helicopters now are staged at a hastily organized air base on the west side of Highway 89. The fire base has completely moved from the dusty, crowded field station to the large stretch of grassy ranchland, about two miles north of the air base, where Kirkendall had earlier set up his tents. Scores of tents from Type 2 and Hotshot crews are fast going up, and the command tents are in place and arranged to create a "Main Street" where the fire managers can mix with other team members to talk shop and strategy. A cluster of big truck trailers from Big Sky Catering has started feeding what likely will be a force of 1,500 people within another 24 hours.

Logistics director Ruth Lewis, a friendly, short-haired woman in her fifties, found this spot after it became clear the field behind the fire station would never do, if only because a cattle guard there restricted traffic flow to one lane. "That alone would have delayed getting crews to the fireline by an hour and a half," she tells me as we walk around the new camp. She'd taken a drive a few days before, scouting locations, and had found a good one in a meadow. "But the owner was smart enough to not let us have it," she says with a chuckle. Then she found this spot. Snakes aside, it is almost perfect—an open field more than a half mile long and 200 yards deep, strung along a lightly traveled gravel road that permits several drives where visitors and base traffic can enter and exit. Crew tents are set up on the south end, with showers and a medical tent nearest them. To the north of the command center tents rows of school buses and other vehicles sit parked, among them big National Guard trucks serving a contingent of troops that have been called in. Thirty phone lines run into camp, plus lines for Internet use. Power lines are strung for lighting, computers, and printers. A supply cache fast fills up with cases of MREs, piles of Pulaskis and shovels, rows of Mark III pumps, and boxes full of Nomex shirts, sleeping bags, backpack pumps, and other equipment. Trucks from Livingston run between clusters of Porta Potties, emptying and cleaning them. And water tanker trucks drive up and down the frontage road, spraying the dusty gravel with water and creating a fine slurry of reddish-brown mud that coats my rented Intrepid a half inch thick, to the later horror of the Avis supervisor who checks it in.

Despite the reinforcements, however, the Fridley Fire remains largely uncontained—it is just too big to encircle, and there still aren't enough crews. Large stretches of the fire's perimeter haven't even seen a fire crew—fire maps show a wishful "Division C" or "Division X" drawn along a portion of the perimeter, but there are no crews to dispatch to these areas, so the fire burns unchecked. By now it has grown from 4,000 acres to more than 30,000, and it retains plenty of potential. "We're stretched real thin," Frye says to me when asked about progress. "It has been a struggle to get the resources that would allow us to attack this fire the way we'd like to attack it."

Plus, the weather has been bone-dry, with humidity levels in the teens during the day and no higher than 30 percent even during the cool mountain evenings, a time when Tobin, the meteorologist, normally expects to see humidity close to 50 percent. Tobin's weather maps show another dry cold front sweeping in from the west. Although the wind direction will be a little different from that on August 23, when the fire made its big run, he still expects a reprise: afternoon winds, perhaps again hitting 40 miles per hour. That worries Frye; the Fridley Fire still has plenty of potential to grow. In particular, it has shown considerable liveliness near its origin point, working its way out of the hills and moving to the east toward Highway 89. At its northern end, the fire has the potential to jump the perimeter and Trail Creek Road and make a run toward Bozeman, damaging the city's watershed and maybe even hitting the outskirts of town, only 15 miles distant. A fast-moving fire could get there in three days, maybe two.

The next day, Ron Hvizdak voices those concerns during the morning briefing. "We could be off to the races again if it spots across French Creek," he tells team bosses crowded around him near the camp parking lot as the sun peeks over the Rockies. To show where his concerns lie, he points to a spot on the southeast corner of the fire perimeter, now nearly 50 miles in circumference, in what has been dubbed Division A. "The RH [relative humidity] got down to just 23 last night, which isn't very good. So keep your heads up out there, and stay alert to the safety zones. Let's try to hang on to what we've got."

I again join Kirkendall. We head to the fire's southern end, driving up a long, winding road that climbs high above the Paradise Valley, allowing us to look east across the valley and south to the border of Yellowstone National Park. We can see a smoke pillar rising from a fire near the park border that started two days earlier when a vehicle drove through a patch of dry grass, sparking a blaze with its hot muffler. Called the Little Joe Fire, it has grown quickly, and has hit 1,500 acres in just a day while threatening to cross over into the park.

But our concern is closer at hand. As Kirkendall's truck crests a ridge, a large hunting cabin appears, swathed in silvery fire wrap that can reflect the heat from a fire for up to an hour. Located on a block of private land in one of the characteristic "checkerboard" private tracts that break up so much of the national forests, the cabin—more of a house, really—already has consumed a fair amount of the firefighters' energy. Its owner has over the years cut down scores of lodgepole pine trees that surrounded it. Then he largely left the logs where they fell, surrounding his cabin with piles of dry cordwood. Kirkendall can barely hide his disgust. "We've spent five fucking days on this place," he growls. "This guy really ought to be made to pay for this." Crews with bulldozers have been working to move as much of the dry, downed timber away from the cabin as possible. Downhill from it a ridge of toppled logs stands 20 feet high.

West of the ridge crest and the cabin, opposite the direction from which we came, the ridge drops steeply 1,000 feet or more into a heavily wooded valley, then climbs back up to crest at another, higher ridge. The day before, the fire had marched over that distant ridge, and now it is backing down the slope. The wind is calm, but in the growing heat from the sun the fire moves steadily. While Kirkendall checks with a Hotshot crew from Georgia that had been detailed to hold the ridge, I walk up to a rocky promontory to watch a conga line of helicopters shuttle up and down the valley, dropping buckets of water on spot fires emerging downslope from the main blaze as burning embers and chunks of wood roll downhill.

A half hour later, Kirkendall and I drive south from the cabin along a road that side-hills a ridge above and perpendicular to the threatened valley. A crowd is forming—Hvizdak and Parkinson are there, and soon we are joined by some division chiefs working in the area. There isn't much for them to do. They still lack sufficient ground crews to send into the valley and attack the fire directly. Plus, even if those crews are available, the threat of a sudden shift in the wind makes a full-on attack untenable. This is instead a spectating outing, and the road overlooking the burning ridge and the valley between the blaze and the ridge where it could break out and race to the east and north is a perfect place for an informal grandstand.

At a time like this, it is hard not to be utterly fascinated by a wildfire, much as one is fascinated by hurricane-driven waves crashing into a jetty, or a tornado skimming a cornfield. From our vantage point we can see a long, curving arc of smoke rising from the forest in the valley below us. The blaze has crowned in places out a mile or so away, where I've just watched the helicopters work. Closer to us, as I look downslope, I see a line of orange and red through the dark green of the trees: a stealth fire, sneaking along below the tree-tops with a crackling sound audible a half-mile away.

This part of the fire is at the moment doing precisely what fire ecologists want fire to do—working its way along the undergrowth, cleaning up brush and downed timber while not doing the upper trees much harm. That can't last, though. As we watch, clouds herald-ing the leading edge of the cold front appear in the west. Moreover, lodgepole pine forests of this type just don't lend themselves to nice, clean understory burns. They go up with a *whoosh*.

By early afternoon, this fire begins to do exactly that. The winds remain fairly calm, but the fire is hitting friendlier ground. Clumps of lodgepoles burst into flames with a sound like jet engines. Worse, the fire has by now backed almost all the way down the east-facing slope, and smoke is billowing from hot spots on the west slope, a half mile or so from the hunting cabin and equally close to a notch in the ridge that the fire could leap through and hit yet more timber. A steady roar comes from a half-dozen helicopters—little Hueys, a thundering Black Hawk, a fat Sikorsky—as they fly repeatedly over the hot spots, dumping buckets of water on the rising smoke. From our vantage point, it is easy to see which pilots are most effective, and which are a little hasty to drop and scram. "A lot of good that's doing," sneers one bystander as a helicopter dumps its load of water from hundreds of feet up. "That won't even moisten the ground."

Hvizdak, Kirkendall, and the other division supervisors and line operations chiefs have larger concerns than the hunting cabin, but

A Black Hawk helicopter ferries a bucket of water to a fire in Montana.

from where I stand it sure looks as if that is the focus of this aerial bombardment. About $60,000 spent, I figured, because somebody wants a cabin in the woods and decided the feds will bail out his ass when it is crunch time. But had it burned, it would have been the headline in every paper from Missoula to Billings: "Fridley Fire Takes Structures."

But by late afternoon, the fire clearly is gaining the upper hand. Earlier in the day, crews had worked in the bottom of the valley's V, cutting some timber in an effort to create a firebreak. But it isn't working. "The fire has jumped the line," I hear over someone's radio. "The fire has jumped the line." Kirkendall, Hvizdak, and the division supers ponder their next move. One option is to send crews downhill to attack the fire directly, a plan quickly discarded as too risky. So, too, is the idea of starting a backfire to rob the big fire of fuel—should the winds pick up as forecast, the backfire itself could grow out of control. For now, it will be up to the helicopters to hold the line.

And they manage to do just that. By 5 P.M., after dozens of helo trips, the smoke plumes that had been clambering up the wooded ridge are largely out; the fire has been held to near the small stream that flows down the valley. New weather reports, moreover, say that winds will not be nearly so severe as predicted. It is something of an anticlimax, like watching a movie and having the projectionist lose the last reel. Kirkendall makes plans with a Hotshot crew supervisor to stay on the site overnight, watching for flare-ups and burning out a section of dry grass for a firebreak. We get into the trucks and drive back to base. Show over.

The next morning, I point the mud-caked Intrepid north up Highway 89, then west on I-84 toward Seattle. The worst danger from the Fridley Fire apparently has passed. But it will be more than two weeks before the last crews pack up and leave the now-footbeaten grassy field that has become a temporary home for 1,270 people. Before it finally is extinguished, the Fridley Fire consumes 26,373 acres—moderate by today's standards, and most of that in the fire's one big run. The final cost: $10.6 million.

As sometimes happens in these weeks-long, siege-style firefights, dollars alone aren't the only expense. As I drove past the helicopter base my last morning there, I spotted a twin-rotor, red-and-white Vertol flown by crews from Portland, Oregon–based Columbia Helicopters. I'd seen the big craft often over the summer—its size and bright paint made it hard to miss. For the past week, however, it had been grounded because of mechanical problems. *That's good,* I say to myself idly as I watch the big helicopter skim overhead. *They've got it flying.*

Two days later, on a test flight after routine maintenance, that same Columbia Helicopters Vertol crashes in the hills just outside the heli base, apparently because the forward rotor spins off when an attachment bolt fails. The accident gets no more than a few paragraphs in most newspapers the next day, but its death toll is nearly as great as that in the Thirtymile Fire. Three die: the pilot, 37-year-old Rich Hernandez, copilot Santi Arovitx, 28, and Kip Krigbaum, the 45-year-old crew chief.

Meanwhile, farther north, Glacier National Park is now threatened by the Moose Fire. Like the Fridley, it blows up, consuming thousands of acres a day in late August. And it will continue to do so for two weeks, before mid-September rains calm it and finally extinguish it after it has burned nearly 70,000 acres. Across the West, 20 other large wildfires burn, as some 8,000 firefighters work to extinguish them. Another season of fire is coming to a close, but it is not doing so quietly.

Chapter 12

▲ ▲ ▲ ▲

The Fires Next Time

As is so often the case, it's early September that proves to be the peak of the burning season. The Moose Fire in particular shows itself to be a formidable blaze. Burning along Glacier National Park's western boundary, it blows up each afternoon for days, shooting up huge columns of smoke and ultimately taking out nearly 70,000 acres, making it one of the largest fires of the season. But by early October, autumn's cool weather and showers have largely brought the fire season to an end. Even then, though, fire teams still are out, either keeping a watchful eye on, or actively digging line around, fires in Montana and California.

As cottonwood trees begin to turn golden, I am back in Montana. Not for a fire, but to see the aftermath of one. I meet again with Kevin Ryan, the fire-effects specialist from the Fire Sciences Laboratory in Missoula. But rather than get together at the lab, I drive south of Missoula along Highway 93, dotted with log-home makers, as it skirts along the Bitterroot National Forest. After a long, winding climb through steep, wooded mountains, the highway emerges on a broad, grassy plain—the Big Hole Valley. Long a ranching area, the Big Hole often sprouts 10,000 or more haystacks as ranchers lay in supplies for cattle. In its middle is the tiny town of Wisdom: a few hotels, the inevitable bar, a restaurant, some houses. It's the kind of place that brings to mind what Montana was like long before Ted Turner became the biggest landowner in the state—open, isolated, quiet. Incredibly quiet. To stand on Wisdom's main street at midnight and look into the hard, dark sky is to hear . . . absolutely nothing. These days, the effect is frankly creepy. Once, the entire West was like that.

The next morning, along with two young women researchers—Sharon Hoad and Kate Dircksen—Ryan and I drive west of Wisdom and up into the Spanish Peaks. We wind through stands of ponderosa and lodgepole pine, dust rising in our wake on the dry gravel road. Then the occasional blackened tree appears. Then entire stands of them. We pass a stream that courses quietly through banks of ashes and piles of charred limbs. "No fish in there," Ryan says. "That creek was boiling just over a year ago."

We're now passing through the burn-over from the Mussigbrod Complex, a 56,000-acre cluster of fires that hopscotched through these peaks and forests for more than a month during the summer of 2000. It had hardly rated a mention when it burned, as during August of that year it seemed as if all of western Montana had been on fire. On the night of July 21, thunderstorms touched off 78 fires in the space of a few hours. Conditions had been incredibly dry, with no significant rain for months—so dry that any lightning bolt that struck the ground had close to a 90 percent chance of touching off a fire.

While the Mussigbrod grew quickly, the largest of these fires burned about 20 miles farther west, in the Bitterroot. Steve Frye's

crew had been called in to manage that burn, dubbed the Valley
Complex. It arrived on August 2, when 13 significant fires were eating their way through forests of mostly overgrown ponderosa pine
and were threatening to merge. Ron Hvizdak, the fire-behavior analyst, knew immediately that this collection of still-small fires, totaling a relatively insignificant 8,000 acres, had the potential to turn
into something enormous. He'd been working a fire called Little
Blue in July, where moisture levels in "1,000-hour fuels"—the heavy
timber and wood that can give a fire great intensity—had hovered
around 8 percent, an incredibly low level. That put even big chunks
of wood on par with "10-hour" fuels such as grass, the hour label in-
dicating how long it takes for the moisture to penetrate the fuel
when the weather changes.

Armed with the knowledge that fuel moisture in this new group
of fires was similar, if not lower, Hvizdak spent his first day at the
fires flying the terrain in a small plane. That evening, he talked with
people who were familiar with the Bitterroot National Forest, where
the fires were burning, and began to go over maps to estimate how
large the fire might grow. He didn't need the usual United States
Geological Service quadrangle maps. Instead he got out a table-size
map of the whole forest and began to trace his fingers around a
likely perimeter, where rivers, mountains, or firebreaks such as roads
would likely halt the fire. The circle he traced out encompassed a
quarter million acres.

Hvizdak's estimate was depressingly prescient. Over the rest of
August, the Valley Complex ripped through almost the exact amout
of acreage he had forecast. The weather was relentlessly dry, giving
beleaguered firefighters no respite as the blazes consumed forest at
a steady mile-per-hour pace—at least, when the wind wasn't blowing. When it was, things were much worse. A few days after Hvizdak and the rest of Frye's team arrived, for instance, strong winds

out of the west and northwest pushed several of the fires together, forming an enormous 160,000-acre fire that during the day and night of August 6 burned 73 homes and outbuildings near the towns of Conner and Medicine Springs. Firefighters were helpless to do much about the damage; the fire was too big, and with only a few hundred firefighters on the scene due to the enormous demands a hot fire season had placed on resources, Frye didn't dare ask his forces to be more aggressive. Crews were stretched so thin, in fact, that even managers pitched in. The night of August 6, as the fire neared the town of Connor, Hvizdak himself pitched in to help a squadron of bulldozers punch some fireline through. The Valley Complex burned through August, finally eating through some 212,000 acres of forest.

Ryan's interest in the Mussigbrod fire, and by extension the nearby Valley Complex, is in finding a way to determine if a fire-damaged tree will survive, or if it will die from injuries caused by the fire, or succumb to insects in its fire-weakened state. It's an interest that's partly academic and partly practical. The academic portion is fed by Ryan's intellectual curiosity—his professional focus long has been on the impact fire has on trees. From a practical standpoint, a test that could tell a doomed tree from one that will live, even though it appears to have had similar fire damage, may give forest managers the ability to remove fire-damaged trees from a burned forest in order to extract some economic value from them without massacring healthy trees, as happened in the wake of the "salvage rider" in 1996.

Such triage may become depressingly common in the years to come. Big fires are not new to the West, of course. Big fire years took place in 1910, 1919, and 1934. The fires of 1934, in fact, so devastated the Selway National Forest that it was effectively disbanded and became the Selway-Bitterroot Wilderness, which laps over the Idaho and Montana border west of Highway 93. In Oregon a year earlier, the infamous Tillamook Burn consumed 240,000 acres. What was particularly striking about that fire was that it occurred in the wet coastal range of the state, not its dry, ponderosa-pine-dominated eastern half.

Still, what has been striking about the past two decades is the increasing size and severity of fires, and their tendency to erupt into giant fires such as the Valley Complex. Certainly the Valley Complex's size and fierceness was a result of the thick fuel loads on the forest floor, fuel that would likely have been burned off by frequent small fires in the years prior to the 1930s or 1940s.

But while fire managers, environmentalists, and others talk about restoring a "historic" fire pattern to the West's forests, such objectives beg several questions: What was fire's historic role? What did forests really look like 100 or 200 years ago? And how will the planet's apparently changing climate affect fires?

At Northern Arizona University, researcher Scott Anderson tries to predict future fires by studying those in the present. Anderson, a boyish-looking 50-year-old with thinning light blond hair, is a specialist in paleoecology—the study of ancient environments. Like many scientists who scrutinize the distant past, his primary tool is the fossil record, bits of long-dead plants and animals now frozen in stone. But no dinosaur bones for Anderson. Instead, he seeks more subtle reminders of a bygone world—ash, charcoal and pollen—that show how living plants have had their worlds changed by fire.

In his fieldwork, Anderson has pulled cores from bogs and lake beds throughout much of the western United States, as well as parts of Alaska and Mexico. In these wet areas, layers of airborne dust or waterborne silt build up like a layer cake over thousands of years. In the case of Anderson's samples, back 13,000 years, to the end of the last ice age and the beginning of what scientists call the Holocene

era. Or, put more simply, until modern times. We still are in the
Holocene, an epoch marked by relatively stable temperatures and
climate.

From his samples, which range in length from a few feet to nearly
10 feet, Anderson takes subsamples of individual layers, some just
fractions of an inch thick. These are run through a series of sieves
that remove any unwanted sand or grit. Left behind are bits of charcoal washed into a lake from surrounding hills after a fire, or even the
ash deposits in a wetland that burned when summer's heat dried it.

From these samples, one thing is clear: Fire has been a part of
the West's environment ever since the giant glaciers of the last Ice
Age receded 16,000 years ago. "The older cores are just loaded with
charcoal," Anderson says. "You look at them, and come away with
the clear impression that the past 100 years are a world away from
anything we have seen since the last glacial episode. It's not a far cry
to suggest that man has had a tremendous impact on the environment, and has changed the landscape itself."

Still, Anderson himself concedes that while his approach can reveal broad changes in the West's fire and forest environment, it's less
good at pinpointing exactly what an ecosystem or forest once looked
like. It's like measuring the exhaust from a passing car, and using
that information to determine the car's color and how many passen-
gers were inside.

But the whole idea of what constitutes a "normal" forest, defined
by most people studying the question as a forest before white settlers began to have widespread impact on the environment in the
last half of the nineteenth century, is almost impossible to pin
down. In the past century humans have inflicted profound change,
and profound damage, on the landscape that so awed Lewis and
Clark in their travels across the northern half of the West, and later
John Wesley Powell as he explored the Grand Canyon and the great

Colorado Plateau. To this day, environmentalists trying to understand the West before 1900 often make a pilgrimage to the Powell Plateau, a table-topped mesa that made such an impression on Powell that he named it after himself when he first saw it in 1871. Located off the north rim of the Grand Canyon, it remains today one of the last pieces of ponderosa pine forest that is widely thought to look much like what most of that ecosystem resembled 100 or 150 years ago. There, the pines are widely spaced, with plenty of blue sky visible between the tree crowns, and the forest floor parklike in its natural tidiness. Here, fires still pass through on occasion as they did for thousands of years, burning off dried grass and low brush, pruning the lower branches of the trees, but otewise doing the forest no harm.

That's in sharp contrast to a fire that burned near Flagstaff in 1977. The Radio Fire, visible from Flagstaff, burned with ferocious intensity, destroying even the organic material in the soil. A lodgepole pine forest might have survived such a burn—its seedlings prefer soil that doesn't have much organic material. But not a ponderosa. Twenty-five years later, few trees have returned to the site of the fire. Had such blazes been burning over the past 10,000 years, the entire West literally would have been a wasteland by 1800, not the verdant landscape enjoyed by thousands of Native Americans and later explored by white trappers, miners, and settlers.

Century-old photographs give good hints as to what the West once looked like. Invariably, the more open, meadowy landscape shaped by frequent fire has been replaced by a much more overgrown, densely wooded terrain. But photos show only so much. Across the West, a number of researchers are working to create an accurate picture of the forest that our grandparents knew well but that today is such a cipher. What's most striking is the degree to which forests seem to have taken over large tracts of the West—

often in areas where no forests existed for hundreds of years previous. Emily Heyerdahl, a researcher with the Fire Sciences Lab in Missoula, has in recent years conducted fieldwork in Utah aimed at determining just how great this forest spread has been and what it means for the current state of forests and fire. There's evidence that woodlands cover 10 times the area of Utah that they did a mere century ago—an amazing expansion, if true. Heyerdahl is looking for signs that fire frequency changed since around 1880 or so, and whether this actually caused the expansion of ponderosa pines and other trees, or if a change in climate precipitated the forest march.

It's a difficult detective problem. Trees that were growing before the middle of the nineteenth century show ample signs of fire, and scientists can determine what years those fires burned and even how widespread a particular fire might have been. With fires much less frequent, those scars are more difficult to find and cross-reference. So in some cases, Heyerdahl infers a fire's occurrence by clusters of trees that like lots of light and open space for germination—conditions most apt to occur after a fire.

Among the wild cards Heyerdahl's work contends with is not just the modern influence of humans. It's the influence of humans from long ago. That's because it is well-documented that Native Americans were enthusiastic users of fire, setting fires clear across North America to manage the landscape for their benefit. In present-day Oregon and other states, for instance, fire was used to clear forests of trees to improve grazing conditions for deer, elk, and other game. In California's Yosemite Valley, the Miwok Indians who once lived there set fires aimed at destroying conifer trees in order to allow more oaks to grow, as the Miwoks used the acorns as a food source.

The implication is that the landscape white settlers found when they first came west may not have been as "natural" as it's now viewed. In the same way that the current landscape is the product of fire suppression, it's possible that the landscape of 120 years ago was the product of fire *creation,* as it had been shaped by centuries of regular burning practiced by Native Americans. Yet even that landscape might not have shown the full impact of humans on the landscape going back thousands of years. Writing in the March 2002 issue of *The Atlantic Monthly,* writer Charles Mann cited anthropologists who believe that North America before its first contact with Europeans in 1492 was a very different place than what is widely believed. Some, such as Clark Erickson of the University of Pennsylvania and William Balee of Tulane University, say that the continent was once much more heavily populated than it was in 1800. By then, diseases unwittingly introduced by Europeans had wiped out millions of Native Americans. Sometimes those mass annihilations occurred even before the people responsible for them made an appearance. The viruses they carried traveled overland faster than the Europeans did.

In parts of Bolivia there is evidence that natives there managed the landscape on a massive scale, diverting water and setting huge fires so aggressively that they actually created an ecosystem rather than adapting to an existing one. While little concrete evidence supports the notion that the same thing occurred in North America, it's possible that the landscape seen even by Lewis and Clark was morphing into a less managed, less fire-frequent state, a change greatly accelerated by the arrival of settlers with their sheep, and later the Forest Service. The idea also has profound implications for any discussion of managing those western lands still deemed to be wild. What, after all, does "wild" mean if human beings might have been enthusiastically shaping it for thousands of years?

Still, even widespread human-set fire perhaps took a backseat to what might be the most powerful engine behind fire: climate. Not weather—the daily or weekly ebb and flow of sun or rain that can spoil a weekend trip or contribute to the perfect weekend—but climate, the slow, gradual tendency toward drier, colder, wetter, or warmer weather that can have a profound impact on the landscape. Anderson's work has shown that the early part of the Holocene was slightly warmer and drier than it has been in the past several thousand years, leading to more frequent fires. That warmer, drier weather would lead to more fires might seem intuitive enough, but it's also true that *wetter* weather can lead to more fire. How? By encouraging greater growth of grass, brush, and even young trees. Outside Flagstaff, in the Fort Valley Experimental Forest, established in 1909 as one of the first efforts to understand how forests actually work, stand thickets of ponderosa pines crammed not a foot apart. Similar pockets of trees are found elsewhere in this part of Arizona. All germinated in 1919, a year when the meteorological stars aligned for pine seedlings, with the ideal amount of rainfall and sun. That doesn't mean these are healthy trees, though. Their crowding ensures that none get sufficient moisture in leaner years, while their close proximity to one another and stumpy size makes them exceedingly vulnerable to fire. In the same way, a year or two of heavy rain can yield a bumper crop of grass and brush, material that turns into a superb fire fuel when it dries out during a drought year.

These patterns of wet years and dry years are in turn driven by several factors. One is El Niño/La Niña, the pattern of ocean warming in the central Pacific that can alter climate over much of the globe. In the United States, an El Niño season can lead to drier, warmer years in the Northwest and wetter, cooler ones in the Southwest. A La Niña, in which the central Pacific Ocean cools, causes more rain in the Northwest while drying out the Southwest. Particularly in the Southwest, based on tree-ring records, several wet years followed by a dry year or two equals a severe fire season.

Those events in turn play out against the backdrop of phenomena such as the Pacific Decadal Oscillation (PDO), a roughly 20-year pattern in which subtle changes in the Pacific Ocean lead to noticeable "flips" in the climate pattern over land. The last two decades of the twentieth century, for instance, seem to have been dominated by a PDO pattern that led to warmer, drier seasons, something that indeed may have contributed to a cluster of bad fire years during the 1980s and 1990s and up until 2000. What causes the PDO is a mystery; nor are climate researchers able to tell when a change might occur.

El Niño and La Niña, meanwhile, seem to be more common than they were a century ago. And the reason for that may be found in the greatest climatic wild card of all: global warming. The vast majority of climate scientists now say the Earth clearly is heating up, and that the billions of tons of emissions from cars, factories, and charcoal grills that enter the atmosphere each year are almost certainly the cause of that warming. Probable indications of warming are widespread—mid-elevation plants creeping into the high mountains, birds and insects laying eggs earlier, coral reefs dying as water warms.

But the effects of global warming aren't straight-line; they won't translate neatly into something such as the mean August temperature of Seattle rising from its current 64.7 degrees Fahrenheit to something like 68. Such a change might indeed take place, but along with it will come wild variations in weather—extremes of heat, extremes of rainfall. And that, in some areas, may be the exact formula required for fires on a scale not yet imagined—or at least fires that regularly match the size and severity of blazes such as the Valley Complex.

The work of another Arizona-based researcher, Tom Swetnam of the University of Arizona, clearly shows the potential. Swetnam is director of the Tree Ring Laboratory at the university and spent years studying tree rings. In particular, he looks for evidence of fire, which often leaves a scar on trees it doesn't kill, a scar that in time becomes enveloped within the tree. Swetnam can extract an amazing amount of data from the concentric circles that form as a tree grows. By starting with rings that can be firmly tied to a date, he can work backward in time, comparing growth patterns, burn scars, and other marks to nail down the particular year a ring was formed in trees as far as 500 miles apart, and dating back hundreds of years. Just about anything wooden can be used—living trees, felled trees, wooden timbers from Anasazi cliff dwellings.

Swetnam's rings show clearly the close correlation between climate and fire. For hundreds of years, whenever dry, warm weather followed wet, cool weather, big fires erupted. The year 1747, for instance, saw tremendous rainfall across much of the West, rainfall that led to fat tree rings from that year. But the next year, 1748, was warm and dry, and enormous fires broke out—fires that perhaps burned across much of the West. That wild swing was a rarity; Swetnam has found only once such incident. But he worries that global warming may make such extremes of wet weather followed by dry weather more common, leading to bigger and bigger fire years that are exacerbated by the unnatural buildup of fuels during the past five decades (and continuing) of fire suppression. "It's a combination that's just right for creating big fires," he tells me when we talk over the telephone.

In the wake of the 2000 fire season, fire managers across the West grimly awaited a repeat in 2001 of conflagrations such as the Valley Complex. None came, but that is hardly to say another will not occur anytime soon. Big fires may well become a fixture in the years to come, with firefighters in two decades looking back at the Valley fires with the same sense of seeing a switch flipped that an earlier generation felt about the 1961 Sleeping Child Fire, which seemed so huge at 28,000 acres. That fire, though, was half the size of the Mussigbrod Complex, which itself was pushed off news pages by the Valley fires.

In the fire-scarred terrain of the Mussigbrod Fire, Ryan, his two student assistants, and I spend a sunny day working our way through draws and over ridges. The fire that burned through here the previous day was a big one, but not one that sent a solid wall of flame roaring across the terrain. The densely wooded valley bottoms got hit hard. But higher up, where we are, it hopscotched here and there, burning one thicket of trees and leaving the next. So the country retains its wooded character, with big old ponderosa pines mixed with some white bark pine and Engelmann spruce. Here and there stand aspen, turning gold now that nighttime temperatures are brushing against freezing. Ryan always has found this part of his work the most enjoyable—free from the office, hiking through a forest, reading it like most people read a book. It also was far from Washington, D.C. There, when called to testify on forest health in August, he'd been overshadowed by the debate over whether environmental considerations had outweighed safety ones in the Thirtymile Fire. "That was a mess," he says of the D.C. trip.

With human impact on western forests so widespread, Ryan tells me, just about anything we do now could have further damaging effects. Logging fire-damaged trees scars the landscape and changes the character of a forest shaped for centuries by fires that form a complex pattern of old and new trees. Leaving them, particularly if they are killed or damaged in a fire that's the result of our meddling, may have its own consequences. The weakened trees may encourage insect infestations. Bugs such as pine beetles, along with fires, are one of two ways trees in the West die natural deaths. But even the bug outbreaks are no longer natural. The denser forests that now prevail owing to fire suppression, meanwhile, have a tremendous impact on forest hydrology. Trees soak up huge amounts of water, of course—hundreds of gallons a year for a mature ponderosa pine. If too many trees crowd the hills, that water does not find its way into streams and rivers. Too few, and flooding can take place.

Toward the end of the afternoon, Ryan finds a cluster of trees that includes trees that are clearly dead owing to the previous year's fires, some that are clearly not, and several in between. He helps his students measure out a plot, which they'll use as a frame to encompass the trees to be watched. They'll watch how the damaged trees fare, whether they attract insects, whether those insects dine primarily on the damaged trees, or look farther afield and munch on healthy ones too. This project may last for years, and may turn out to be inconclusive. "We just don't know how fast the damaged trees will die, and whether insects like the pine beetle can establish a life cycle of their progeny before they do," he says, referring to the beetles' need to lay eggs in live trees. "We're not even sure what trees the beetles will prefer."

Back in Wisdom, after dinner in the one small restaurant, Ryan and I talk outside our rooms, in the parking lot, under a dark, hard sky littered with stars. Like most people who study fire, he has some notions as to the shape of the big patterns. But plenty of uncertainty remains about the future. "Prescribed burning," for instance, is seen by some as the fix for western forests—deliberately setting fires that burn off the volatile fine fuels. But that has its costs, and risks. A prescribed fire in May 2000 set off one of the worst fires of the year, a blaze that nearly took out the national laboratory at Los Alamos. "We just don't understand a lot of the natural processes," Ryan says. "People talk about bringing fire back into the forest. But what happens in a lot of cases is that fire brings with it an infestation of insects that eat the dead and damaged trees. So is that what people mean when they say we should restore forest health? I don't think so."

On the other hand, he says, it's foolish to think that if we simply leave forests the way they are, nature will sort things out. "It's naive to think that everything will simply adjust itself," Ryan says to me. "That's a theological position. There's no data to support it— not a bit."

Chapter 13

▲ ▲ ▲ ▲

Finding a Fix

Ryan's statement, spoken into the cold night air of Wisdom, cuts to the heart of what might be the biggest question of all: Can we manage fires without mounting the equivalent of a D day invasion every time one breaks out?

Walking away from the problem—simply admitting that fires are beyond our control, so we should let them burn—is not the answer. To do that may well be to condemn the ponderosa pine ecosystem to death by fire. Certainly that's what Wally Covington believes. "If we don't have this worked out by 2010 or 2015, we're not going to have any natural ponderosa pine forests left," he says to me. "We'll have pines, but not 500-year-old ones. And people just won't know what a natural forest looks like."

William Wallace Covington—"Wally" to everyone—is founder and director of the Ecological Restoration Institute at Northern Arizona University, perhaps the most influential site in the field of shaping forests to prevent catastrophic fires. He is 55, a tall, affable man with a broad, handsome face and light brown hair and the impressive title of Regents' Professor and Director of the Ecological Restoration Institute. Nattily dressed in a brown checked long-sleeved shirt and brown slacks, he looks more like a successful pediatrician than a forester, a class of academic that's usually a pretty grubby specimen. Covington has been at Northern Arizona since 1975, after a short stint in medical school before switching to the nascent field of ecological studies. He majored in forestry at Yale, specializing in how forests recovered from clear-cutting. How they recovered—or didn't—from fire was a natural progression, particularly in light of the vast imbalance that Covington and other forestry experts began to see in ponderosa pine forests. And beginning in the 1980s, Covington began to conduct research and publish papers that made a bold assertion: It was true, said the onetime medical school student, that the West's forests were sick. But they could be *cured!*

Covington came to that conclusion after deciding the conventional wisdom wasn't that wise. Since the 1970s, it's been widely believed by many that simply reintroducing fire into forests, either by allowing natural fires to burn or starting new ones, will in time solve the problem of excess fuels. "I tried that," Covington says, as we talk in his comfortable, wood-paneled office on the second floor of Northern Arizona's School of Forestry, one window nicely framing a view of San Francisco Peak's pyramidal summit. "And it just doesn't work." He had his epiphany about prescribed fire as the sole treatment for overgrown forests in 1980, while running a prescribed fire on a Forest Service site near Chimney Springs, Arizona. He had set what's called a "ring fire," which consists of a dab of flame in the middle of a circle, then a ring of fire dropped around it with a drip torch. The middle fire pulls the surrounding heat into a rising cone, killing low trees but in theory not harming larger ones. "Not only did we get heat up into the canopy, we got fire up into the canopy," Covington said. "We had winds of around 10 miles per hour—had they been 15 or 20, we would have lost it."

"That," he says, "scared the pee out of me. And I started to think about whether there's a better way to do this."

Covington decided that in order for fire to begin functioning naturally in a ponderosa pine forest, the dense thicket of trees that now existed had to be thinned out—by hand. Covington developed a precise model for how to do this. He chose as his starting point the "presettlement" forest, the forest as it existed before the first white settlers. By counting stumps from trees that had been logged during the late nineteenth century and early twentieth—before grazing and fire suppression had dramatically altered the forests' nature—he and researchers working with him estimated that a typical ponderosa pine forest had about 30 or 40 trees per acre. To mimic that tree density in today's overgrown forests, Covington advocated an approach in which researchers identified an old, logged tree stump, circumscribed around it a circle with a 60-foot radius, then removed most of the trees within the circle. Left behind for each presettlement stump were anywhere from 1.5 trees—on average—to three trees. Allowing for tree mortality due to insects, windstorms, or perhaps even a fire, Covington reasoned, that should in time create a forest that closely duplicates what once existed. And once a forest was sent down that path to normalcy, then fire could again be welcomed as a regular visitor.

But forestry is littered with the rubble of right-sounding ideas that came to grief. Forestry in fact is a cruel field to study; even a fast-growing Douglas-fir takes 50 or 60 years to reach young maturity, and a forest—as opposed to a tree farm—develops over literally hundreds of years in a slow-motion ballet of trees that grow and die, fall back to earth and wipe out nearby siblings, burn in some places but not in others, and come to mirror the underlying topography, the soil and water, and exposure to sun or shade. So theories that sound great require decades to prove, and often are overtaken by new premises even before the old ones get thumbs up or down.

Moreover, the very idea that better forest management also may be used as a tool to allow logging, grazing, or other "industrial" uses of the West's much-abused forests is enough to make some go ballistic. Today a discussion that is vitally important for the West—how to bring some natural balance to the fire-prone forests—takes place against a background of deep suspicion between federal land-management agencies such as the Forest Service, and the environmental community.

Much of that distrust is fairly recent, going back to 1994, a year of severe fires in Washington State. Those came at a propitious time for logging supporters—and for a Forest Service eager to show that it still mattered in the wake of a federal judge's 1991 decision that the agency had ignored its own environmental guidelines, a decision that all but shut down the Forest Service as a tree-cutting outfit.

But even before that, since around 1976, so-called salvage logging had accounted for a growing portion of the trees cut on federal lands. Salvaged trees typically were burned trees—even severe fires burn through a forest quickly, damaging trees enough to kill them but doing little harm to the merchantable portion of a log. Such tree-cutting seemed to make sense; the forest already was badly damaged, so why not extract some economic value from what was by most accounts a bad situation?

There were two problems with that approach, however. For one thing, salvage logging was analogous to peeling a scab off a deep wound. A burned forest has enormous potential for rebirth, but in the months and years immediately after a fire it is exceedingly fragile. The scorched soil, stripped of a protective layer of pine or fir needles, grass and duff, can erode easily. Salvage logging often meant adding another insult to this injury as loggers dragged downed trees across the landscape and cut new roads. Slash and debris left behind after even scrupulous logging loads the forest floor with a layer of kindling, raising the risk for yet another high-intensity fire. And the urge to salvage ignored the fact that forests had evolved with fire for thousands of years, finding ways to recycle burned trees as nutrient sources and shelter for wildlife. If forests were so dysfunctional, why were they also so ubiquitous when whites first came on the scene?

What was perhaps worse, though, was the deep level of cynicism shown by the Forest Service's salvage-logging efforts. It was a way to dress up what was by most accounts an ordinary clear-cut in the guise of forest health. And it proved to be yet another variation on what had become a longtime Forest Service belief: that a forest can't be allowed to behave naturally and must be "improved," usually by extracting economic value from it. Soon, salvage became a term that cast an impressively wide net. In 1992, the Associated Press got hold of a Forest Service memo that read: "Even if a sale is totally green [live trees], as long as one board comes off that would qualify as salvage on the Salvage Sale Plan Fund, it should be called salvage."

In July of 1995, salvage-logging regulations, Clinton's inability to make peace in western forests, and the previous summer's fires resulted in a ploy that to this day infuriates environmentalists. It was the "salvage-logging rider"—an amendment to a must-pass budget measure that the newly Republican Congress was determined to force down Clinton's throat. For a two-year period, the rider opened up huge chunks of Forest Service land to logging, removed appeals processes, and speeded up review of proposed harvests. The rationale was to remove burned and dead trees left by fires that burned in

1994. But the rider was written in such a way that thousands of live trees also fell under its umbrella. In fact, according to language in the rider, if a tree was so much at risk of burning down it might be deemed "salvageable." Some 4.5 billion board feet were released for logging, more than had been cut on Forest Service land in years. In 1996, Vice President Al Gore called the salvage rider "the biggest mistake" of the administration.

The rider left environmentalists more distrustful than ever of the Forest Service and further tarnished the idea that "salvaging" burned logs accomplished much aside from boosting the Forest Service's timber-cutting budget. So salvage proposals remain bitterly contested. In Montana, for instance, a 46,000-acre tract in the Bitterroot National Forest that burned during the 2000 fires was proposed for salvage in December 2001. But that led to a near-war between the Bush administration and environmental groups, who filed suit to stop what would have been the single largest salvage operation ever proposed by the Forest Service. A federal judge blocked the salvage plan, but the fight over it and other proposals is sure to continue.

That suspicion of proposals to fix burned or threatened forests has spilled over into the large debate over forest restoration. In Arizona the Southwest Forest Alliance (SWFA)—a group that includes such mainstream green groups as the Sierra Club and Audubon chapters—has bitterly opposed the work of the Grand Canyon Forest Partnership where it has tried to put Covington's ideas into practice. One plot recently thinned near Flagstaff as part of the parternship's demonstration of Covington's ideas has become the Forest Alliance's poster child. The Alliance's Web site shows a photo taken shortly after the site was thinned. A few forlorn-looking semi-mature trees stand in a sea of raw red earth, while in the background the unthinned forest looks green and verdant. Another, taken from the air, shows the test tracts as relatively open areas that stand out against the dense surrounding forest. By comparison, the treated sites look beaten-up and abused.

Just a few miles from where the Grand Canyon Forest Partnership is running its test plots a competing set of plots has been established by the SWFA. "I've been fighting Wally on this issue for what seems like geologic time," says Sharon Galbreath, a cheerful, hazel-eyed woman in her forties with short brown hair and a humorous manner far at odds with the excessive earnestness sometimes found in the environmental community. She's the Southwest Forest Alliance's executive director, and like Covington and others from Northern Arizona University lives in Flagstaff. "The sorts of things he's proposing are very well-intentioned. But they can do just as much damage as the practices used by the Forest Service that got us here in the first place."

In the past few years the Southwest Forest Alliance has been doggedly critiquing the Grand Canyon Forest Partnership—and the work of Covington in particular. In Galbreath's eyes, the proposals espoused by Covington (and rapidly becoming dogma in western forestry circles) are not only wrongheaded, they're dangerous. "He's seeking to turn the forest back to a single point in time—whenever he says that natural fire was disrupted," says Galbreath. "Our belief is that you can't do that because the old-growth trees that were the cornerstone of the forest system no longer exist. So now we're fighting over how many little trees it takes to end up with a few big trees."

On a different visit to Flagstaff, I visit another set of plots with Galbreath, a former director of the SWFA named Martos Hoffman, and a young forester named Brian Nowicki. In Galbreath's Explorer we drive west of Flagstaff on I-40 and into the Kaibab National Forest. There, the three walk me through their own test plot—which, though ironically also monitored by Covington for his own studies, is one they are using to refute the Ecological Restoration Institute and its forest-health models. The forest alliance doesn't dispute the need for forest treatment. Indeed, the Southwest Forest Alliance group was an early advocate of Covington, and Galbreath, among others, still admires him deeply for his commitment to halting old-growth ponderosa pine logging. The group even followed closely his presettlement thinning model for treating a plot in the Kaibab. And they were appalled at the result. "It sounded really good on paper," Galbreath tells me. "But when we tried it, we said to ourselves, 'Oh my God—this is not a good thing.'"

So alliance members set about developing their own approach to restoring ponderosa pine forest health, one that in 1999 was applied to the 38-acre site we visited. The alliance isn't a group of unalloyed tree-huggers—it came in and logged with considerable enthusiasm, reducing the number of standing trees on the site from about 150–200 per acre to around 100. But the group didn't apply an arbitrary formula for coming up with how many trees stood here before, say, 1900. They could have—the site is littered with waist-high stumps, telltale signs of logging that took place nearly a century ago when two-man "misery whips"—cross-cut saws—were still used to fell trees. But instead, the group sought a gentler approach, one that didn't try to bludgeon the forest into its pre-1900 shape all at once, but rather aimed to set it down a road that, it is hoped, eventually will lead toward something approaching the forest's natural, happily fire-prone state. Says Galbreath: "We're trying to figure out what's the least we can do to reintroduce fire to this area."

Galbreath says the Alliance's approach has several advantages over Covington's. For one, it's more respectful of what actually exists, not some idealized notion of what was on the ground before 1900. Because even pre-1900 forests weren't homogeneous; they reflected a natural pattern in which some wet years led to an explosion of seedling growth, and some dry years led to catastrophic fires even in "adapted" ponderosa forests. Moreover, the alliance's approach seems to allow more flexibility in treating an area. Covington distinguishes between his "strict sense" restoration based on a firm presettlement formula, and compromise approaches that allow extra trees to screen a house from a highway or give migrating elk extra shelter. But even that, says Hoffman, is too dogmatic—at best a two-size-fits-all, or fits most, approach to forest restoration. "But there are 27 different ponderosa pine forest types just in Arizona," he says. So the Southwest Forest Alliance believes its approach allows for greater sensitivity to a particular forest, although I wondered how, with 95 percent of the old-growth ponderosa pine forests wiped out, anyone can know 27 distinct varieties once existed.

Perhaps most important, the alliance's forest-health prescription is simply less labor-intensive than the approach espoused by Covington and the Ecological Restoration Institute. Forest treatment isn't cheap—on average about $100 an acre. Extrapolate that across the West, and the tab comes close to $10 billion. In their Kaibab plot, the Southwest Forest Alliance took down fewer trees and left less slash than under the Ecological Restoration Institute's strict approach, requiring less cleanup afterward, or, if fire is used to remove slash and debris left by thinning, it results in a less hot fire, killing fewer of the remaining trees. In ERI-prescribed areas, "we've seen 25 or 30 percent of the trees killed by the first fire to go through there," Hoffman says as we walk through the test plot. "Here, we think it would be more like 10 percent."

Alliance members say their claims aren't simply an intellectual exercise. They point to one of the handful of large-scale efforts to apply Covington's prescriptions as proof that they're right. That example is the Mount Trumbull site in the northeast corner of Arizona, where the Bureau of Land Management has carefully followed Covington's model for the treatment of a 3,500-acre tract of ponderosa pine forest that had become badly overgrown after pre-1900 sheep grazing, then post-1900 fire suppression. In the eyes of the Southwest Forest Alliance, the effort is a disaster. "It's heinous," Galbreath says to me as she aims her car along the highway. "They've cut 28-inch-diameter trees down, then left six- and eight-inch-diameter trees. It'll never be used as a national model. It's just too extreme." After touring the Kaibab plot, Hoffman shows me slides he took at Mount Trumbull. They show plots largely stripped of vegetation, with thick mats of slash that had been tamped down by bulldozers. In some places, trees that perhaps topped 100 years in age have been cut down, while a much smaller tree just a few feet away has been left in place. Why? "Because the larger tree fell outside the circle they drew around a presettlement stump," he says. Alliance members believe that as the word gets out about just what "forest restoration" means, there will be as much outrage over it as there was over clear-cutting 20 years ago.

Covington, for his part, scoffs at that notion. In his eyes, the challenge posed by the Southwest Forest Alliance has little to do with real forestry science. "We were all great friends until 1994," he says of his relationship with local environmental activists. "That's when I came out and said that we had to look at ways other than prescribed burns for bringing these areas back. Well, what I was recommending proved to be beneficial to some of the traditional economic interests—logging, livestock, and water and power. And groups like the Alliance couldn't stand that. They figured that if these old foes were for what I wanted to do, then they couldn't possibly be for it. It's a kind of shallow analysis that's so common today—'Don't

Logs are stacked near an experimental forest plot being thinned in an effort to forestall catastrophic wildfire. Such treatment projects are controversial, with some people claiming they do more harm to a forest than good.
(Martos Hoffman)

bother me with details, just tell me where my opponents stand, and I'll tell you my position.'"

Covington also is convinced his use of around 1880 as his target for a "typical" ponderosa pine forest is correct. "That argument is a red herring," he says of efforts to cast doubt on presettlement conditions as a good yardstick. "The results we get from that approach are generalizable—we see them across the West, from up in British Columbia to down in Mexico, and in places like the Powell Plateau. It would be great to be able to look back 10,000 years, but we just can't do that."

The controversy, which given its huge implications for Western forests has remained remarkably localized, has gotten nasty in recent years. Covington accuses Southwest Forest Alliance members of attacking him personally—"all these *ad hominem* attacks," as he puts it. And after the alliance bought a full-page ad in the *Arizona Daily Sun* in advance of an August 2001 visit by Secretary of the Interior Gale Norton—an ad that was harshly critical of Covington's methods—he was said to have referred to alliance members as "Nazis," a charge he sharply refutes (while referring to what he saw as the agitprop approach of some green groups, he told me, he "had pointed out that the evils of propaganda are best illustrated by Nazi propaganda techniques"). "It's too bad," Galbreath tells me, as we eat lunch in one of the new semi-chic restaurants popping up in Flagstaff as that town's clean air, temperate climate, and rustic atmosphere become discovered. "I used to see Wally around town, and he'd give me a hug, and then we'd just find something else to talk about," she says. "Now we'll just ignore each other."

When I visit the participants in this debate, it isn't clear who has the upper hand. Covington certainly has a strong deck; he and the Ecological Restoration Institute are gaining nationwide renown, and two days after I speak with him he flies to Utah to meet with an array of western governors and members of the Bush administration. His institute is awash in grant money—it raked in some $10 million in 2001, for instance—and has published an impressive array of papers. Covington also is doing well in the arena of public opinion; I've quoted him myself in articles I've written for *The Economist,* and his name also appears regularly in publications ranging from *The New York Times* to *Scientific American.* When Gale Norton visited in August, Covington was her chief tour guide to several test plots, and she had high praise for Covington's approach. He's intelligent, approachable, and has found a delicate balance that allows him to both be harshly critical of the U.S. Forest Service ("they're very adept at hijacking terminology, such as 'ecosystem restoration'") and yet appear balanced and open to a range of viewpoints. I found him persuasive, knowledgeable, and a seeming breath of reason in an arena that often is bitterly polarized.

The Southwest Forest Alliance, meanwhile, was beset by funding problems and squabbling among its charter members, several of whom dropped out when the alliance wouldn't adopt a "no-cut" stance on the subject of forest restoration. Still, while their Web site presentation was a red herring—in effect, their aerial photos seemed intended to make a badly out-of-whack forest look preferable to a serious effort to restore it—their own test plots and well-thought-out critique of Covington's position make sense. It took more than 100 years to get ourselves in this fix, and getting out of it may well take another 100 years—or at least longer than it would take to race through nearly 100 million acres of Western woodlands, drawing circles with old stumps at the midpoint, and leaving 1.5 trees behind.

No one denies, though, that something should be done to help forests, particularly the ponderosa pine forest. The day I tour the SWFA's test sites, I later go on Highway 180, toward the Grand

Canyon, pull off on Forest Service Road 245, and bounce down a gravel road to the Kendrick Mountain Trailhead. There I hike up the trail, breathing hard in the thin air at 8,000 feet. In June 2000 the Pumpkin Fire burned here, sweeping over 14,000 acres of forest that by any standard is typical of the forests now found in much of the West. Here, the trees are packed closely together, and burned readily. In places the damage was not great—the pines' lower trunks were badly scorched, but the upper branches were green and needle-covered, and most of the trees almost certainly will live. But elsewhere the trees were torched, burned from base to top, leaving a blackened mass of twigs branching out from a charred trunk. Here, as at the nearby Radio Fire in 1977, the fire was so hot that it literally cooked the soil, sterilizing it. Only an occasional sprig of grass pokes up from the ground. It will be many years, and perhaps decades, before this ground recovers. Some ponderosa pine samples suggest that big, old trees survived perhaps 200 fires before finally succumbing to old age or insects. On Kendrick Mountain, the first fire that large stands of seemingly healthy trees faced proved fatal for many of them.

I stop at a switchback in the trail and look down across an expanse of blackened trees, and at the patches of green that sweep across the lower foothills toward Flagstaff. There, the forest looks fine. That's what is so deceiving in this debate. People see a green, thick forest, and come to believe that's both normal and healthy. But hardly any people younger than 60 have seen a "normal" ponderosa pine forest. Except for relict fragments such as those on the Powell Plateau, north of the Grand Canyon, and a handful of other locations, few examples of what once covered the West remain. Perhaps, if hit by a fast-moving crown fire that originates in a neighboring forest, even they may be destroyed.

Chapter 14

▲ ▲ ▲ ▲

Mopping Up

Fire seasons don't cross a finish line, or pass some date after which they cease to exist. In the fall of 2001, as in every year, it winds down slowly; the preparedness level at the fire center in Boise drifts down from the Level 5 of late August, to Level 4 by early September, then Level 3, and by the end of September Level 2. But fires keep starting—even on October 5 the daily situation report lists three new large fires in the northern Rocky Mountains and California, and forests remain extremely volatile across the entire West. Only autumn's cooler temperatures and dearth of thunderstorms keep fire starts low.

That October 5 situation report lists another activity: support in New York City, by then trying to pick up after the catastrophes of September 11. The West's fire community contributes to the effort, sending incident command teams to organize the massive cleanup and search effort, and logistical crews to manage the flood of equipment and supplies pouring into the city and lapping at the edges of Ground Zero.

Also by October, fire managers in the West are tallying up the figures for 2001. It has been an "average" year when compared with the previous 10. Acres burned: 3,570,911, a bit less than the 10-year norm of just over 4 million. Number of fire starts: 84,079, again just a little below other recent years. Big fires have included the Moose Fire, which burned 70,000 acres near Glacier Park in Montana; the Virginia Lake and Rex Creek Fires in Washington, which burned 58,000 and 41,000 acres, respectively; the 49,000-acre Sheepshead Fire in Oregon; and the 35,500-acre Blue Complex near Alturas, California, which profited so handsomely from the blaze. There is no monster fire such as the previous year's Valley Complex, but nearly all the significant fires of 2001 have burned at the same time, putting firefighters and fire managers in a short frenzy of activity as the national fire center zooms from Level 1 to Level 5 preparedness in a matter of a few weeks.

Some 730 "structures" are listed as burned in the year's final tally, but only a small fraction of these are homes—maybe 50 or 60. The rest are wood sheds, garages, outhouses, and buildings long ago abandoned. I think of a story I hear but cannot confirm, of the fire crew that was diligently wetting down a barn in advance of an approaching fire when the barn's owner arrived. "What the hell are you doing!" he demanded to know. "If that burns, I'll get $200,000 insurance money for it!" I figure the tally for keeping the hunting cabin on the edge of the Fridley Fire safe easily tops $100,000, money that paid crews who cleared the cabin's property of downed timber, bulldozers that dug a fireline around it, helicopters that kept the fire at bay as it crept up the slope beneath the cabin. No doubt that expenditure was repeated dozens of times throughout the summer. Almost the entire $9.8 million bill for the Green Knoll fire in Wyoming, for instance, can be attributed to efforts to save homes.

In May, while talking with Kevin Ryan at the Fire Sciences Laboratory, he suggested I'd be wise to rent a hotel room in Wenatchee, Washington, for around early August. I didn't, but it wasn't bad advice, as eastern Washington has had one of its hottest fire seasons since 1994, with a half-dozen big fires burning at once there, and dozens of smaller ones. The eastern half of Oregon has been hit hard as well. Idaho and Montana, which had suffered so during 2000, get off relatively lightly. Conditions are ripe for big blazes almost the entire summer, but the lightning gods take it easy on those states, sparing them the parade of dry thunderstorms that spark big bursts of wildfire. (Human-set fires, while nothing to cheer about, typically happen individually. Lightning-set fires come in batches than can overwhelm fire crews.) Arizona and New Mexico, hard hit as well in 2000, also get off relatively lightly due to heavy, late snow and early-spring rain. But that isn't necessarily good news. The summer of 2001 is a fabulous growing season for cheatgrass, piñons, juniper, and other readily combustible stuff, ensuring that those states will be pasted the following year.

The year 2001 isn't average in one regard, however: cost. Despite the somewhat mild burning season, the National Fire Plan ensures that plenty of money gets thrown around. In part, that is an aberration—the millions slated for reducing flammable conditions in forests often wind up in suppression budgets. That is because the national forests don't have time to go through the sometimes two-year process required to get permits for thinning, prescribed burns, and other antifire measures. But it also means that with 5,000 new firefighters and twice the number of helicopters as in previous years, fire managers sometimes get all the resources they ask for, particularly for midsummer fires such as Green Knoll and Fridley, which don't have much competition. Just about any fire that tops 10,000 acres manages to hit the $1-million-a-day-mark for suppression costs. One lightning-set fire in Oregon, the Olallie Lake Fire, costs $4.3 million despite the fact that it never gets larger than 2,400 acres. The Arthur Fire in Yellowstone is not cheap either, racking up a $4 million bill yet burning only 2,800 acres. The much larger Moose Fire near Glacier National Park in Montana, at 70,000 acres, is a relative bargain at $11.9 million.

One fire, though, becomes the poster fire for the lunacy shown at times by fire managers. It's the Craggie Fire, started September 17 when lightning hits the dried trunk of a long-dead tree in a remote section of Oregon's Kalmiopsis Wilderness, in the southwest corner of the state. As fires go, it's as innocuous as they get. It burns in a wilderness area, miles from the nearest home, in forests that likely will benefit from a little fire-induced fall cleanup. And the chances the fire will make any sort of a run are pretty near zero, given the shorter burning period in the autumn sun and the near certainty the usual Oregon October rain will wrap it in a soggy blanket.

No matter. The Craggie Fire warrants a full-scale firefighting assault. By September 22, 395 people and an incident command team are assigned to it, along with seven heavy helicopters. The helos do their thing, dropping buckets of water, making a lot of noise, and racking up one hellacious bill. The little Craggie Fire, which never gets beyond 279 acres—it's barely 12 football field lengths across— nonetheless costs $2.2 million to fight. At $7,899 per acre, the Craggie Fire earns the distinction of being the most expensive fire, on a per-acre basis, of the summer—its per-acre bill totaling seven times the national average of $1,164 per acre.

Going into 2001 the Forest Service had budgeted $469 million for fire suppression. That at least represented a halfway realistic estimate. In years past, the Forest Service essentially pretended there wouldn't even *be* a fire season, at least in terms of budgeting for it. Then, when fires broke out, it simply spent money until the rains started, afterward asking Congress to pick up the bill. In 2000, for instance, a paltry $122 million had been set aside for fire, a figure promptly sent up in smoke as fire costs hit the $1.1 billion mark. But despite the extra dough in the 2001 account, it too proves insufficient. The Forest Service finally figures its costs for the year at $700 million, give or take a few dozen mil. Less than 2000, true, but on a cost-per-acre basis, far more. The 2000 season saw three times the acreage burned, yet cost less than twice as much as 2001. The glaring disparity even frustrates Forest Service officials. One, Harry Croft, the deputy director of the Forest Service's National Fire Plan, offers the candid observation that "if I was in business, I'd be out of business. Everywhere I've been, everyone says the same thing—the system is broken, and we've got to change it. Whether they are going to want to fix it is another issue." And those figures don't even take into account the money spent on retardant dropping military C-130s used in Oregon and Washington in August, or the National Guard teams put to work at the Fridley Fire and others. Different budget—Pentagon budget—and they don't show up on Forest Service ledgers.

But there is no call to fix things. By late fall, the National Fire Plan is rebudgeted for 2002, with another $2 billion allocated for fire suppression, fire prevention, and assistance to communities seeking to fireproof themselves a little.

In short, the long-established tradition of blank-check firefighting emerges unscathed from 2001. The Pentagon cancels over-budget weapons that don't perform well (rarely, but it does). State governments that don't have enough money lay off teachers and highway patrol officers. Cities that haven't got enough cash to pay all the bills leave potholes unfilled. But forest fires operate under no such rules. Fire camps never are shut down when it is obvious that little real progress can be made stopping a fire. Helicopters aren't grounded because they've exceeded the budget for a fire. And the Forest Service and other land-use agencies that fight fires never have a problem refilling the firefighting coffers after a summer's blown budgets. In the case of the Forest Service, it will even raid the budgets of individual forests—money earmarked for trail rehabilitation or even prescribed burning—to make sure it has enough for the suppression machine.

It's madness, say longtime critics of the nation's firefighting efforts. Some, such as University of Maryland economist Robert Nelson, contend that the Forest Service today simply has no other mission aside from firefighting, and it is botching that mission so utterly that the agency should be abolished. "The Forest Service is so disoriented and confused that it doesn't do anything," Nelson tells me. "That is, except during fire season, when it doesn't have to write an environmental impact statement."

But not only isolated self-described rabble-rousers such as Nelson take the Forest Service to task. The General Accounting Office weighs in as well, with a scathing indictment of the nation's fire effort. In late fall it lambastes the Forest Service for failing, since the 1995 revision of the Federal Wildland Fire Management Policy, to develop fire management plans for more than half of the land it controls. It is the lack of a fire plan, for instance, that led the agency to throw so many resources at the Craggie Fire. The GAO also lashes the Forest Service and other agencies for failing to inventory communities at risk of fire; for failing to develop criteria for what constitutes an "urban wildland interface" (in Arizona, almost entire national forests have been declared hazardous to nearby communities); and for continued coordination problems between agencies such as the Forest Service, the Bureau of Land Management, and the Department of Interior.

But the fire's influence on the nation's politics is deeply entrenched. The Forest Service, for instance, is one of the most D.C.-savvy agencies in the nation, having successfully reinvented itself repeatedly since its inception to tailor its self-appointed "mission" to suit the prevailing mood about how to manage national forests. Today, as Robert Nelson suggests, it has become almost entirely a fire-prevention and fire-suppression agency, and is quick to co-opt suggestions about managing lands to prevent fires and embed them in its bureaucratic structure.

Even if it chooses to, however, it's unlikely that the Forest Service can free itself from the very perception it worked hard to create— that fire poses an imminent threat to the West. It declared war on fire from its earliest days, developed a militarylike infrastructure to carry out that war, created a nomenclature in which fires are "attacked" and "contained," and developed one of the most effective propaganda campaigns the United States has seen in the past 100 years—Smokey the Bear, of course. Fire invariably is seen as the enemy, something that can only do harm.

Some progress in correcting that image has been made, and the Forest Service itself has helped with that effort. Many of its field people believe strongly that fire has a role on the landscape, and in many cases fires are left to burn with little more than a handful of fire specialists to watch them and make sure they don't make an unwanted run. But these instances of "wildland fire use," while commendable, are drowned out in the roar of helicopters fanning out to douse some other blaze. So dollars keep getting thrown at firefighting—dollars that add up to a higher bill each year, so that even an average fire season can see more spent on a per-fire basis that an earlier one viewed widely as catastrophic.

And, of course, those dollars reflect only part of the cost in the 2001 fire season. In addition to the $700 million, 16 people die. Three die in the helicopter flying near the Fridley Fire that I saw two days before it went down. Two more are killed in California when two firefighting planes collide, others in vehicle crashes while traveling to fires. And there are the four who died in early July at the Thirtymile Fire.

Those deaths weigh heavily on the season. The numbers aren't as high as at Mann Gulch or Storm King, perhaps, and everyone recognizes or at least pays lip service to the notion that walking into a forest full of burning trees carries with it some unavoidable risks. And that, of course, also is part of the work's appeal. But Thirtymile carries with it a particular kind of sadness. In part that's because three of the dead were so new to firefighting. Children, really, who died trying to make a few bucks for college. Then there is the manner in which the disaster played out, with the firefighters nervously awaiting their fate, milling around a narrow road like sheep. At Mann Gulch and Storm King, at least, the firefighters were moving, trying to get away.

In late September, I sit in a meeting room at the Forest Service's Region 6 headquarters in Missoula, waiting for a live video feed from Yakima, Washington. There, Jim Furnish, the Forest Service deputy chief who led the investigation into the Thirtymile tragedy, is about to review the report's findings. Furnish looks a little unsettled as he stands on a stage before a room packed with media and family members; in Washington State, the Thirtymile incident had remained big news throughout the summer. "The Thirtymile Fire tragedy could have been prevented," starts Furnish. "This tragic accident was the result of many factors—factors that are agonizingly familiar."

Over the next 15 minutes, Furnish ticks off a list of mistakes made that day that probably seem astonishing to casual observers, but sound familiar to the thousands of people who confront wild-land fire each summer and often make decisions that in the wrong circumstances would haunt them. Still, what happened in the Chewuch Canyon that day almost defies description. Firefighters are drilled regularly on the 10 standard fire orders—the guidelines for safe conduct that command firefighters and their leaders to en-sure a path of retreat, watch the weather and fire behavior, and stay in touch with one another and superiors. Every one of the 10 rules, Furnish says, was broken. The firefighters were working in unfamil-iar terrain, without scouts to keep an eye open. They ignored changes in the temperature and humidity, changes reflected in the fire's in-creasingly aggressive behavior. No escape route was established, or safety zone identified. Worst of all, they lost track of where the fire was in relation to the road, allowing the fire to cut them off when it started to move. Ignored as well were 10 of the 18 "watch out" situ-ations, scenarios in which firefighters are advised to exercise cau-tion, such as when unburned fuel is between firefighters and the fire, or when weather conditions are changing. The firefighters and their team leaders were tired, which clouded judgment, and not mindful of how the lowering humidity and increasingly aggressive fire behavior posed a threat.

Those up the chain of command are sharply criticized for failing to understand the potential of the Thirtymile Fire and doing a poor job of keeping tabs on the crew's progress against the fire. The delay in getting a helicopter to the fire because of environmental concerns is discounted; more serious was the failure of the pumps to perform properly, as they could have put far more water directly on the fire than a helicopter could.

In particular, the report singles out Ellreese Daniels and Pete Kampen, the Thirtymile crew's bosses, for ignoring clear warnings given by the fire that it had the potential to turn into something big. "No one associated with this fire gave it the respect it deserved," Furnish says. Worse, Kampen and Daniels literally led their teams into a trap, traveling north up the Chewuch River Road even as the fire threatened to spot across the road and cut off their only escape route. And when Daniels was finally trapped by the fire, along with 13 of his crew members, he did little to help them prepare for the approaching fire. He gave no directions to rookie crew members desperate for guidance and failed to take rudimentary steps, such as clearing the area where the crew was gathered of flammable material and advising firefighters to prepare their shelters for deployment.

In the absence of leadership, the Thirtymile crew had to make its own decisions. Some made the right ones—those such as Nick Dreis and Matt Rutman, who started to think about the need to deploy their fire shelters, and stayed on the road where the bare gravel could protect them. But others were not as conscientious, and gathered with friends from their home units rather than the squad members they were working with on the fire. This, Furnish says, played a role in why firefighters from Yakima were the ones sitting on the rocks above the road when the firestorm hit. Moreover, the report suggests, the firefighters on the boulder field uphill from the road apparently ignored orders from Daniels to come down to the road.

The report is instantly controversial, largely because of its effort to hold those who died at least partly responsible for their own deaths. But the suggestion that the four dead were at least in part responsible for their deaths infuriates family members. "Tom disobeying an order? That's ridiculous. You tell Tom to do something, and he does it," says Evelyn Craven, Tom Craven's widow. "They're trying to make Tom a scapegoat."

Perhaps more disheartening to family members of the dead firefighters, however, is that the report calls for no punishment for the crew's leaders. Within the Forest Service, I'd been told, keen competition for promotion spots leads to furious infighting and mudslinging in an attempt to gain the upper hand. But in public the agency closes ranks in a manner not seen even in the military, with its well-established court-martial procedure for command mistakes. Despite obvious blunders in 1994 at the Storm King fire, for instance, no one ever took the rap—some of the same fire managers who put 14 firefighters in death's path are still managing fires years later.

For a time it appears that the Thirtymile managers will lead a similarly charmed life. But the too-familiar pleas that the Forest Service has "learned its lesson" this time, seven years after it has supposedly learned and relearned its lessons, stick in the craw of people with influence. Maria Cantwell, a member of the U.S. Senate from Washington, keeps pressure on the Forest Service to do more than verbally wrist-slap those responsible for the deaths of four people. She gets help in that cause from the Occupational Safety and Health Administration, which blasts the Forest Service for its handling of the Thirtymile Fire, hitting it with citations for two "willful" violations—an administrative step away from shutting down the whole Forest Service firefighting operation. The Forest Service, the OSHA report says, had not provided a workplace free of obvious hazards—a finding based on the wholesale violation of the fire orders. The agency also took the Forest Service to task for failing to inspect its firefighting operations. Not long after the report appears, 11 Forest Service employees—not named in a heavily self-censored report issued by the agency, but including Ellreese Daniels and Pete Kampen—are hit with sanctions ranging from firing to letters of reprimand.

Meanwhile, the Forest Service pursues something at which it has gotten all too much practice: building memorials. At the site of the burn-over where Devin Weaver, Jessica Johnson, Tom Craven, and

Karen FitzPatrick died, a concrete memorial wall is started, one that will contain the etched faces of the four dead. And at the four firefighters' home base, the Naches Ranger Station, a memorial garden also proceeds. These newest memorials join those already in place at Mann Gulch and at Storm King Mountain. Meant to honor firefighters who died in the line of duty, they stand primarily as monuments to either ignorance or incompetence in the face of one of the great forces of nature. The idea of a memorial for the Thirtymile firefighters, while surely appropriate, seems to ring particularly hollow. The four were sitting, waiting for a fire to bypass them as they and their leaders surely thought it would—"sitting on a goddamn rock waiting to die"—an angry Ken Weaver, father of Devin, said to me during a telephone conversation.

Moreover, while the Forest Service investigation team altered its report to tone down accusations that the four dead firefighters had ignored orders, it is clear that the Thirtymile Fire is something that Mann Gulch and Storm King really were not: survivable. Ten members of the fire crew trapped in the Thirtymile Fire lived—as did two civilians with absolutely no training or protective gear who squeezed into Rebecca Welch's shelter. The road, with its smooth surface that could work with the fire shelters to create a seal against the fire's superheated gases, clearly should have been a place where all the firefighters gathered. That 10 did, but four did not, speaks to a lapse in judgment. I had taken the same rookie training as FitzPatrick and Weaver, and had been made fully aware that a rocky field was far from ideal for shelter deployment, particularly when flat ground, free of woody debris, lay so near. When I last speak with Kathie FitzPatrick, Karen's mother, she tells me that one of the fire crew now says that Karen had a premonition of death on the Chewuch Road, and was sitting in the rocks engrossed in prayer when she died. Perhaps. But why would any God chivvy four people away from the group, allowing them to make a fatal mistake? Instead, it all seems like such a waste.

Perhaps a better memorial to the four dead than a slab of etched concrete will be a better fire shelter. Clearly, the shelters saved lives on July 11. But their poor design and documented flaws—their inability to seal over an irregular surface, the tendency of the laminate to come unglued in high heat—also contributed to the four deaths. Over the fall and winter of 2001, technicians at the Forest Service's Missoula Technology and Development Center evaluated proposals for new designs, finally settling on one of their own making in June of 2002. The new shelters, slated for deployment over the 2003 and 2004 fire seasons, are slightly heavier than the older models, but offer better protection against both hot gases and direct flame contact, and provide much better coverage than the older shelters. Still, the firefighter's best friend, as it always has been, continues to be the wisdom to know when it's time to leave a fire.

By fall, as the fires burn out, the firefighters head home. Steve Frye returns to Glacier National Park, to his neat clapboard house inside the park's employee compound in West Glacier, to begin a round of planning for the 2002 season and catch up on park business.

Rebecca Welch, who emerges from the Thirtymile Fire as a true hero because of her thankless willingness to share a fire shelter with two others, returns to California to plan a wintertime trip to Europe, a trip financed with her fire earnings. Immediately after Thirtymile, she'd taken two weeks off to recover from the burns she suffered. That was it, she'd told herself. No more fires. But she misses her crew, and by late July returns to Naches to finish her summer of duty. She soon has one enormous hurdle to cross. Her crew boss puts her team through a shelter-deployment drill, and she has to crawl back inside one of the devices in which she nearly died. It is a harrowing moment for her. It's a hot early-August day, and the temperature inside the shelter, well over 100 degrees, is eerily reminiscent of that awful afternoon near the Chewuch River. Welch begins to sob, but somehow maintains enough self-control to stay inside the shelter until her crew boss gives the okay to leave it.

Not long after that, her crew is assigned to a fire. Another hurdle—it's in a canyon, much like Thirtymile. Welch is scared half to death, but gets a reprieve when the crew is sent to a smaller fire in a safer, more open area. She spends a night digging line, staying within a few feet of her squad boss, and gradually begins to feel more comfortable. She works on two more fires that summer. But she dreams about her dead friends, particularly Jessica Johnson.

And on a sunny, cool day in Eugene, Oregon, I sit on a bench and talk with Matt Rutman. Rutman, who had documented what it was like inside the Thirtymile Fire both in his journal and with a disposable camera, is in this university logging town to plan a winter trip to Guatemala, packing with him a mass of computer equipment for that nation's impoverished schools. He had a harder time of the summer than Welch. Mainly, that was because he'd begun to do some whistle-blowing in the wake of the Thirtymile Fire, talking with reporters about the fire and writing letters to supervisors about ways to improve training and preparedness for firefighters caught in situations like Thirtymile. For the most part, his efforts to improve firefighter safety fell on deaf ears. He was even encouraged to get out of firefighting, and was offered jobs in fish and wildlife or trails work. But he stayed with the fire crew, going only to two tiny fires over the balance of the summer.

The experience has left him bitter and depressed. He is critical of the Forest Service's report on Thirtymile, especially the version that says the firefighters on the boulder field were ordered to come down to the road. He never heard such a command, and believes its inclusion in the report is part of a calculated whitewash. And he is angry that at the time no one in charge of the Thirtymile firefighting operation was so much as disciplined. But mainly he is acutely aware of now narrowly he escaped death. Months after the fire, he has nightmares and thinks often about death. He thinks as well about the four dead firefighters, all around his age, and what their dreams and aspirations for the future might have been. The Thirtymile tragedy also is a lesson to him, though. That life is short, and if you want to make a difference in the world you had better start now. So he redoubles his efforts to collect equipment for Guatemala. On the way back to Seattle from our visit, I stop at a Fry's Electronics store and buy a case of computer mice, which I ship to him when I get home. More Matt Rutmans, I think, likely would make the world a better place.

Whether the nation's wildland firefighting apparatus can draw any lessons from Thirtymile, or anything related to its primary mission, remains to be seen. It's difficult to be optimistic, as the current system is utterly dysfunctional. One could argue that for the $1 billion or so a year now spent to put fires out, taxpayers get nothing in return but the risk of worse fires later. It's true that initial attack crews corral about 97 percent of all fires, but in so doing they often simply set the stage for worsening those 3 percent of fires that require a multiday effort.

A rational discussion about changing our approach to fires, though, will be difficult to come by. On the one hand, there's Smokey the Bear, with his clear message that fire is a terrible thing. And as a terrible thing—it cannot be left to its own devices. The West's entire firefighting apparatus is predicated on the assumption that the vast majority of fires should be extinguished as quickly as possible. At the other extreme is the modern environmental movement, which wants forests left "natural" and places special emphasis on the "ancient" forest, when in fact few American forests are all that ancient and insects almost invariably take them down in time if fire does not. Almost no forest standing today is natural; fire suppression has taken care of that, and it may be incumbent upon humans to physically attempt to reshape forests into a more natural form. The deep reverence for the ancient forest, meanwhile, seeks to embalm them so that they never change, at least at the hand of humans.

I came away from the summer of 2001 certain of one thing: Neither approach works. The continuing war on forest fires is a waste of time, money, and lives. It often damages the forests it claims to protect. It puts thousands of young people in harm's way. It strips money away from other important considerations on federal lands (even as the Forest Service budgets ever more for fires, it increasingly seeks to charge parking fees to hikers and others who use tax-supported land). And rarely achieves its objective.

On the other hand, we can't simply walk away from western forests and let fires sort things out. Drought and lightning and the very nature of forests all contribute to fires. Those factors alone will create the occasional enormous fire. But statistics make it clear that fires are getting bigger and hotter because of our own past intervention. So we have a responsibility to try to ameliorate the problem, at least in some areas. Lodgepole pine forests probably should be left to their own devices—if they burn, they burn. As Yellowstone proves, for these forests a good fire causes little if any real harm. In other cases, particularly in the ponderosa pine forest, human intervention may be all that will save many of those forests from their utter annihilation at the hands of fire.

My own belief is that better managing wildfire must begin with coexistence. That may be a difficult habit to acquire, when fire has been so completely characterized as the enemy. Fire engenders panic in a way that floods or perhaps even hurricanes do not. The reaction to them seems more analogous to how people view tornadoes: wildly unpredictable, immensely destructive, utterly terrifying. And when that panic sets in, any talk that it's a fire that's simply inevitable gets lost in the roar to do something. Still, people living in hurricane- or flood-prone areas in the United States seem to have largely come to terms with the possibility that one or the other will smite them. Fires could surely be viewed the same way. Towns and communities should draft good, workable plans for making people and homes fire-safe, while those individuals who insist on living right on the edge of a fire-prone forest should be given no more sympathy than someone who insists on waterfront property on the Gulf Coast. Sooner or later, in both cases, a big fire or a big storm is going to do some damage.

The next step must be some sort of effort to fireproof certain forests, an effort commensurate with our current effort to extinguish fires. Wally Covington's proposals may be too extreme, but the time is rapidly approaching when forest thinning must be accomplished. The difficulty here will be in deciding *which* forests to thin. Treatments that may well help a ponderosa pine forest will not help elsewhere. And it's completely unclear how to manage forests where a mixed-conifer stand of trees, flammable and crowded, has replaced forests where ponderosa pine once dominated. Some, perhaps, nature will have to handle as best it can. Others may require an effort to restore some competitive balance between the ponderosa and encroaching trees such as Douglas-fir, even if that means logging some healthy, large firs. How we'll get beyond the current poisoned atmosphere between environmentalists, the Forest Service, and the logging industry is beyond me. And the more conservative George W. Bush administration, with its knee-jerk reactionism on environmental issues and its penchant for end runs around carefully developed rules, is not apt to become the arbiter that is needed. But some credible party must emerge, one without axes to grind or political points to score, and show the way. I believe that this generation must accept the fact that for 30 or 40 years forests will not look as "pretty" or as natural as they would like, due to the aftereffects of mechanical thinning and even selective logging. But 100 years from now, if that work is performed carefully and for the right reasons, the West's forests may come much closer than they are now to the way they appeared 100 years ago.

The third step must be to rein in the firefighting machine. It is ludicrous to believe that every large fire must have every available dollar spent on it. In some manner, a sense of proportion must be restored to firefighting. That can never be accomplished in the heat of the moment. The only way to achieve that goal is to force firefighting agencies to adhere to some semblance of an actual budget. One solution may be to cap the number of firefighters hired each year at a level below what was reached in 2001. Cap as well the number of helicopters, aircraft, food contractors, and others who are on call. Close the smokejumping bases—all of them. Smokejumpers are a reminder of the once-romantic past of wildland firefighting. But they have no role in the modern fire world. Using DC-3s to ferry small teams of smokejumpers to fires within view of interstate highways, an all-too-common occurrence, is simply absurd.

Reducing the dollars spent on firefighting will of course mean that some large fires will not get the same number of firefighters that they received in 2001. But otherwise the cost of fighting fires will simply continue to grow. And it's a receding target—without a concerted effort to reduce the buildup of fuels in the forests, it is impossible to catch up to the number and severity of fires that can be expected.

A firefighter in Oregon throws dirt on a spot fire near a lightning-set blaze.

The seemingly Draconian notion to put a lid on firefighting, however, need not cause harm to Western forests. On the contrary, we have or are very close to having the capability to use limited resources in a way that will result in better fire management and even fire control, not worse.

Here, science may be of considerable help. On a hazy day, while at the Fire Sciences Lab, I watched lab researcher Colin Hardy and University of Montana forestry professor Lloyd Queen working around what looked like one of the large, flat griddles popular in Korean-style restaurants. Next to it stood a wading pool. Both devices, the griddle heated to 200°C and the pool cooled to 20°C, were wired to record their precise temperatures. An orbiting Cessna, outfitted with infrared sensors, flew overhead, checking the temperature picked up from the air with the actual temperature of the pool and griddle. Queen and Hardy plan to use the airborne infrared sensors to build an accurate thermal image of fires—how hotly they burned, and for how long—and compare that to other data about the fuels and forest conditions known to exist on the fire's site. Hardy, like Kevin Ryan a fire-effects specialist, also is hoping to use data gathered from the air to determine if a fire is hot enough to kill trees, or merely scorch their needles, information forest managers may use to determine whether to salvage dead trees or allow them to recover.

Remote sensing—the use of infrared scanners or devices such as LIDAR (Light Detection and Ranging) to study a fire's intensity and its emissions from a distance—is fast coming into its own. Such applications are not new; for several years, infrared images have helped fire managers spy on a big fire by peering through its smoke and haze to pinpoint its location and size. Satellite imagery also has helped determine the location and size of fires. "But," says Queen, "those methods basically give us pictures, not real data. What we're trying to do is say more than 'here is a fire.' We want to understand its thermal characteristics; therefore, this is the effect it might have."

Such data also is a step toward what fire scientists view as their current Holy Grail—knowing what a fire will burn before the fire burns it. Atop the fire lab's 42-year-old burn chamber, for instance, sits a new white dome. Inside, a satellite dish tracks the National Aeronautic and Space Administration's Terra satellite, launched in December 1999 as part of a 15-year project to collect data about the Earth. Each day, Terra makes three orbits that pass over North America. With each pass, its MODIS unit (Moderate Resolution Imaging Spectroradiometer) scans the planet's surface, gauging snowfall or melt, cloud cover, the spread of green grass each spring. With its fairly rough 10-meter resolution, MODIS also can pick up hot spots—fires—and relay that information in the dish atop the burn tower, and from there to an array of Compaq servers in a room on the fire lab's second floor. There, within minutes of the satellite's pass, researchers can spot a fire that has erupted since the satellite last was overhead.

At face value that seems like a terrific thing—the ability to detect new fires regardless of weather conditions, time of day, or whether any human is nearby. But fire detection really isn't the problem. "We already do a great job at fire detection," says Ryan. "If anything, we're too good at it—with cell phones and the like, hardly any fires burn for more than a few hours before they're spotted."

Instead, the MODIS data may allow scientists to combine news that a fire exists with information about the fuels around the fire, the terrain across which it is burning, and what the weather will do. With that, fire scientists may be able to tell fire managers within hours of a fire's start exactly how that fire will behave, how much damage it will cause if left to its own devices, and where it might

Smoke pours from the fireline of a California blaze.

make the most sense to try to stop the fire. Or that a fire may actually benefit an area that is in need of fire yet not so overgrown that a
fire would become catastrophic. Or that forest conditions and terrain are such that a serious effort to extinguish a fire should be
made. At least that's the tantalizing prospect. Whether fire managers and the politicians to whom they answer ever will feel completely comfortable allowing a computer model to make the call on
how to manage a fire remains to be seen. But surely it can't handle
things any worse than they've been handled the past 50 years.

Such information might have made a big difference in how the
Thirtymile Fire was tackled. Fire managers on July 11 wanted to
keep trying to catch it, for fear that it might grow rapidly and sweep
up the Chewuch River Valley. But the odds that they could do so
were low from the start, something that they hadn't quite been able
to calculate. The fire had chugged and puffed along the moist valley
floor for a few days, but by the time the Northwest Regular Crew
No. 6 arrived it was beginning to move into mixed forest of lodgepole pine, subalpine fir, ponderosa pine, and Douglas-fir. The area
had not burned for many years, and was due for a big fire. In the narrow valley of the Chewuch, with hot, dry air and drought-parched
fuels, that big fire was imminent. An extra push was made against
the Thirtymile Fire because it was human-caused. But that implies
a moral value—that a human-set fire is somehow worse than a
lightning-caused one. It's the Smokey mentality, so deeply rooted
that even the best-trained fire managers can't see it.

Fire is simply fire. It has no sense of morality, has no persona,
does not wish to do good or bad, is neither deliberately enemy nor
friend. It is a piece of the western landscape, as much as the West's
mountains and rivers and forests. Indeed, it should be viewed as a
component of those forests, as much as the ponderosa pine and
Douglas-fir are components. There is nothing to "fight," no war in

which to engage. Or, if there is, it is of our own making. We created an enemy of fire, defined its nature, arrayed forces against it. Like Canute, we have tried to stop the tide, and failed. It is time to learn from that failure. With every summer now a season of fire, there is no other choice.

Acknowledgments

▲ ▲ ▲ ▲

In December 2000, an e-mail popped into the computer at my home office. It was signed by someone named Jamie Watkins, who said she worked for a New York literary agent. Jamie said she had seen a recent article of mine in *Business 2.0* magazine, liked it, and wondered if I had any book ideas rattling around.

To which I replied: Yeah, right. Who are you *really?*

Thankfully, Jamie was not entirely put off by that rude response, fostered by my belief that she was fronting for something akin to a vanity press. And a week later, she, her boss Jim Levine, and I were talking about a book on forest fires. I'd been thinking about the idea for several months, since the enormous fires of the previous summer, and had even talked with a couple of fire researchers about what might go into such a book. Within a month, with Jim's encouragement, I had a proposal in the works. This book owes much to Jamie and to Jim. In particular, after Jamie left James Levine Communications to pursue a career with The Dalton School in

New York City, Jim did fantastic work shepherding the proposal through its formative stages and getting it before the right pairs of eyes.

Two of those eyes belonged to Wendy Hubbert at the Tarcher imprint of Penguin Group (USA) Inc. Wendy was instrumental in giving the book its final shape, and through her good advice and patience saw the manuscript through several rough patches. I owe a huge debt to her as well.

Out west, where the fires were burning, the list of people who loaned a hand is long, and I surely will miss some names. At the top, however, belongs Don Smurthwaite, a media relations officer for the National Interagency Fire Center in Boise, Idaho. Don was a constant source of advice, information, and leads. Without him, I also would never have gotten my firefighting "red card," as the bureaucracy in the Forest Service—in which Washington, D.C., headquarters staff defers all decisions to local forests, where staff members promptly dive for cover—thwarted me at every turn. Others at the fire center who were immensely helpful include Neal Hitchcock, manager for the center's National Interagency Coordinating Center (NICC), the nerve center of the operation; Rick Ochoa, fire center meteorologist; and Linda Bass, manager of the supply center.

In Montana, Kevin Ryan at the Fire Sciences Lab in Missoula took hours away from his work to talk fire and let me tag along on research projects. Michael Harrington, like Ryan a fire-effects specialist, also was generous with his time and knowledge. Don Latham, who runs the lab's fire behavior department, helped explain the workings of fire and his staff efforts to better understand it. Fire lab researchers Bret Butler, Colin Hardy, and Mark Finney also were a wealth of knowledge. In Arizona, Pete Fulé and Wally Covington were immensely helpful.

Out in the field, I am deeply indebted to the incident command team directed by Steve Frye. Steve and his entire team were unfailingly helpful, particularly fire behavior analyst Ron Hvizdak and meteorologist Bob Tobin. Media officer Bob Summerfield helped coordinate outings with Hotshot teams and other fire units. And Jack Kirkendall let me tag along during a crucial day at the Fridley Fire in Montana.

Many people helped me reconstruct the events in the Thirtymile Fire. Among them: Matthew Rutman, Rebecca Welch, Thom Taylor, and Nick Dreis. Kathie FitzPatrick, Karen FitzPatrick's mother, was a constant source of both information and inspiration. Her generosity of spirit is rare.

Thanks as well to Jack Hart, my editor many years ago when I worked for the Sunday magazine of the *Oregonian* newspaper (Portland, Oregon). His continued influence is reflected in this book's most successful passages.

Finally, a heartfelt thanks to my wife, Jane Kilburn, who read drafts, caught many typos, and provided much-needed encouragement. She also showed considerable patience while I chased fires hundreds of miles away within 48 hours of the wedding of our son, Justin, and daughter, Jennie. On the other hand, what were they *thinking* of, getting married six weeks apart? Kids these days . . .

Index

Numbers in *italics* indicate illustrations

About the Author

▲ ▲ ▲ ▲

Douglas Gantenbein is the Seattle correspondent for *The Economist* news magazine. He has written for publications including *The Atlantic Monthly, The New York Times Sunday Magazine, The Wall Street Journal, Outside, Travel & Leisure, Scientific American,* and *Backpacker.* Author of the *Outside* magazine column "The Gear Guy," he teaches nonfiction writing at the University of Washington and is a member of the Seattle Mountain Rescue, the oldest and largest volunteer wilderness organization in the United States.